MW01165769

Why Do You Need a College Degree?

More people are receiving college degrees than ever before. In 2000, more than 1 million students earned their bachelor's degree. By 2001, 58 percent of all individuals between the ages of 25 and 29 had completed some part of a college education. The National Center for Education Statistics reports that 29 percent of this same age group held at least a bachelor's degree.

With a larger number of college graduates entering the workforce, many employers now require a college degree for jobs that previously had lower educational requirements. This "educational upgrading" has occurred primarily in occupations that are considered desirable and are high paying.

Employers want workers with good communication, teamwork, and problem-solving skills. They want workers who are able to learn quickly, workers who can adapt and adjust to workplace challenges, and workers who have the desire to excel and achieve. Above all, they want college graduates.

This book does more than tout the importance of a college degree. Also included is information on how to define and evaluate your skills and interests, how to choose a major, how to make the most of your college program, and how to turn your college degree into a satisfying job. In particular, this book focuses on students interested in studying economics and those who already hold an economics degree.

The following is a brief description of the contents.

SECTION I

Introduction: Meet the Economics Major provides an overview of the typical college experience for economics majors. It also provides basic information on colleges and universities, suggested courses, skills, potential employers, starting salaries, and further avenues for exploration.

Chapter 1: Your High School Years will help you select a major and prepare for college study while you are still in high school. You will read about suggested courses, self-assessment tests, methods of exploring your major of interest, and how to choose a college.

Chapter 2: Making the Most of Your Experience as a Economics Major will help you make the best use of your college years—even if you are not sure of a major. Topics include typical economics curricula, the benefits of a minor, methods of exploring careers, and preparing for the workforce.

Chapter 3: Taking Your Economics Degree to Work offers tips on finding direction after graduation, conducting a job search, improving your resume, applying for jobs online, successful interviewing, and the benefits of a graduate degree.

Section I also includes informative interviews with college professors and working professionals in the field that will provide further insight on the economics major and its career options. You will also find helpful sidebars that provide further information about issues in the economics field, top employers of economics graduates, fun facts about money, and top graduate programs.

SECTION II

The second half of the book features profiles of 35 careers in the field of economics. Each article discusses the occupation in detail.

The **Quick Facts** section provides a brief summary of the career, including recommended school subjects, personal skills, work environment, minimum educational requirements, salary ranges, certification or licensing requirements, and employment outlook. This section also provides acronyms and identification numbers for the following government classification indexes: the *Dictionary of Occupational Titles* (DOT), the Guide to Occupational Exploration (GOE), the National Occupational Classification (NOC) Index, and the Occupational Information Network (O*NET)-Standard Occupational Classification System (SOC) index. The DOT, GOE, and O*NET-SOC indexes have been created by the U.S. government; the NOC index is Canada's career classification system. Readers can use the identification numbers listed in the Quick Facts section to access further information on a career. Print editions of the DOT (*Dictionary of Occupational Titles*. Indianapolis, Ind.: JIST Works, 1991) and GOE (*The Complete Guide for Occupational Exploration*. Indianapolis, Ind.: JIST Works, 1993) are available from libraries and electronic versions of the NOC (http://www23.hrdc-drhc.gc.ca/2001/e/generic/welcome.shtml) and O*NET-SOC (http://online.onetcenter.org) are available on the World Wide Web. When no DOT, GOE, NOC, or O*NET-SOC numbers are listed, this means that the U.S. Department of Labor or the Human Resources Development

Canada have not created a numerical designation for this career. In this instance, you will see the acronym "N/A," or not available.

The **Overview** section is a brief introductory description of the duties and responsibilities involved in this career. Oftentimes, a career may have a variety of job titles. When this is the case, alternative career titles are presented.

The **History** section describes the history of the particular job as it relates to the overall development of its industry or field.

The Job describes in detail the primary and secondary duties of the job.

Requirements discusses high school and postsecondary education and training requirements, certification or licensing, if necessary, and any other personal requirements for success in the job. The majority of the careers in *Top Careers for Economics Graduates* require a minimum of a bachelor's degree, but we have also included a few careers that may have a minimum educational requirement of a graduate degree. For example, the career of economist will require a master's or doctorate degree, but an individual with a bachelor's degree may be able to work as a research assistant.

Conversely, the book includes a few careers that require less than a college degree; however, some college-level economics courses are highly recommended for these positions. Examples include the job of buyer, commodities broker, cost estimator, and franchise owner.

Exploring offers suggestions on how to gain some experience in or knowledge of the particular job before making a firm educational and financial commitment. While in high school or the early years of college, you can learn about clubs and other activities, for example, that will give you a better understanding of the job.

The **Employers** section gives an overview of typical places of employment for the job and may also include specific employment numbers from the U.S. Department of Labor.

Starting Out discusses the best ways to land that first job, be it through a college placement office, newspaper ads, or personal contacts.

The **Advancement** section describes what kind of career path to expect from the job and how to get there.

Earnings lists salary ranges and describes the typical fringe benefits.

The **Work Environment** section describes the typical surroundings and conditions of employment—whether indoors or outdoors, noisy or quiet, social or independent, and so on. Also discussed are typical hours worked, any seasonal fluctuations, and the stresses and strains of the job.

The **Outlook** section summarizes the job in terms of the general economy and industry projections. For the most part, Outlook information is obtained from the Bureau of Labor Statistics and is supplemented by information taken from professional associations. Job growth terms follow those used in the *Occupational Outlook Handbook:*

- Growth described as "much faster than the average" means an increase of 36 percent or more.
- Growth described as "faster than the average" means an increase of 21–35 percent.
- Growth described as "about as fast as the average" means an increase of 10–20 percent.
- Growth described as "more slowly than the average" means an increase of 3–9 percent.
- Growth described as having "little or no change" means an increase of 0–2 percent.
- "Decline" means a decrease of 1 percent or more.

Each career article concludes with **For More Information,** which lists organizations that can provide career information on training, education, internships, scholarships, and job placement.

Whether you are a high school student who is unsure of a college major, a college student interested in learning more about careers, or an adult thinking about returning to school, this book will help you learn more about the economics major and the career options available to those with this background.

MEET THE ECONOMICS MAJOR

WHAT IS ECONOMICS?

French writer Albert Camus once said, "Economics is the art of trying to satisfy infinite needs with limited resources." This is a fairly accurate description. *Economics* is the study of the systems and structures in society that are in place to balance the supply of goods and services with people's needs. When problems in these systems arise, economists help to pinpoint the imbalance and reestablish stability. To do this, economics professionals use their combined knowledge of history, philosophy, and mathematics to develop formulas and theories. Economics can be narrowly focused, such as the study of how a household balances its budget, or it can have a broad scope, studying global problems such as unemployment, starvation, inflation, and environmental destruction. This distinction has developed two branches of economic study: micro- and macroeconomics. *Microeconomics* is the study of a small economic system, such as that within a particular company or employment industry. *Macroeconomics* is the study of a much larger economic system, such as that within a country. Because of this wide scope, those who study economics can work in many different jobs, from business and politics to academia.

According to the U.S. Department of Education, 18,441 students graduated with a bachelor's degree in economics in 2000. In the same year, 2,168 students earned master's degrees, and 851 students were granted doctorates.

Because of the relative popularity of economics as a course of study, many colleges and universities offer economics as a major. To view a list of colleges offering bachelor's degrees in the liberal arts and humanities (which includes economics), visit Universities.com (http://www.universities.com). You can also research graduate school programs in economics at the master's and doctorate level at Gradschools.com (http://www.gradschools.com).

WHAT COURSES WILL I TAKE?

Because an economics major is applicable in so many arenas, courses will cover many disciplines. Typical course loads include classes in micro- and macroeconomics, mathematics (calculus, in particular), and statistics. In addition, classes in sociology, philosophy, and business are also included in most programs. Many schools require students to take a core curriculum in the liberal arts before declaring a major. These classes will include English, history, science, and foreign language.

WHAT WILL I LEARN?

Because of the broad spectrum of classes included in the economics major, students learn a variety of skills in areas such as problem solving, public speaking, report writing, teamwork, analytical and critical thinking, observation, and research.

Economics majors should stay up to date on changes in technology. Graduates in this field will likely be expected to be familiar with several computer software programs, including word processing (Microsoft Word) and spreadsheet (Microsoft Excel) programs, as well as more technical statistics programs (SAS or SPSS, which are programs for managing small and large sets of data).

INTERVIEW: Dave Zobrist

David Zobrist is an associate auditor with Deloitte & Touche in Chicago. He spoke to the editors of Top Careers for Economics Graduates *about his work experience and educational background.*

Q. What is your main job responsibility?

A. My main responsibility is to test financial statements and write a report stating that the information provided looks okay. I continue testing until my superiors are comfortable enough to sign off on the report.

Q. How long have you been working as an auditor?

A. I've worked in this job for a year. I previously worked for two years at Bank One as a commercial lending analyst.

Q. How did you train for this job? What was your college major?

A. I majored in economics and Spanish literature. The knowledge I learned in accounting classes was very transferable to this job. The method of thinking that was taught in my economics classes has also been very applicable and useful. As for the technical aspects of my job, classes in econometrics (applying statistics to study economic problems) have helped me to understand sampling methodology that is used to test financial statements.

Q. Did this major prepare you for your career or, in retrospect, would you pursue another major?

A. Yes and no. The major gave me an edge when dealing with sampling techniques. However, many elements of economics are unrelated to accounting.

Q. What is the most important piece of advice that you have to offer economics majors as they graduate and look for jobs?

A. Network, network, network—especially with other alums from your college. I've gotten all my jobs through alumni.

Q. Are there any misconceptions about your job that you'd like to clear up?

A. One misconception: I know a lot about taxes. The reality is, I don't do taxes. We're number crunchers. The hardest mathematical function I do is division.

Q. Is attending graduate school a good way to advance in your particular career?

A. Honestly? No. Once you get your CPA, additional education is not really necessary unless you plan on doing something totally different.

WHERE WILL I WORK AND HOW MUCH WILL I EARN?

An economics major can be useful in a variety of industries, from the media to politics to business. Many of the careers in this book, such as auditor, intelligence agent, and statistician, require a bachelor's degree as a minimum requirement.

Large cities provide the most opportunities for work in this field. The area of economics you choose to pursue may influence where you choose to work. Cities such as New York, Los Angeles, and Chicago offer the most opportunities in business. Washington, D.C., offers the most opportunities in politics and law. Seattle and San Francisco offer many opportunities in technology and consulting. However, most areas of the country have a demand for individuals with an economics background, since all towns and cities need teachers, accountants, and local government officials.

Earnings levels will vary depending on industry. Banking executives and judges will earn more than high school teachers and writers. However, most jobs in economics provide for a comfortable living. According to the *Summer 2003 Salary Survey* by the National Association of Colleges and Employers, the average starting salary offer for an economics major was $40,084. Those with graduate degrees earned an average of $53,183.

You can use the Internet to learn more about the economics field. There you will find information about college programs, local and national organizations that support the industry, job-hunting advice, and job listings. The following are a few good sites to explore as you get to know this field:

About: Economics
http://economics.about.com

Creighton University: Economics
http://cujobs.creighton.edu/Economics.htm

Fed 101: The Federal Reserve Today
http://www.kc.frb.org/fed101

Great Economic Lessons (includes websites for all ages)
http://ecedweb.unomaha.edu/ecedweek/lessons.htm

The Economics Website
http://www.mcwdn.org/ECONOMICS/EconMain.html

The U.S. Mint
http://www.usmint.gov

CHAPTER 1

YOUR HIGH SCHOOL YEARS

Figuring out what to do with your life is quite a daunting task, but there's no need to stress. Whether you realize it or not, some important changes are already taking place during your high school years. As you take more high school classes, you are learning more about what you like and don't like to do, which will help you narrow your career choices. With that in mind, this chapter will help you learn more about yourself, about economics, and help you know what to look for when choosing a college.

SUGGESTED COURSES

Taking specific courses in high school will help you determine your interests before it's time to choose a college and a career. If you think you might be interested in economics, there are several high school classes you can take to prepare.

Mathematics (especially calculus) and business are among the most important courses that will prepare you to study economics in college. Of course, be sure to take economics classes if your high school offers them. In addition, you should take a college preparatory course load, including history, government, science, social studies, foreign languages, and English literature and composition classes. The days of writing college application essays and lengthy term papers are just around the corner, so high school is the time to sharpen your writing skills. Be sure to take computer science so that you will be able to do research, write papers, and even apply to college online.

Meet with your guidance counselor to make sure you take all the classes that will help you get into college and prepare you for a major in economics.

ASSESSMENT TESTS

Assessment tests can be invaluable tools to help you choose a college, plan your courses, and pick a major. Although questions vary depending on the test, most focus on your academic strengths, values, interests, and personality, and they help you evaluate your college and career options. The following are some of the most popular tests available (Note that some of these tests require a fee. Talk to your high school guidance counselor or adviser for more details.):

- Scholastic Aptitude Test (SAT): The SAT is a three-hour test measuring verbal and mathematical reasoning skills. Many colleges and universities use the SAT as one indicator of academic performance, in addition to your grades, class rank, extracurricular activities, personal essay, and teacher recommendations. Visit http://www.collegeboard.com for more information.
- American College Testing Program (ACT): Similar to the SAT, the ACT is designed to assess high school students' academic abilities and estimate their college performance. The test covers four basic areas: English, math, reading comprehension, and scientific reasoning. For details, visit http://www.act.org.
- Kuder Career Planning System: The Kuder test helps individuals evaluate their interests, skills, and values. Suggested college majors and careers are ranked based on survey responses. For sample tests and more information, visit http://www.kuder.com.
- Myers-Briggs Type Indicator: This assessment test identifies an individual's personality type using four general, but opposite, dispositions: extraversion/introversion, sensate/intuitive, thinking/feeling, or judging/perceiving. Based on responses to test questions, the individual is characterized as one of 16 personality types. Although most organizations charge a fee for this test, you can visit http://www.humanmetrics.com/cgi-win/JTypes1.htm for a free test based on the Myers-Briggs Type Indicator. Also visit http://www.cpp-db.com for details.
- Career Key: Developed by Lawrence K. Jones, a college professor specializing in career counseling and development, this website hosts a quick and easy assessment to help you explore jobs that fit your career type, such as artistic or enterprising. After answering questions about your interests and skills, the Career Key develops a list of appropriate jobs that fit your responses. Visit http://www.careerkey.org.

- Armed Services Vocational Aptitude Battery (ASVAB): The ASVAB, administered by the U.S. Department of Defense, is a multi-aptitude test available at over 14,000 high schools nationwide. The tests evaluate students' vocabulary skills, reading comprehension, math skills, math reasoning, general science knowledge, shop and technical skills, mechanical knowledge, and knowledge of electronics. Scores are combined to reveal three general scores for verbal, math, and academic ability. See http://asvabprogram.com for more information.
- Princeton Review Career Quiz: This quick and easy multiple-choice survey will help you determine your worker "type" (such as careful/orderly or quick/random) and your main work interests (such as artistic/creative or mechanical/technical). To try it out, visit http://www.princetonreview.com/cte/quiz.

EXPLORE AND GET YOUR FOOT IN THE DOOR

You can learn a lot about the field of economics long before you decide to major in it. By participating in some of the following activities, you should get a sense of whether or not this field is right for you.

Join a Club

Join your school's economics or business club. Clubs are great places to meet like-minded people and explore your interest in economics. Extracurricular activities also look great on college applications. If your school doesn't offer an economics or business club, check out the Junior Achievement (JA) organization (http://www.ja.org) and see if there is a chapter near you to join. JA encourages business leaders in the community to talk to groups of students about how they got started in their careers and how to be successful in economics and business in the future.

Become a Newsie

Writing and editing for your school's newspaper will teach you how to gather information, conduct interviews, analyze and assess information, meet deadlines, and work with others—skills that are useful to economics majors. If your school doesn't have a newspaper, talk to school officials about helping to start one.

INTERVIEW: Alok Bohara

Alok Bohara teaches economics, particularly statistics and econometrics (using statistics to solve economic problems), at the University of New Mexico. He also conducts research in environmental economics, poverty and health, and conflict and human rights violations. Bohara was kind enough to speak to the editors of Top Careers for Economics Graduates *about his background and experience.*

Q. How long have you been teaching economics?

A. I have taught at the University of New Mexico for the past 15 years.

Q. For what careers does an economics major prepare students?

A. At the undergraduate level, economics majors can have an advantage in getting into and doing well in law and business school. They can also seek a job at a local or federal government agency. In the private sector, economics majors can work for banks, insurance companies, brokerage firms, and even nongovernmental organizations.

Q. What are the most important personal and professional qualities for economics majors?

A. Undergraduates in particular will need good computer skills to be able to understand databases, merge different files, and conduct statistical analysis.

Having an open mind and being curious are important traits to be a good economist. Curiosity combined with the analytical tools taught in economics will empower you to see things differently.

With an open mind, students can be aware of, for example, the power of the free market to solve socio-economic problems. For example, in our global economy, if we are too protective of our computer sector (i.e., not allowing other countries and economies to manufacture memory chips and software), we would not be able to afford cheap computers for our homes. This could compromise our productivity.

Economists must also maintain a balanced view. For example, pouring money into public education without any accountability is not useful. However, destroying what is one of the best things in this country, our free public education, is not wise either. These are the types of problems that economists face. To work towards solutions, economists must weigh both sides of every issue.

Q. When the average student enters your program, what are their expectations?

A. I don't think new students come into economics with any expectations, at least not the way business students do. One of my biggest challenges in teaching economics is to convince new students that an economics degree can allow them to do everything that a business degree can do . . . and more. Furthermore, a solid degree in economics allows you to venture into different policy areas: environment, development, poverty, social programs, international banking, you name it.

Q. What advice would you offer new graduates?

A. Recent graduates need to keep an open mind about the free market without losing a sense of social responsibility. Big government is not necessarily a solution to every social problem that we face today. Government policies are essential on a certain level, but there are plenty of market solutions that can be made on the private level—economics professionals just need to have an open mind to look for them.

In addition, if you want to work as an economist in other countries, always keep in mind that what may work in the United States may not work elsewhere. History, local customs, and the political-economic environment of other countries are important to consider before prescribing Western policies. Necessary institutions (e.g., legal and political) may not be in place for such borrowed policies to take root. To be a good economist, you need to do your homework and take cultural differences into perspective.

Q. What are common misconceptions about the economics major?

A. Economics is not all about math, statistics, and modeling. Increasingly, the field of economics has become more interdisciplinary. Understanding a problem from the economics point of view and finding policy solutions is a fun and rewarding part of the field. For example, protecting the environment for our future generation is essential. Economists can work towards developing public policies that look into alternate fuel sources and promote scientific innovations.

It is also important to note that the study of economics is a global one. The work of economists can be used to help protect and improve the life for workers in struggling countries. For example, economists have developed policies to promote fair trade in coffee production by pairing up American buyers with local farmers in Central American countries. These farmers receive good wages to produce quality coffee for export to the United States. This is done without the involvement of big corporations and distributors; the American buyers visit these farmers annually and deal with them directly. Not only does this bring quality coffee to us inexpensively, such initiatives save these small farmers from many woes. They don't have to give up their family life and cross into the United States illegally to find work.

Q. What are the top industry segments for economists?

A. There are so many areas that are quite promising for economics majors: environmental, public finance, international trade and finance, labor economics, and development, just to name a few. The health sector will become a promising area for economics majors. The growing need to organize health-related information is opening up opportunities for those with an economics background. Many public health programs have started offering fields in health care information. Economics majors can move into this field with an added advantage: their ability to model and estimate economic relationships.

Q. What is the future of your school's program?

A. We have reorganized our graduate program to include a field in international and developmental economics in addition to environmental economics, public finance, and labor. Plus, students can now concentrate in two fields. We also have moved away from requiring students to take a field exam by offering instead the option to write a field paper. This way, students can begin working on their research early on in their studies.

Undergraduate students are also bound to benefit from developments in our graduate program. These students can take advantage of our mentoring and tutoring programs and can also help out in research.

Participate in Student Government

Many economics graduates work in government, so experiencing firsthand how government works will give you an advantage as you prepare for college. Getting involved in student government will show college admissions workers that you are a strong communicator and a leader. If you aren't involved in student government, you can become more familiar with politics and government by attending school board and city council meetings or helping a local politician with his or her campaign. You can also check out the Youth Leadership Initiative (http://www9.youthleadership.net/youthleadership), a program sponsored by The University of Virginia Center for Politics, which helps middle and high school students learn more about our political process. Participating in one of these activities will help you to develop your critical-thinking, leadership, organization, and information- and people-management skills. College admissions officers also like to see participation in activities such as student government on college applications.

Take the Economics Challenge

If you are taking general or advanced placement economics classes at your high school, you might be eligible to demonstrate your knowledge of economics by competing in The National Council on Economic Education (NCEE)/Goldman Sachs Foundation National Economics Challenge. The Challenge is a state, regional, and national competition for high school students that is designed to increase their knowledge of economics and finance. In each competition, your team will be asked questions on microeconomics, macroeconomics, and international economics. The final round of competition consists of an oral quiz-bowl format. Winners receive U.S. Savings Bonds. For more information on the Challenge, visit http://economicschallenge.ncee.net.

Have Some Fun

The World Wide Web provides many interesting and fun ways to learn more about economics. Try the following games, exercises, and simulations to learn more about economics and financial management.

- It All Adds Up (http://italladdsup.org). This website, sponsored by the American Express Foundation and the NCEE, is geared toward high school students who want to get a head start on their financial futures. It offers online games and simulations that will teach you about paying for college, buying a car, credit management, saving, and investing.
- Gazillionaire (http://www.gazillionaire.com) is described on the website as "a cross between *Monopoly* set in outer space

and Wall Street in wonderland." You'll use economic tools and principles to compete with others to build a top company.

- Peanuts & Crackerjacks (http://www.bos.frb.org/peanuts) teaches about economics by applying its rules and principles to professional team sports. Visitors to the site (sponsored by the Federal Reserve Bank of Boston) play a nine-inning baseball game in which they are asked up to nine randomly selected questions per inning. Each question, depending on its level of difficulty, is worth either a single, double, triple, or home run. Every correct answer you make earns you a hit and the possibility to score runs. Wrong answers earn you an out, and if you're familiar with baseball, you only get three of these an inning. Even if you're not a sports fan, you can still read the Sports Page section to learn the basics of economics.

Volunteer

Community service is a great way to help others, meet new people, learn career skills, and test your interest in a field. Volunteering at a local business, bank, or even a place that is seemingly unrelated to economics, such as a hospital, will help you to develop leadership, organizational, interpersonal, and other skills that you will need to be successful in any field.

Get a Job

A summer or part-time job, whether it's working as a bank teller, a cashier in a fast food restaurant, or as a runner at a financial exchange, will teach you time-management skills, responsibility, and how to get along with others. It might also help you save money toward college tuition and related costs. You'll also get a chance to meet people who are interested in business and economics, and you might even make such a great impression that you'll be considered for positions in the future. College admissions officials will be impressed by the fact that you excelled at your studies while holding down a job.

Talk to the Experts

Ask your guidance counselor or your economics or business teacher (another expert resource for information on this field) to set up an information interview with an economist, financial analyst, or another worker with an economics background. Compile a list of questions before the interview to ensure that you will make good use of the worker's valuable time. Suggested questions include: What are the pros and cons of your job? Can you describe a typical day on the job? What other fields can I work in with an economics degree?

Do Some Research

You can also learn more by reading books on economics. Read books such as *A Student's Guide to Economics* (ISI Guides to the Major Disciplines) (Wilmington, Del.: Intercollegiate Studies Institute, 2000); *Naked Economics: Undressing the Dismal Science* (New York: W.W. Norton & Company, 2002); and *Basic Economics: A Citizen's Guide to the Economy* (New York: Basic Books, 2000). Your school or public librarian can help you locate these and other books on economics.

You can also read the business section of your local newspaper and check out print or online versions of specialized business magazines such as *Business Week* (http://www.businessweek.com), *Fortune* (http://www.fortune.com), *Money* (http://money.cnn.com), and *Forbes* (http://www.forbes.com).

Additionally, Junior Achievement offers *Onpoint Economics,* an online newsletter for middle and high school teachers and their students that focuses on economics topics and activities. Visit http://www.ja.org/about/about_edu_newsletter.shtml to read sample issues.

INTERVIEW: Warren Hrung

Warren Hrung has been a financial economist in the Office of Tax Analysis at the U.S. Department of the Treasury for four years. Hrung spoke to the editors of Top Careers for Economics Graduates *about his job and educational background.*

Q. What is your main responsibility at the Treasury?

A. I estimate the impact on federal revenues of changes to various individual tax items, including tax-preferred savings incentives and the charitable giving deduction.

Q. How did you train for this job? What was your college major?

A. I majored in economics in college, and then went straight to graduate school. I received my Ph.D. in economics from the University of California at Berkeley.

Q. Is having a Ph.D. in economics a good way to advance in your career?

A. Yes, my doctorate is useful for advancement, although for most jobs, a master's degree is probably sufficient.

Q. Did you participate in any internships while you were in college?

A. Though I didn't work in a formal internship, I did work for an economics professor while in college. This job allowed me to meet and work with economics graduate students, who gave me valuable advice about which courses to take to prepare for graduate school. Because of their help, I wasn't overwhelmed by the workload once I entered graduate school.

Q. What are the most important personal and professional qualities for economists?

A. Organizational skills are crucial because many issues come up on a moment's notice that require immediate attention and a quick solution. You can't waste time trying to locate materials and information. Economists in my office must also be comfortable working with large amounts of data, so it's also important to be able to navigate an Excel spreadsheet.

Q. What advice do you have for recent economics graduates?

A. No matter what kind of job you end up landing, keep thinking like an economist. Examining issues in terms of price-quantity/supply-demand will come in handy in many fields.

THE FINAL STEPS . . . AND BECOMING A FRESHMAN AGAIN

Once your junior year of high school arrives, there's no more avoiding it: You must narrow down school possibilities and tackle the college application process. If the whole ordeal has your stomach knotting up, take a minute to relax, and remember that there are many resources to help with your decision.

CHOOSING A COLLEGE

Selecting a college is one of the most important choices you will ever make. After you finish high school and begin a new chapter of your life, what sorts of things do you hope are in store for you? Have you always dreamed of going to college far away from home, or would you prefer a school that's close to your current stomping grounds? Is a small school more your style, or would you feel most at home in a larger environment?

The right college will provide you with the tools for academic and career success. It will also introduce you to excellent instructors and professors as well as a whole new group of friends that you may keep your entire life. Picking the wrong college is not the end of the world, but it might delay your education or simply make you frustrated or unhappy. So, how should you learn more about colleges so that you make the right decision? You can learn about college from the following sources:

Guidance Counselors

Your guidance counselor is a great resource for information on colleges and universities, including application deadlines, financial aid, and academic programs. When deciding on a college, there are many factors to consider, such as academic programs offered, reputation or ranking, atmosphere (small, intimate college or large, active university), location, costs, and clubs or other student activities.

Sit down with your guidance counselor and make a list of what you're looking for in a school. Save the list and refer back to it so you don't forget about the most important factors. Keep all your college information organized in a folder or binder so that you can find the appropriate information when you need it.

If college seems out of reach financially, talk to your guidance counselor about financial aid packages. A multitude of scholarships, grants, and loans are available.

College Recruiters

Your high school should host recruiters from colleges and universities. These recruiters will give presentations on their colleges, providing information on everything from admissions and academic offerings to student housing and extracurricular activities. Recruiters will also provide information on tuition, financial aid, and scholarships available. Sign up for all the recruiter visits that you are interested in—you will learn valuable information that should help you start narrowing down your list of school possibilities. Prepare a list of questions to ask the recruiter. This is your chance to ask specific questions, so make sure that you really think about what to ask so you don't end up inquiring about general information that is already addressed in the college's brochure or at its website.

College Fairs

Another helpful way to learn about colleges is to attend college fairs. Representatives from colleges and universities all across the country attend college fairs to inform and recruit students. Each school's representatives usually set up an information booth, where they hand out information packets and answer students' questions.

The atmosphere at a college fair is fairly relaxed; you should feel comfortable walking up to representatives from all sorts of schools and asking lots of questions. However, it is a formal gathering, so it is a good idea to get a little dressed up (don't wear jeans and a T-shirt). College fairs vary in size—there may be 25 schools represented at one college fair and 200 at the next. Your guidance counselor should have information about fairs, and be sure to read your local (or school) newspaper for announcements about upcoming fairs.

Before going to a college fair, be sure to make a list of what you are looking for in a school (see "Guidance Counselors"). In addition, prepare a list of questions to ask representatives—they should be able to inform you about financial aid, first-year classes, computer facilities, student housing facilities, extracurricular activities, and almost anything else about the school.

Some suggested questions are

- What are the two or three most popular majors at your school?
- Can you tell me about the economics department at your school?
- What first-year courses would I take if I were to major in economics?
- Does your school help students find internships?
- What is the student-to-faculty ratio at your school?
- What percentage of students receive financial aid?
- What kinds of extracurricular activities does your college offer?
- What is your school's job placement rate (particularly for economics majors)?

Bring writing materials to the college fair so that you can keep track of everything you learn. You may also find it helpful to bring a backpack to hold all the college pamphlets you'll gather. For a list of college fairs, visit http://www.nacac.com/fairs_ncf.html.

Contact Colleges Yourself

Contact college admissions offices directly to obtain their catalogs. You can also view catalogs and other information on colleges at their websites. Visit CollegeSource Online (http://www.collegesource.org) to view over 25,000 college catalogs.

To view a list of colleges offering bachelor's degree economics programs in the United States, visit http://edirc.repec.org. Schools offering master's degrees and Ph.D.'s in economics are listed at Gradschools.com (http://www.gradschools.com).

Campus Visits: Giving Schools a Test Drive

You probably wouldn't buy a car without at least sitting in it and taking it for a test drive. This same philosophy should apply when you pick a college, since you'll be investing lots of money and plenty of time in your decision. Thus, the campus visit is an important and worthwhile part of the college-selection process.

Touring a campus will show you much more than what is covered in the college's brochure. For instance, seeing a school's layout, facilities, and student body firsthand will have a larger impact on you than the few pictures listed in the college's brochure. Almost all schools look appealing in their brochures, so only by covering some ground on the campus will you get a true feel for what the school is like. Consider the following points before you make your first campus visit:

- Research before you go. Learn as much as you can about the college before you visit. Read the institution's brochures and visit its website. Talk to your friends, teachers, and parents about the school. Some colleges even have programs in which you can talk to currently enrolled students or alumni about their experiences.
- Make a list things you would like to learn about during your visit. These might include academics, financial aid, student housing, the library, the school newspaper, and extracurricular activities.
- Schedule a formal tour. It is important to schedule a campus tour in advance; you won't learn nearly as much if you just

show up and wander around the school. Contact the school's admissions department to arrange this appointment. This might even lead to a short interview with an admissions counselor during your visit. Again, be prepared with a list of questions for the counselor. You might also want to schedule a meeting with a financial aid officer to discuss your financial aid options. Once the formal tour is over, feel free to check out any other areas of interest that you haven't seen yet, such as the soccer fields, the churches, a dorm, or a lecture hall that is used for economics classes.

- Spend a day and night on campus. If possible, try to spend at least a full day on campus, and take your tour when classes are in session. This will give you the opportunity to visit the library, sit in on a class, and visit the economics department. Visiting a school when no one is around can really take away from the school's atmosphere and affect your opinion toward it.
- Stay in a dorm. Most schools give you the option of staying overnight in a college dorm, which is a good learning experience. A dorm stay will give you a preview of what your living quarters may be like as well as a chance to try the meals, check out the laundry facilities, and meet a few people.
- Take notes. Be sure to bring a pen and paper so that you can take notes during your visit. Chat with former students and ask questions. You might even want to bring a camera to snap photos of important sites on campus as a way to jog your memory once you return home from your visit.
- Keep an open mind. Approach campus visits with an open mind, but remember that no college or university would employ a guide who hated the school. Each college aims to present itself in the best possible light to encourage interest. Be sure to balance what you learn on your campus tour with information from other resources, such as college guidebooks, fellow students, guidance counselors, your parents, and your own observations.

If a college visit is not an option for you, check out CampusTours.com (http://www.campustours.com). This website provides virtual campus tours of more than 850 colleges and universities.

LAST, BUT NOT LEAST

Parents, guardians, and teachers will also be willing to help with and give input on your college decision. Take their advice, but be sure the decision you make is truly yours.

For more information on choosing the right college, visit

Adventures in Education (See "Find the Right School" in the "High School" section)
http://www.adventuresineducation.org

College Board
http://www.collegeboard.com

College Is Possible
http://www.collegeispossible.org

CollegeNet
http://www.collegenet.com

Colleges.com
http://www.colleges.com

CollegeLink
http://www.collegelink.com

CollegeNews
http://www.collegenews.org

Princeton Review
http://www.princetonreview.com

CHAPTER 2

MAKING THE MOST OF YOUR EXPERIENCE AS AN ECONOMICS MAJOR

Once you have decided on a college, there are a few things to keep in mind as you plan your college experience. As an economics major, you will have to stay focused and work hard in your classes while at the same time participating in outside activities. Employers will be impressed if you earned straight As, but they will be even more impressed if you also gained some real-life experience. This chapter will help you to get the most out of college and the opportunities available to make contacts and learn more about your chosen field.

SUGGESTED COURSES

Given the variety of courses that most colleges offer, picking classes can be almost as overwhelming as picking a school. But you won't have to face these decisions on your own: Most colleges will assign you an academic adviser to guide you through registering for classes. Your first year or two, your main concern will be to satisfy your core curriculum requirements that all students, regardless of their major, have to fulfill. This will include survey and introductory-level classes, such as English 101. After you've declared your major, your adviser can help you choose classes that are required for the major and electives that might interest you.

The typical course load for economics majors includes classes in business, statistics, calculus, computer science, and of course, economics. School programs differ, but your major classes should cover micro- and macroeconomics, accounting, finance, economic history, international trade, economic thought, and public policy.

In today's workforce, almost every employee needs some computer knowledge. Economics professionals are no exception—in fact, they work with pretty complicated software, such as SAS and SPSS, when studying statistics; these programs organize and help disseminate data sets of all sizes. Computer science classes can introduce you to these programs and give you experience working with them.

DON'T FORGET A MINOR

If you know exactly what you'd like to do after you graduate, consider choosing a more specific minor to supplement your economics degree. For example, if you are set on working in the government, a minor in political science or law would be beneficial. Even if you're unsure of what to do after college, a minor will make you a more marketable job candidate. Just be sure to consider how your minor will fit into the schedule for your major.

CONSIDER A DOUBLE MAJOR

Another way to prepare yourself for noneconomics careers is to pursue a double major. A double major is the simultaneous pursuit of two distinct majors. Students who complete the requirements of a double major receive one bachelor's degree that states that they majored in two disciplines.

Majoring in one discipline is hard enough, so before you double major, be sure to do the following:

- Ask your academic counselors for advice on pursuing a double major. They may be able to recommend complementary majors and steer you clear of double majors that might not be as marketable as other combinations.
- Research your school's requirements for completing a double major.
- Talk to fellow students who are currently pursuing a double major and ask what the experience is like for them.

Some of the pros of a double major are that it

- allows you to explore two distinct majors while most of your classmates only explore one major
- makes you a more marketable job candidate (only, of course, if you maintain a high GPA)
- improves your chances of getting into graduate school

Some of the drawbacks of a double major are as follows:

- It is very difficult to study two subjects at once. Your social life might suffer as a result of the extra work you need to do to maintain your grades.
- While you can complete some double majors in four years, others will require an extra semester, or even another year, to complete the course work. Of course, pursuing a double major will require that you spend more money and time than you would if you just pursued a single major.
- A double major will reduce the number of credits you have available to explore other subject areas.

INTERVIEW: Caroline Hoxby

Caroline Hoxby has been a professor of economics at Harvard University for the past nine years. She specializes in labor economics, public economics, and the economics of education. Hoxby was kind enough to speak to the editors of Top Careers for Economics Graduates *about Harvard's program and to share advice for future economics students.*

Q. For what types of jobs does an economics major prepare students?

A. A major in economics prepares students for any job that requires analytic thinking and the skills to digest and prepare evidence. The economics major is ideal for someone who wants to become a policy maker (legislator or other), an attorney with a complex practice, or a manager/administrator in any complex business (an administrator of a major hospital, for instance). While many of our economics majors do go on to become economists, financiers, or business people, we also educate many people who go into public health, education policy, urban policy, regulation, labor policy, and so on.

Q. What are typical misconceptions about the work of economists?

A. If your idea of an economist is the person you see on television (someone discussing the Federal Reserve's setting the discount rate or a financial firm's predictor of next week bond market moves), then you have too narrow a view of the economics profession. Economists *are* important in setting macroeconomic policy and predicting what will happen to the capital markets. However, economists are also at the forefront of devising policy in many realms: anti-poverty programs, development of poor countries, world trade policy, industrial regulation (think telephones and media), education (think school choice and school finance), and health care. Moreover, much of the interesting work in economics is theoretical and even experimental: wouldn't you like to know how people make spending decisions or hiring decisions? Today, economists learn about such behavioral decisions in a variety of ways, including labs where people participate in what look like psychological experiments.

Q. What types of skills do economics majors need to be successful?

A. An economics major must be willing to submit real-world situations to rigorous analysis. This requires both logical skill and objectivity. While economists are increasingly sympathetic to psychology (behavioral economics is currently very popular), a person who does not have detachment is unlikely to become a good economist.

Q. What does the typical economics major in your program expect to learn by studying this field?

A. The average student wants economics to explain the world around him or her. This is a realistic expectation and it is mostly fulfilled. However, some students have read or learned confusing "pop" economics before they enter the program. After learning more rigorous tools, they usually are able to sort out strong and weak economic reasoning. Also, students are sometimes surprised to find that mathematics and statistics are vital tools of the economics trade.

Q. How can economics students prepare for the work world?

A. Do a project in which you must do some original economic analysis of an industry, policy, or area. Then, you will have the experience of setting up an analytic project from scratch, assembling your evidence, and having your report subjected to constructive but acute criticism. This is great experience for work and it is also something that you can describe to prospective employers, to explain your skills.

Q. What is the current state of the job market for economics majors?

A. Economics majors usually enjoy a strong job market, even during recessions.

Q. What is the future of your school's program?

A. At Harvard University, economics is one of the largest majors and our offering of classes is very diverse. We are currently focused on offering more small-group classes and more opportunities for students to do original research in advanced classes. We are very proud of our thesis program, in which seniors write a very serious research thesis with an individual faculty member. This cooperative effort has produced publishable research that has influenced the economics profession and policy makers.

EXPLORE AND GET YOUR FOOT IN THE DOOR

Picking the right classes (and hopefully doing well in them) is only a part of what you should focus on while in college. Though it will be tempting to spend all of your free time going to parties with friends, you should spend some of it getting experience that will complement your economics education. Employers will expect that you've already gotten some work experience in the economics field, even if you were a full-time student. Here are a few ways to gain some workplace skills.

- Work or volunteer for a politician, lawyer, judge, accountant, or anyone working with economics.
- Get involved with business-related clubs and organizations.
- Read several newspapers daily and all kinds of books.
- Read other related publications, such as *The Economist* (http://www.economist.com) and *The Wall Street Journal* (http://online.wsj.com).
- Contact professional organizations that offer opportunities for you to attend conferences and meet workers in the industry. Some of these associations offer student memberships. A few examples are the American Economics Association (http://www.vanderbilt.edu/AEA), the American Agricul-

tural Economics Association (http://www.aaea.org), the Association of Environmental and Resource Economists (http://www.aere.org), and the National Association for Business Economists (http://www.nabe.com).

- Compile a portfolio containing samples of your writing. Include any projects or papers that represent your best work.
- Create a website dedicated to your interests in economics.
- Run for student government.
- Participate in social justice groups such as Bread for the World (http://www.bread.org). This group encourages students to write their elected officials about supporting hunger-fighting legislation.
- Join organizations committed to preserving and protecting the environment, such as the Sierra Club (http://www.sierraclub.org) or the Nature Conservancy (http://nature.org).
- Contact the chair of your economics department to see if any of the professors hire student assistants. You could help with photocopying or even assist with a research project.
- Join a campus or community organization that encourages entrepreneurial or leadership skills. Colleges may give these clubs different names, such as Young Entrepreneurs or Young Leaders.

Also check out some of the following online resources:

Exploring Economics
http://www.economics.neu.edu/exploring

One Line Economics (humor)
http://aris.ss.uci.edu/econ/personnel/kawa/aphorism.html

Study Tips for Economics
http://dos.cornell.edu/CLT/campus/learn/Study%20Skills%20Content/Econtips.pdf

PREPARING FOR THE WORKFORCE

In addition to doing well in classes and participating in student clubs, there are several things that you can do to prepare for a career in economics. During the last two years of college, you should prepare for your career by networking and gaining firsthand experience of the working world.

Using Your Connections

One of the most important things to do in college is make contacts within the economics department. Faculty members will be able to offer you advice on your job search, and you may need them to write recommendation letters for job interviews or graduate school applications. Most professors are glad to write recommendation letters, but only if you have made a point to get to know them and have proven that you are dedicated, talented, and a hard worker.

Internships/Job Training

Internships are key to obtaining work in the field of economics. If a hiring decision comes down to two applicants with similar education and work experiences on their resumes, one candidate's having completed an internship can be the deciding factor. Students studying economics can inquire directly with the organization where they hope to intern, check postings at their school's career placement center, contact alumni for ideas, and search the Internet for opportunities.

Many internships are unpaid or pay very little, so you should be prepared for this reality. To make the most of your internship, ask to sit in on meetings. Your responsibilities as an intern may range from filing papers and getting coffee to researching and helping to write reports. Some companies offer competitive salaries and let their interns assist with special events.

Obtaining an internship does not guarantee you will be offered a full-time position, but it is good experience that shows potential employers you are familiar with working in the field.

The following websites can teach you more about internships:

InternshipPrograms.com
http://internships.wetfeet.com

Internships.com
http://www.internships.com

InternWeb.com
http://www.internweb.com

Rising Star: Economics Internships
http://www.rsinternships.com/econ.htm

Job Fairs and Corporate Recruiters

Job fairs are great opportunities to meet employers and make contacts in the economics field. These events enable you to see which employers are hiring and, perhaps more importantly, to meet working professionals and ask them questions about their field. In fact, some job fairs are purely educational. Companies send representatives to these fairs just to promote their business and drum up interest among soon-to-be graduates and job seekers. Similarly, you should use these job fairs to get your name out there and let companies know about you. Here are a few tips for success at job fairs:

- Bring 15–20 copies of your resume (printed on quality paper) and pass them out to employers that interest you.
- Bring letters of recommendation (see "Using Your Connections") to pass out to recruiters. The more information recruiters have about you, the better your chances of getting noticed.
- Bring a pen and paper so that you can take notes on your conversations and contacts.
- Make an effort to be conversational and enthusiastic. Depending on the size and turnout of the job fair, you may get only a minute or two to make an impression on a recruiter.
- When you speak to a corporate recruiter, ask for his or her business card if it seems appropriate. If your conversation was especially promising, make a note to stay in touch with the recruiter and pursue the company further.
- If you set up an interview with a recruiter, send a note to say thank you for his or her consideration, and be sure to mention your interest in the company.

To find a job fair in your area, and to learn more about preparing for them, visit the following websites:

CareerFairs.com
http://careerfairs.com

CollegeGrad.com
http://www.collegegrad.com

JobExpo.com
http://candidate.jobexpo.idealhire.com

JobWeb Online Career Fair
http://www.jobweb.com/employ/fairs

The Job Fair, Inc.
http://www.thejobfair.com

Information Interviewing

As you narrow down your career possibilities in college, you will come across questions that may be best answered by workers in the industry. Going straight to the source, by conducting an information interview, is a great way to learn more about careers firsthand.

Information interviewing is a job search tool that is growing in popularity. The purpose of this interview is not to get a job, but instead to learn about the field or a particular position. Instead of sitting in the hot seat, you're in the driver's seat, asking for job advice but not for a job.

First, do some research and locate several professionals that you would like to interview. Your family members, friends, and neighbors can even be good interview subjects. Regardless of whom you ask, make it clear that you are not looking for a job. Prepare for an information interview by learning all you can about the position and the company beforehand. Here are some recommended questions to ask:

- I have done some research about this position, and _____ is what I've found. Can you tell me more about what sort of work is done here?
- Can you describe your typical workday?
- Why did you decide to work for this organization?
- Who are your major clients? Major competitors?
- What are the most rewarding aspects of your job? Most challenging?
- How have you been able to balance the demands of the office with your personal life? Do you often find yourself bringing home additional work that you didn't finish at the office?
- How can you advance in your job?
- When you hire new employees, what skills do you look for in candidates?
- Has your company hired economics graduates in the past?
- How do you suggest that students find jobs in this field?
- What additional training or education should I pursue to enhance my chances of finding a position within this field?

- What is the future employment outlook for your career?
- Who else can I talk to for more information on this career/field?

Bring along paper and a pen so that you will be able to take notes during the meeting. Even though the interview is informal, you should dress and act as if you were going to an actual job interview. When the interview is complete, be sure to thank the interviewee for his or her time, and follow up with a written thank-you note. These interviewees are not only great sources of information, but they may come in handy as a source for future job leads.

For more tips on information interviews, visit the following websites:

About.com: Information Interviewing
http://jobsearch.about.com/cs/infointerviews

Career Key: Information Interviewing
http://www.careerkey.org/english/you/information_interviewing.html

Quintessential Careers: Informational Interviewing Tutorial
http://www.quintcareers.com/informational_interviewing.html

INTERVIEW: Rebecca Pasquesi

Rebecca Pasquesi is a commercial loan officer with The Northern Trust Company in Chicago, Illinois. She has been working in the banking industry for four years. She was spoke with the editors of Top Careers for Economics Graduates *about her work and educational experience.*

Q. What are your primary and secondary job duties as a commercial loan officer?

A. Primary: My most important job is to bring in new business to the bank. Secondary: I manage a portfolio of 25 commercial clients. This involves tending to all their commercial banking needs, helping them establish credit, and advising on their financial performance. I also promote services and products of other areas of the bank with the ultimate goal of obtaining a more extensive banking relationship (both commercial and personal) with our clients.

Q. How did you train for this job? What was your college major? Did you participate in any internships?

A. I trained as a credit analyst in commercial lending at another bank in the Chicago area. However, my finance major and additional classes in management and economics also gave me a good foundation for my work.

I did an internship during college, working one summer as a financial analyst for a manufacturing company. It was a good experience.

Q. What are the most important qualities for people in your career?

A. To work with clients, I feel you need to be personable, organized, flexible, dedicated, driven, and focused.

Q. What advice would you offer college students as they graduate and look for jobs in this field?

A. When it comes to a new or challenging job, one thing I've learned is to just give it your best. If it doesn't work out, you need to remember that you are not locked into a job. Life is way too short to be unhappy. Look elsewhere for the right job for you. Because even in a tight economy, there are still many opportunities out there.

Q. Where do you see yourself in the future?

A. I'd like to stay in commercial lending. The usual path of advancement in my department is from commercial loan officer to second vice president, vice president, senior vice president, etc. . . . each position handling a larger portfolio of clients.

CHAPTER 3

TAKING YOUR ECONOMICS DEGREE TO WORK

As college draws to a close, you may be feeling somewhat lost now that it's time to enter "the real world," where people go to bed before 2:00 A.M. and diets consist of more than just pizza. Rest assured, it is normal to feel this way. Many new graduates feel a sense of confusion and anxiety once they've stepped off the stage with their diploma. They might ask themselves, what are my strongest job skills? Where should I go from here? What type of company do I want to work for?

Before you try to answer these questions, you'll need to do a little self-assessment. You've probably taken the tests before (see Chapter 1), whether it was the Myers-Briggs or another formal assessment. This time, your career should be the focus. Write down your interests and skills, and then think about particular jobs that might fit your strengths and preferences. Are your writing skills strong, or are you more confident in analyzing statistics? Perhaps it's a combination of both?

After writing down and evaluating your skills and interests, ask yourself the following questions:

- Do I enjoy working independently (as an information broker, writer, etc.) or as part of a team (as a college administrator, demographer, economist, etc.)?
- Am I a self-starter, or do I need more interaction and supervision to stay motivated and focused?
- Are financial rewards (i.e., a higher salary) important—out of either necessity or desire? Or am I more concerned with finding a job that is fulfilling—regardless of the size of the paycheck?
- Does the location of a job matter? Do I want to stay close to family and/or friends? Would I rather work in a city, suburb,

or rural environment? Would I rather work in an office (as an actuary, financial analyst, or research assistant), in a classroom (as a liberal arts teacher), in another country (as an accountant, export-import specialist, or reporter), in a courtroom (as a lawyer or judge), or in the halls of Congress (as a lobbyist, press secretary, or political consultant)?

- Do I need or want a flexible working schedule? Am I willing to work occasional long or irregular hours or on weekends (as a business manager, editor, or government official)?

Continue to think of more narrowly focused questions, and read through the careers in this book to see which ones match your interests. These answers should lead you to answer the biggest question of all: What do I want to do with my life? The key is to keep in mind your given strengths and interests—and be true to them.

JUMP START YOUR JOB SEARCH

Now that you've narrowed down your list of job possibilities, it's time to plunge into the job search and see what your options are. Start researching on the Internet, in newspapers, and over the telephone; your focus should be on finding companies that are hiring. You may want to start a database at this point and record the actions that you take (sending resumes, attending interviews, making calls, sending thank-you notes, etc.) to stay organized because you never know how long and involved the job search might get. Note when employers call you back and when you find out that positions have been filled, so you're not keeping your hopes up for positions that are no longer open.

NETWORKING

Once you have a good idea of what you want to do, contact the network of people that you know within your field. Don't be afraid to let anyone and everyone know that you are looking for a job, because telling people about your situation is the only way they'll have the chance to help.

Start with family, friends, and professors. Call up old bosses from summer jobs and internships to touch base and let them know you are now looking for a job. Other alumni in the economics field may also have tips or job leads. Most colleges keep track of alumni activity and can likely offer you information about where economics students have found positions in the past. Your school's alumni network should also be able to give you contact information so that you can call up an alum and arrange to meet and talk about jobs. Alumni contacts are especially important because established economics workers from your school may be able to put in a good word for you with their bosses.

Try the Liberal Arts CareerNETWORK

If your school is a member of the Liberal Arts CareerNETWORK, finding job leads will be even easier. The CareerNETWORK works like this: employers of liberal arts graduates submit information on internships and full-time and summer jobs to one of the colleges in the consortium, and then these listings are forwarded via the Internet to the career services offices of all the other consortium schools. Students at participating schools can review the opportunities and submit their resumes when they find promising positions.

Members of the Liberal Arts CareerNETWORK include Amherst College (Mass.), Bates College (Maine), Bowdoin College (Maine), Brandeis University (Mass.), Carleton College (Minn.), Clark University (Mass.), Colby College (Maine), Colgate University (N.Y.), College of the Holy Cross (Mass.), College of Wooster (Ohio), Connecticut College (Conn.), Hamilton College (N.Y.), Hartwick College (N.Y.), Hobart and William Smith Colleges (N.Y.), Hope College (Mich.), Macalester College (Minn.), Middlebury College (Vt.), Mount Holyoke College (Mass.), Oberlin College (Ohio), St. Lawrence University (N.Y.), Skidmore College (N.Y.), Smith College (Mass.), Trinity College (Conn.), Union College (N.Y.), Vassar College (N.Y.), Washington and Lee University (Va.), Wellesley College (Mass.), and Wesleyan University (Conn.). For more information, visit http://www.lacn-group.org/barter.html.

Look for Economics Jobs on the Web

The World Wide Web is a great place to search for economics-related jobs. Visit the following websites to start your job search:

Chronicle of Higher Education: **Career Network**
http://chronicle.com/jobs

Economics Research Network's Job Openings
http://www.ssrn.com/update/ern/ernjob/ern_job.html

H-Net Job Guide for the Humanities and Social Sciences
http://oldwww.matrix.msu.edu/jobs

Job Openings for Economists
http://www.aeaweb.org/joe

USAJOBS (official job site of the U.S. Federal Government)
http://www.usajobs.opm.gov

CREATING A RESUME THAT GETS RESULTS

Before you follow up with all these contacts, you need to shape up your resume. The content, length, and format of your resume will depend on the type of job you are seeking. Regardless of the position, the resume and cover letter may be your one chance to grab a potential employer's attention, so be sure they shine.

- Load up on content. Don't be afraid to list a few extracurricular activities. Employers in the economics field are looking for well-rounded people who did more than just study throughout college. List all of your leadership positions, internships, and volunteer and work experiences on your resume. In addition, be sure to include the job skills you possess (detail-oriented, strong communication skills, teamwork, etc.) as well as the computer knowledge you've gained.
- Proofread. A sharp, professional resume can make all the difference when an employer is deciding whether to call you in for an interview. In many cases, your resume is your only chance to make an impression on an employer, so it must be perfect. Most employers will immediately toss a resume if it has grammatical errors or misspellings, so make sure to have several people read over yours before it's sent out.
- Creative several versions of your resume. Tweak your resume slightly according to what each individual employer is looking for. For example, if a job ad asks for candidates with international experience, be sure to list the year that you spent studying international economics abroad in Brussels, Belgium. However, this information should be played down on your resume when you are applying for a position with the U.S. Department of Labor, which focuses on forecasting and analyzing labor trends for the U.S. workforce.
- If you're a recent college graduate, move the education section to the beginning of your resume. Include classes that are relevant to the position. If you don't have relevant employment experience, you might want to create a section called

Resume and Cover Letter Dos and Don'ts

DO

- Include a cover letter with every resume that you send
- Tell the truth at all times when you are creating a resume
- Ask trusted friends and family to look over your resume before you send it out
- Keep your resume to two pages or fewer

DON'T

- Lie about or embellish your work experience, employment dates, and educational background
- Submit your resume without first reading it closely and having trusted friends also look it over
- Fold or staple your resume

"Experience" to replace the "Employment" section. That way you can list internships, class projects, independent study, and other applicable experiences.

- Show your stuff: Don't be modest when creating your resume, because other job candidates won't be. Be sure to include all important and relevant information on your resume, but try to do so in minimal space.
- Some employees may require more than just a resume, such as samples of your writing. Be prepared to provide these upon request.

WRITING A COVER LETTER

Always include a cover letter with your resume. As with your resume, the cover letter must be polished and tailored to the job for which you are applying. Address the cover letter to the individual in charge of hiring. If a name is not included in a job listing, call the company to inquire, or visit the company's website and check the staff listings. If you still can't find what you're looking for, addressing the letter to "Human Resources" should get it into the hands of the right person. The heading of the letter should include your

Resume Advice from Those Who Trash Them

Companies receive resumes by the handful. Make that piles. Or perhaps tons. Especially during times of slow economic growth, the number of resumes that come across a typical hiring manager's desk can be overwhelming. Fortunately for them (but not for the job seekers), there are many glaring errors that applicants commit that send their resume right into the trash bin. According to monster.com, here's a list of the top 10 resume mistakes from the recruiters and hiring managers who see them each and every workday.

1. Problem: Spelling errors, typos, and just plain bad writing.

   Fix: Read your resume over carefully, use spell check, and have friends and family members look it over for mistakes you might have missed.

2. Problem: Too many duties, not enough explanation.

   Fix: Instead of simply listing your previous job descriptions, describe your accomplishments. Employers don't need to know exactly what you did at your last job, but instead, they want to hear about the direct results of your efforts. For example, list any improvements you brought to your previous job or department.

3. Problem: Employment dates are wrong or missing completely.

   Fix: Include time ranges in months or years for all work positions. Explain any gaps in your work history in your cover letter. Employers need dates to verify your experience and gain a sense of your overall work history.

4. Problem: You don't seem to know your name and address.

   Fix: Double-check your contact information each and every time you update your resume. The whole point of the resume is to get a phone call asking for an interview. Employers will not look you up to contact you.

5. Problem: Converted or scanned resume shows formatting errors.

   Fix: If you are emailing your resume, make sure it is saved and sent in plain text (ASCII) format. Even if you send your resume by fax or mail, use plain text because some employers scan resumes for easy browsing. Fancy fonts, boxes, or colors are unnecessary on a professional resume and will only cause problems.

(continues)

Resume Advice from Those Who Trash Them

(continued)

6. Problem: Organized your resume by function.

   Fix: Most employers prefer a chronological resume, where work and school experience is listed by date, over a functional one, where experience is listed by skills or functions performed. Month- or even year-long gaps in employment (which becomes obvious in chronological resumes) are more common now than in previous years and can be filled with volunteer work or continued education.

7. Problem: Too long.

   Fix: Highlight only your work and educational experience that is most prevalent to the job at hand. Recruiters simply don't have the time to read through long resumes.

8. Problem: Too wordy.

   Fix: Similar to #7, pare down your work, school, and other descriptions to include just the most important highlights.

9. Problem: Unqualified.

   Fix: Apply only to jobs for which you are qualified. You're not only wasting the employer's time, you're wasting your own when you apply for positions that require higher degrees or more work experience than you have.

10. Problem: Too personal.

    Fix: Include your fondness for stamp collecting if you are applying to work in the post office. Otherwise, leave it off your resume. In other words, list only information that's pertinent to the employer and the open position. Listed activities and interests should be included only if they are related to the job.

name, address, and phone number, as well as the same for the person to whom you're sending it.

Your cover letter should also be concise. The body of the letter should contain three short paragraphs, as follows:

- The first paragraph should mention the position for which you are applying and where you saw the job listing.

Employers like to keep track of how and where their applicants learn about positions. For example, a good first paragraph might simply state, "I am applying for the position of Advertising Assistant, which I saw advertised in *The Daily Bugle* on 22 March 2004." If a friend or associate recommended you for the job, you can mention that here, but only if that person gives you permission to do so.

- In the second paragraph, state briefly why the job interests you and why you will be a valuable addition to the company. Do not restate the contents of your resume here: simply touch on one or two of your strongest skills and what you can bring to the position. Most importantly, write with confidence. Avoid phrases like "I think I would be . . ." or "I feel that I. . . ." Rather, state simply, "I will be . . ." and "I am . . . ." Clear and definitive language, as opposed to cluttered equivocation, is more likely to grab the attention of the person reading your cover letter and resume.
- In the third paragraph, encourage the employer to review your resume and provide any additional information that may have been requested in the job listing, such as salary requirements, ability to travel or relocate, etc. Here you can also state that you will follow up on your resume submission, but do this only if you honestly plan to do so by phone or letter. Do not include such a statement if the job listing states that only suitable candidates will be contacted. This is the employer's way of saying, "Don't call us, we'll call you."

If you are applying for a position in academia, you will need to prepare a cover letter that is slightly different than the traditional business cover letter. Visit Academic Cover Letters (http://owl.english.purdue.edu/handouts/pw/p_covseek.html) for more information on creating this type of cover letter.

In addition, hundreds of books and other resources are available for resume assistance, many of which include examples of resumes that work. The following are a few sites to explore for more information:

For more information on resumes and cover letters, visit the following websites:

Career-Resumes
http://www.career-resumes.com

CollegeGrad.com
http://www.collegegrad.com/resumes

JobStar: Resumes & Cover Letters
http://jobstar.org/tools/resume

JobWeb Guide to Resumes and Interviews
http://www.jobweb.com/Resumes_Interviews

Monster.com: Writing Cover Letters
http://content.monster.com/resume/samples/coverletters

Resume.com
http://www.resume.com

The Resume Place, Inc.
http://www.resume-place.com

APPLYING FOR JOBS ONLINE: SERIOUS INTERNET SURFING

The Internet has added a whole new dimension to the job search—it is full of job postings and job advice, and getting your resume to employers is now less time-consuming. Thanks to the World Wide Web, you can apply for jobs while in your pajamas at 3:00 A.M. without having to leave your house. While some employers still prefer to receive resumes through the mail, many now prefer or require that applicants submit resumes via email. Here's a checklist to follow when applying online.

- If submitting your resume online, save it as "Text Only" to convert it into ASCII format. This is the only way to guarantee that the recipient of your resume will read it in the manner and format in which you intended. Fonts and automatic formatting that you may have used in a word processing program may not be converted correctly when the resume reaches the desk of an employer. Sending your resume in text-only format also ensures that employers receive your information free from possible attachment viruses. Only send your resume as another type of attachment, such as Microsoft Word, if the ad explicitly states that you should do so.
- Once you save your resume as text, clean up the body of the email, watching out for new line and section breaks. If you used bullets, use asterisks (*) instead. If you used formatted section breaks, use dashes (—-) to separate sections.

- When you prepare your email to send to the employer, write your cover letter in the body of the email, then attach the text-only version of your resume. When the employer reads your email, your resume will actually be viewed in the body of the email instead of as a separate attachment.
- Make sure this text-only resume is as clean and error-free as your original. As one recruiter on the monster.com website puts it, "Do you know what we call people who submit electronic resumes with typos? We call them unemployed."
- Be sure to mention the name of the position, any job codes that may have been mentioned in the ad, and the words resume and cover letter in the Subject line of the email. The latter is just in case the employer automatically looks for an attachment and overlooks your cover letter in the body of the email.

Some employers enable you to apply for jobs directly from their company websites. If this is the case, follow the directions on the site very closely, and have your cover letter and resume in plain-text format at the ready.

THE PRESCRIPTION FOR A PERFECT INTERVIEW

Once you have sent out your resumes you can gear up for the interview process. Once you have been contacted for an interview, the first step is to perform some research about the company. Learn as much as you can through websites, magazine articles, and other sources. The interviewer may say, "So tell me what you know about our company," and a deer-caught-in-the-headlights stare is probably not a good answer. Here are some other tips to help you ace interviews:

- Be on time. Being late for the interview makes a very bad (and perhaps irrevocable) impression on the potential employer. If an emergency arises and you can't possibly get to the interview on time, be sure to call the employer and explain the situation. Don't just stroll in 15 minutes late and expect the employer to sympathize with you. If you are unfamiliar with the location of the interview, you may find it helpful to drive or walk to the site beforehand so that you're not lost and nervous on the big day.

- Dress for the part. Always wear a conservative business suit to interviews, and make sure your suit is clean and wrinkle free. Even if you feel overdressed once you get there, it is better that the employer remembers you as professional (and not as the one who didn't care enough to dress up).
- Come prepared. Bring several copies of your resume in case you are interviewed by more than one person. Also, bring two pens and a pad of paper to take notes. When you walk out of the interview, you won't remember everything that was covered, so notes will be helpful for future reference. It is also a good idea to bring contact information for several people (your former employers, teachers, friends, etc.) in case the employer asks for personal references.
- Ask lots of questions. Have at least five sample questions ready when you walk into the interview, and think of more as it proceeds. Ask questions about the specific job as well as about the company and the industry. Don't ask about salary on the first interview unless the interviewer brings it up first, but have a number in mind in case you are asked to suggest a range.
- Respond confidently. It's okay to pause for a minute and think after a question is asked, but make sure you respond in a fairly timely manner and in such a way that shows you are sure of yourself. Sit up straight and use intelligent, well-constructed sentences at an interview, so the employer can tell that you mean business.
- Sell yourself. Have a polite, upbeat, and enthusiastic demeanor throughout the entire interview. There may be hundreds of other qualified candidates applying for the position, but if an employer likes your personality and thinks that you would make a good fit, that may push you ahead of the others.
- Be ready to write/test. For many editing, writing, and marketing positions, you may be required to take a writing or editing test. These tests vary in length and depth, and you may be asked to complete one or more as part of your first interview or at a subsequent interview. In addition, some companies administer basic tests of computer programs, such as Microsoft Excel, at interviews.

- Be grateful. When the interview is over, don't forget to say thank you and let the employer know how much you appreciate the time you were given. Finally, follow up with a thank-you note after every interview.

A NEW BREED OF INTERVIEW: THE SITUATIONAL INTERVIEW

When most people think of a job interview, an image comes to mind of a question-and-answer session between a job seeker and a hiring manager. However, a new trend in applicant evaluation has emerged. Some employers, even those at small design firms or local museums, are now looking at an individual's ethics as much as his or her education and job experience. Employers want to hire good people as much as they want to hire skilled people.

In these situational, or behavioral, interviews, applicants are put through real-life job situations (such as being verbally harassed by an upset museum visitor) and then are analyzed based on their gut instincts, actions, words, and even body language. According to the *Handbook of Industrial and Organizational Psychology,* while the traditional sit-down interview is reported to be approximately 7 percent effective in predicting job performance, the situational interview is approximately 54 percent accurate.

The bad news for job seekers is that, unlike standard interviews, these character evaluations are tough to prepare for. The only thing to do is be yourself, think before you speak and act, and hope your responses reflect your years of education and training.

The following are some online resources for interviewing tips and techniques:

Ask the Interview Coach
http://www.asktheinterviewcoach.com

Collegegrad.com: Interviewing Information
http://www.collegegrad.com/intv

Job-interview.net
http://www.job-interview.net

Monster Interview Center
http://interview.monster.com

YOU HAVE THE JOB . . . NOW WHAT?

Once you've found that first job, it will take some time to settle in and learn the ropes. Employers will not expect you to know everything on your first day, so don't be too overwhelmed. Remind yourself that your employer believes in your abilities, otherwise you wouldn't have been hired.

Soon enough, you will gain confidence, and advancement will become one of your top priorities. There are two main ways to advance: by moving laterally to a similar job (with better pay) within your company or at another company, and by moving vertically to a more authoritative, higher paying position.

THE GRADUATE FACTOR

Depending on the type of job you hope to get, more schooling may be required in your future. For some positions, employers may not even consider applicants who have only a bachelor's degree. Graduate school is not for everyone, but it may be something to think about if you're seeking a very advanced position.

If you are considering graduate school, ask yourself the following questions:

- Why am I interested in grad school? Not knowing know what to do with your life or waiting out a weak job market are not good reasons to invest your time and money in grad school. Grad school is an excellent option if you are committed to learning more about economics or another field and are interested in increasing your marketability.
- What type of career do I want to pursue? While your undergraduate economics degree will help you land many jobs, you will need an advanced degree for some economics-related careers. For example, if you want to teach economics (or another discipline) at the college level, you will need to earn at least a master's degree and preferably a Ph.D. in your chosen field. Other careers that require an advanced degree include economist, judge, lawyer, and political scientist.
- What is the academic quality of the program? Finding the right academic fit is very important when choosing a grad school. To learn more about a program, ask yourself the following questions: What is the reputation of the economics department? What are the interests/qualifications of the faculty? Do their interests match my interests? Does the department have a good reputation for developing mentoring relationships with students?

- How much will it cost? Graduate school is expensive, and if financing is an issue, you need to consider how you will pay back loans and other financial aid after you graduate. Ask yourself, how much does the graduate program cost? How will I fund my graduate education? What are average salary ranges for workers in the field who have graduate degrees? Considering these factors, will I make enough money post-graduation to make it worthwhile to pursue a graduate degree?
- Will I get into the program? Graduate programs are selective, and with grad school application fees averaging $50, applying to too many schools can put a significant dent in your savings. It is better to approach these applications realistically and narrow your choices to a maximum of five graduate programs. Choose two top-rated schools, two mid-range schools, and one school that is further down the rankings. Of course, you also need to factor the academic quality, location, type of college, and other selection criteria into your final choice.
- What is the current and future state of my discipline's job market? If the field you are interested in is glutted with people holding master's degrees or Ph.D.'s, then you might want

Ph.D. Program Rankings from a Different Perspective

You may be familiar with the annual rankings of college programs by *U.S. News & World Report* and other magazines, but you can also learn about Ph.D. programs from the 2000 National Doctoral Program Survey, which is conducted by the National Association of Graduate-Professional Students. Over 32,000 graduate students and recent Ph.D.'s were asked to grade their own doctorate programs. Visitors to http://survey.nagps.org can study report cards for more than 1,300 doctorate programs. You can search and prepare a report for programs using the following criterion: overall recommended practices, information for prospective students, preparation for a broad range of careers, teaching and TA preparation, professional development, career guidance and placement services, controlling time to degree, mentoring, program climate, and overall satisfaction.

to consider studying another field or specializing your graduate education in some way to become a job candidate with a more unique skill set.

If you are really serious about graduate school, take the Graduate Record Examination. This exam is composed of verbal, quantitative, and analytical writing sections on various subjects. Your score on this exam is one of the determining factors as to whether you'll be admitted to graduate school (it is required by most schools). Visit http://www.gre.org to learn more.

For more information on graduate schools, visit the following websites:

Graduate School Directory of Liberal Arts Studies: Gradschools.com
http://www.gradschools.com/listings/menus/liberal_menu.html

Graduate School Guide
http://www.graduateguide.com

The National Association of Graduate and Professional Students
http://www.nagps.org

Peterson's Graduate Schools and Programs
http://www.petersons.com/GradChannel

INTERVIEW: Kishore Gawande

Kishore Gawande teaches at the George Bush School of Government and Public Service at Texas A&M University. His emphasis is in international economics. He shared his experience and advice with the editors of Top Careers for Economics Graduates.

Q. What career options are available to economics majors?

A. An economics major will prepare students for all kinds of jobs requiring an analytical mind. Marketing (sales, advertising, new products), finance, accounting, and banking are a few options. Economics is also a good major for jobs involving numbers and statistics. Government agencies at the federal and state level, such as the Federal Reserve, hire economics majors.

Q. What personal qualities do economics majors need to be successful in their studies?

A. Economics majors need to be able to communicate key points about a topic clearly and have analytical skills, both quantitative and qualitative. Students should also be able to think innovatively and outside the box.

Q. What are your academic expectations for students who enter your program?

A. I teach public policy at the graduate level, so knowledge of basic micro- and macroeconomics is expected. Most students start out semi-prepared, but may not expect the amounts of policy-oriented work that is involved.

Q. What advice would you give new economics graduates?

A. I emphasize the importance of analytical skills and the ability to adapt to a broad range of problems that might develop within the workplace, especially as the nature of their work changes.

One thing recent graduates must be prepared for is working in the trenches. New workers should welcome these starting-level jobs because they provide a firm foundation for their future. I also advise that students get as much technical experience and know-how while pursuing their undergrad to prepare them for later education and work demands.

SECTION II

CAREERS

ACCOUNTANTS AND AUDITORS

QUICK FACTS

School Subjects Business Economics **Personal Skills** Following instructions Leadership/management **Work Environment** Primarily indoors One location with some travel **Minimum Education Level** Bachelor's degree **Salary Range** $29,280 to $59,500 to $100,000+	**Certification or Licensing** Recommended **Outlook** About as fast as the average **DOT** 160 **GOE** 11.06.01 **NOC** 1111 **O*NET-SOC** 13-2011.00, 13-2011.01, 13-2011.02

OVERVIEW

Accountants compile, analyze, verify, and prepare financial records including profit and loss statements, balance sheets, cost studies, and tax reports. Accountants may specialize in areas such as auditing, tax work, cost accounting, budgeting and control, or systems and procedures. Accountants also may specialize in a particular business or field; for example, *agricultural accountants* specialize in drawing up and analyzing financial statements for farmers and for farm equipment companies. *Auditors* examine and verify financial records to ensure that they are accurate, complete, and in compliance with federal laws. There are approximately 976,000 accountants and auditors employed in the United States.

HISTORY

The accounting profession in the United States dates back to 1880, when English and Scottish investors began buying stock in American companies. To keep an eye on their investments, they sent over accountants who realized the great potential that existed in the accounting field and stayed on to establish their own businesses.

Federal legislation, such as the income tax in 1913 and the excess profits tax in 1917, helped cause an accounting boom that has made the profession instrumental to all business.

Accountants have long been considered "bean counters," and their work has been written off by outsiders as routine and boring. However, their image, which was once associated with death, taxes, and bad news, is making a turnaround. Accountants now do much more than prepare financial statements and record business transactions. Technology now counts the "beans," allowing accountants to analyze and interpret the results. Their work has expanded to encompass challenging and creative tasks such as computing costs and efficiency gains of new technologies, participating in strategies for mergers and acquisitions, supervising quality management, and designing and using information systems to track financial performance.

THE JOB

Accountants' duties depend on the size and nature of the company in which they are employed. The major fields of employment are public, private, and government accounting.

Public accountants work independently on a fee basis or as members of an accounting firm, and they perform a variety of tasks for businesses or individuals. These may include auditing accounts and records, preparing and certifying financial statements, conducting financial investigations and furnishing testimony in legal matters, and assisting in formulating budget policies and procedures.

Private accountants, sometimes called *industrial* or *management accountants,* handle the financial records of the firms at which they are employed.

Government accountants work on the financial records of government agencies or, when necessary, they audit the records of private companies. In the federal government, many accountants are employed as *bank examiners, Internal Revenue Service agents,* and *investigators,* as well as in regular accounting positions.

Within these fields, accountants can specialize in a variety of areas.

General accountants supervise, install, and devise general accounting, budget, and cost systems. They maintain records, balance books, and prepare and analyze statements on all financial aspects of business. Administrative officers use this information to make sound business decisions.

Budget accountants review expenditures of departments within a firm to make sure expenses allotted are not exceeded. They also aid in drafting budgets and may devise and install budget control systems.

Cost accountants determine unit costs of products or services by analyzing records and depreciation data. They classify and record all operating costs so that management can control expenditures.

Property accountants keep records of equipment, buildings, and other property owned or leased by a company. They prepare mortgage schedules and payments as well as appreciation or depreciation statements, which are used for income tax purposes.

Environmental accountants help utilities, manufacturers, and chemical companies set up preventive systems to ensure environmental compliance and provide assistance in the event that legal issues arise.

Systems accountants design and set up special accounting systems for organizations whose needs cannot be handled by standardized procedures. This may involve installing automated or computerized accounting processes and includes instructing personnel in the new methods.

Forensic accountants and auditors use accounting principles and theories to support or oppose claims being made in litigation.

Tax accountants prepare federal, state, or local tax returns of an individual, business, or corporation according to prescribed rates, laws, and regulations. They also may conduct research on the effects of taxes on firm operations and recommend changes to reduce taxes. This is one of the most intricate fields of accounting, and many accountants therefore specialize in one particular phase such as corporate, individual income, or property tax.

Assurance accountants help improve the quality of information for clients in assurance services areas such as electronic commerce, risk assessment, and elder care. This information may be financial or nonfinancial in nature.

Auditors ensure that financial records are accurate, complete, and in compliance with federal laws. To do so they review items in original entry books, including purchase orders, tax returns, billing statements, and other important documents. Auditors may also prepare financial statements for clients and suggest ways to improve productivity and profits. *Internal auditors* conduct the same kind of examination and evaluation for one particular company. Because they are salaried employees of that company, a qualified independent auditor must certify their financial audits. Internal auditors also review procedures and controls, appraise the efficiency and effectiveness of operations, and make sure their companies comply with corporate policies and government regulations.

Tax auditors review financial records and other information provided by taxpayers to determine the appropriate tax liability. State and federal tax auditors usually work in government offices, but they may perform a field audit in a taxpayer's home or office.

Revenue agents are employed by the federal government to examine selected income tax returns and, when necessary, conduct field audits and investigations to verify the information reported and adjust the tax liability accordingly.

Chief bank examiners enforce good banking practices throughout a state. They schedule bank examinations to ensure that financial institutions comply with state laws and, in certain cases, they take steps to protect a bank's solvency (or ability to pay debts) and the interests of its depositors and shareholders.

REQUIREMENTS

High School

If you are interested in an accounting career, you must be very proficient in arithmetic and basic algebra. Familiarity with computers and their applications is equally important. Course work in English will also help you develop critical business communication skills.

Postsecondary Training

Postsecondary training in accounting is available through many institutions, such as private business schools, junior colleges, universities, and correspondence schools. A bachelor's degree with a major in accounting, or a related field such as economics, is highly recommended by professional associations for those entering the field and is required by all states before taking the licensing exam. It is possible, however, to become a successful accountant by completing a program at any of the above-mentioned institutions. A four-year college curriculum usually includes about two years of liberal arts courses, a year of general business subjects, and a year of specific accounting work. Better positions, particularly in public accounting, require a bachelor's degree with a major in accounting. Large public accounting firms often prefer people with a master's degree in accounting. For beginning positions in accounting, the federal government requires four years of college (including 24 semester hours in accounting or auditing) or an equivalent combination of education and experience.

Certification or Licensing

Certified public accountants (*CPA*s) must pass a qualifying examination and hold a certificate issued by the state in which they wish to practice. In most states, a college degree is required for admission to the CPA examinations; a few states allow candidates to substitute years of public accounting experience for the college degree requirement. Currently 43 states and jurisdictions require CPA candidates to have 150 hours of education, which is an additional 30 hours beyond the standard bachelor's degree. Five additional states plan to enact the 150-hour requirement in the future. This can be met by combining an undergraduate accounting program with graduate study or participating in an integrated five-year professional accounting program. You can obtain information from a state board of accountancy or check out the website of the American Institute of Certified Public Accountants (http://www.aicpa.org) to read about new regulations and review last year's exam.

The Uniform CPA Examination administered by the AICPA is used by all states. Nearly all states require at least two years of public accounting experience or its equivalent before a CPA certificate can be earned.

Some accountants seek out other credentials. Those who have earned a bachelor's degree, pass a four-part examination, agree to meet continuing education requirements, and have at least two years of experience in management accounting may become a certified management accountant (CMA) through the Institute of Management Accounting.

The Accreditation Council for Accountancy and Taxation confers the following three designations: accredited business accountant or accredited business advisor (ABA), accredited tax preparer (ATP), and accredited tax advisor (ATA).

To become a Certified Internal Auditor (CIA), college graduates with two years of experience in internal auditing must pass a four-part examination given by the Institute of Internal Auditors

(IIA). The IIA also offers the following specialty certifications: Certified Financial Services Auditor and Certified Government Auditing Professional. Visit the IIA website for more information (http://www.theiia.org).

The designation certified information systems auditor (CISA) is conferred by the Information Systems Audit and Control Association to candidates who pass an examination and who have five years of experience auditing electronic data processing systems. Other organizations, such as the Bank Administration Institute, confer specialized auditing designations.

Other Requirements

To be a successful accountant you will need strong mathematical, analytical, and problem-solving skills. You need to be able to think logically and to interpret facts and figures accurately. Effective oral and written communication are also essential in working with both clients and management.

Other important skills are attentiveness to detail, patience, and industriousness. Business acumen and the ability to generate clientele are crucial to service-oriented business, as are honesty, dedication, and a respect for the work of others.

EXPLORING

If you think a career as an accountant or auditor might be for you, try working in a retail business, either part time or during the summer. Working at the cash register or even pricing products as a stockperson is good introductory experience. You should also consider working as a treasurer for a student organization requiring financial planning and money management. It may be possible to gain some experience by volunteering with local groups such as churches and small businesses. You should also stay abreast of news in the field by reading trade magazines and checking out the industry websites of the AICPA and other accounting associations. The AICPA has numerous free educational publications available.

EMPLOYERS

Nearly 1 million people are employed as accountants and auditors. Accountants and auditors work throughout private industry and government. About one quarter work for accounting, auditing, and bookkeeping firms. Approximately 10 percent are self-employed. Nearly 40 percent of all accountants and auditors are certified.

STARTING OUT

Junior public accountants usually start in jobs with routine duties such as counting cash, verifying calculations, and other detailed numerical work. In private accounting, beginners are likely to start as cost accountants and junior internal auditors. They may also enter in clerical positions as cost clerks, ledger clerks, and timekeepers or as trainees in technical or junior executive positions. In the federal government, most beginners are hired as trainees at the GS-5 level after passing the civil service exam.

Some state CPA societies arrange internships for accounting majors, and some offer scholarships and loan programs.

You might also visit the Landing a Job section of the AICPA website, which has detailed information on accounting careers, hiring trends, job search strategies, resumes and cover letters, and job interviews. The section also has a list of internship opportunities for students.

ADVANCEMENT

Talented accountants and auditors can advance quickly. Junior public accountants usually advance to senior positions within several years and to managerial positions soon after. Those successful in dealing with top-level management may eventually become supervisors, managers, and partners in larger firms or go into independent practice. However, only 2–3 percent of new hires advance to audit manager, tax manager, or partner.

Private accountants in firms may become audit managers, tax managers, cost accounting managers, or controllers, depending on their specialty. Some become controllers, treasurers, or corporation presidents. Others on the finance side may rise to become managers of financial planning and analysis or treasurers.

Federal government trainees are usually promoted within a year or two. Advancement to controller and to higher administrative positions is ultimately possible.

Although advancement may be rapid for skilled accountants, especially in public accounting, those with inadequate academic or professional training are often assigned to routine jobs and find it difficult to obtain promotions. All accountants find it necessary to continue their study of accounting and related areas in their spare time. Even those who have already obtained college degrees, gained experience, and earned a CPA certificate may spend many hours studying to keep up with new industry developments. Thousands of practicing accountants enroll in formal courses offered by universities and professional associations to specialize in certain areas of accounting, broaden or update their professional skills, and become eligible for advancement and promotion.

EARNINGS

Beginning salaries for accountants with a bachelor's degree averaged $40,546 a year in 2003; those with a master's degree averaged $42,533 a year, according to the National Association of Colleges and Employers. Auditors with up to one year of experience earned between $29,250 and $40,250, according to a 2001 survey by Robert Half International. Some experienced auditors may earn between $59,500 and $106,500, depending on such factors as their education level, the size of the firm, and the firm's location.

Public and private accountants follow similar salary increases, and generally the larger the firm or corporation, the higher the salary. In public accounting, low mid-level salaries range from $28,200 to $32,000, according to the U.S. Department of Labor, and upper mid-level salaries range from $30,000 in small towns to $75,000 in the largest cities with higher rates from the Big Four firms. Partners earn upwards of $100,000. Mid-level corporate accountants earn from $30,000 to $65,000, and managers bring in $40,000–$80,000. Controllers earn an average of $85,100, and chief financial officers' salaries can exceed $142,900.

Government accountants and auditors make substantially less, though they do receive more benefits. According to the U.S. Department of Labor in 2001, beginning salaries for accountants and auditors were approximately $29,280. Employees with master's degrees or two years of professional experience may begin at $33,254. In 2000, the average annual salary for accountants and auditors employed by the federal government in nonsupervisory, supervisory, and managerial positions was $44,380. Accountants in large firms and with large corporations receive typical benefits including paid vacation and sick days, insurance, and savings and pension plans. Employees in smaller companies generally receive fewer fringe benefits.

WORK ENVIRONMENT

Accounting is known as a desk job, and a 40-hour workweek can be expected in public and private accounting. Although computer work is replacing paperwork, the job can be routine and monotonous, and concentration and attention to detail are critical. Public accountants experience considerable pressure during the tax period, which runs from November to April, and they may have to work long hours. There is potential for stress aside from tax season, as accountants can be responsible for managing multimillion-dollar finances with no margin for error. Self-employed accountants and those working for a small firm can expect to work longer hours; 40 percent work more than 50 hours per week, compared to 20 percent of public and private accountants.

In smaller firms, most of the public accountant's work is performed in the client's office. A considerable amount of travel is often necessary to service a wide variety of businesses. In a larger firm, however, an accountant may have very little client contact, spending more time interacting with the accounting team.

OUTLOOK

In the wake of the massive changes that swept through the industry in the last decade, the job outlook for accountants and auditors is good, with employment expected to grow about as fast as the average through the next decade, according to the U.S. Department of Labor.

Several factors will contribute to the expansion of the accounting industry: increasingly complex taxation, growth in both the size and the number of business corporations required to release financial reports to stockholders, a more general use of accounting in the management of business, and outsourcing of accounting services by small business firms.

As firms specialize their services, accountants will need to follow suit. Firms will seek out accountants with experience in marketing and proficiency in computer systems to build management consulting practices. As trade increases, so will the demand for CPAs with international specialties and foreign language skills. And CPAs with an engineering degree would be well equipped to specialize in environmental accounting. Other accounting specialties that will enjoy good prospects include assurance, forensic, and tax accounting.

While the majority of jobs will be found in large cities with large businesses, smaller firms will start up, and smaller business will continue to seek outside accountants. Accountants without college degrees will find more paraprofessional accounting positions, similar to the work of paralegals, as the number of lower and mid-level workers expands. Demand will also be high for specialized accounting temps; CPA firms have started to hire temps to smooth out their staffing through seasonal business cycles.

The role of public accountants will change as they perform less auditing and tax work and assume greater management and consulting responsibilities. Likewise, private accountants will focus more on analyzing operations rather than simply providing data and will develop sophisticated accounting systems.

Accounting jobs are more secure than most during economic downswings. Despite fluctuations in the nation's economy, there will always be a need to manage financial information, especially as the number, size, and complexity of business transactions increases. However, competition for jobs will remain, certification requirements will become more rigorous, and accountants and auditors with the highest degrees will be the most competitive.

FOR MORE INFORMATION

For information on accreditation and testing, contact

Accreditation Council for Accountancy and Taxation
1010 North Fairfax Street
Alexandria, VA 22314-1574
Tel: 888-289-7763
Email: info@acatcredentials.org
http://www.acatcredentials.org

For information on the Uniform CPA Examination and student membership, contact

American Institute of Certified Public Accountants
1211 Avenue of the Americas
New York, NY 10036-8775
Tel: 212-596-6200
http://www.aicpa.org

For information on accredited programs in accounting, contact

Association to Advance Collegiate Schools of Business
600 Emerson Road, Suite 300
St. Louis, MO 63141-6762
Tel: 314-872-8481
http://www.aacsb.edu

For information on certification for bank auditors, contact

Bank Administration Institute
One North Franklin, Suite 1000
Chicago, IL 60606-3421

Email: info@bai.org
http://www.bai.org

For more information on women in accounting, contact

Educational Foundation for Women in Accounting
PO Box 1925
Southeastern, PA 19399-1925
Tel: 610-407-9229
Email: info@efwa.org
http://www.efwa.org

For information on certification, contact

Information Systems Audit and Control Association and Foundation
3701 Algonquin Road, Suite 1010
Rolling Meadows, IL 60008
Tel: 847-253-1545
Email: certification@isaca.org
http://www.isaca.org

For information on internal auditing and certification, contact

Institute of Internal Auditors
247 Maitland Avenue
Altamonte Springs, FL 32701-4201
Tel: 407-937-1100
Email: iia@theiia.org
http://www.theiia.org

For information about management accounting and the CMA designation, as well as student membership, contact

Institute of Management Accountants
10 Paragon Drive
Montvale, NJ 07645-1718
Tel: 800-638-4427
Email: ima@imanet.org
http://www.imanet.org

ACTUARIES

QUICK FACTS

School Subjects	Certification or Licensing
Business Mathematics	Required
Personal Skills Following instructions Leadership/management	**Outlook** More slowly than the average
Work Environment Primarily indoors One location with some travel	**DOT** 020
Minimum Education Level Bachelor's degree	**GOE** 11.01.02
Salary Range $38,810 to $68,120 to $132,630+	**NOC** 2161 **O*NET-SOC** 15-2011.00

OVERVIEW

Actuaries use statistical formulas and techniques to calculate the probability of events such as death, disability, sickness, unemployment, retirement, and property loss. Actuaries develop formulas to predict how much money an insurance company will pay in claims, which determines the overall cost of insuring a group, business, or individual. Increase in risk raises potential cost to the company, which in turn raises its rates. Actuaries analyze risk to estimate the number and amount of claims an insurance company will have to pay. They assess the cost of running the business and incorporate the results into the design and evaluation of programs.

Casualty actuaries specialize in property and liability insurance, *life actuaries* in health and life insurance. In recent years, there has been an increase in the number of actuaries—called *pension actuaries*—who deal only with pension plans. The total number of actuaries employed in the United States is approximately 14,000.

HISTORY

The term actuary was used for the first time in 1762 in the charter for the Equitable Society of London, which was the first life insurance company to use scientific data in figuring premiums. The basis of actuarial work was laid in the early 17th century when Frenchmen Blaise Pascal and Pierre de Fermat derived an important method of calculating actuarial probabilities, resulting in what is now termed the science of probability.

The first mortality table was produced in the late 17th century, when Edmund Halley noticed the regularity of various social phenomena, including the excess of male over female births. Halley, an English astronomer for whom Halley's comet is named, is known as the father of life insurance. As more complex forms of insurance were developed in the 19th century, the need for actuaries grew.

In 1889, a small group of qualified actuaries formed the Actuarial Society of America. Two classes of members, fellows and associates, were created seven years later, and special examinations were developed to determine membership eligibility. Forms of these examinations are still used today. By 1909 the American Institute of Actuaries was created, and in 1949 these two groups consolidated into the present Society of Actuaries.

In 1911, the Casualty Actuary Society was formed in response to the development of workers' compensation laws. The compensation laws opened up many new fields of insurance, and the Casualty Actuarial Society has since moved into all aspects of property and liability insurance.

OASDI (Old Age, Survivors, and Disability Insurance), now known as Social Security, was created in 1935 and expanded the work of pension actuaries. The creation of this program greatly impacted the development, philosophy, and structure of private pension programs. The American Society of Pension Actuaries was formed in 1966; its members provide services to over 30 percent of the qualified retirement plans in the United States.

The first actuaries were concerned primarily with statistical, mathematical, and financial calculations needed in the rapidly growing field. Today they deal with problems of investment, selection of risk factors for insurance, agents' compensation, social insurance, taxation, development of policy forms, and many other aspects of insurance. Once considered mathematicians, actuaries are now referred to as "financial architects" and "social mathematicians" because they use their unique combination of numerical, analytical, and business skills to solve a variety of social and financial problems.

THE JOB

Should smokers pay more for their health insurance? Should younger drivers pay higher car insurance premiums? Actuaries answer questions like these to ensure that insurance and pension organizations can pay their claims and maintain a profitable business.

Using their knowledge of mathematics, probability, statistics, and principles of finance and business, actuaries determine premium rates and the various benefits of insurance plans. To accomplish this task, they first assemble and analyze statistics on birth, death, marriage, parenthood, employment, and other pertinent facts and figures. Based on this information, they are able to develop mathematical models of rates of death, accident, sickness, disability, or retirement and then construct tables regarding the probability of such things as property loss from fire, theft, accident, or natural disaster. After calculating all probabilities and the resulting costs to the company, the actuaries can determine the premium rates to allow insurance companies to cover predicted losses, turn a profit, and remain competitive with other businesses.

For example, based on analyses, actuaries are able to determine how many of each 1,000 people 21 years of age are expected to survive to age 65. They can calculate how many of them are expected to die this year or how many are expected to live until age 85. The probability that an insured person may die during the period before reaching 65 is a risk to the company. The actuaries must figure a price for the premium that will cover all claims and expenses as they occur and still earn a profit for the company assuming the risk. In the same way, actuaries calculate premium rates and determine policy provisions for every type of insurance coverage.

Employment opportunities span across the variety of different types of insurance companies, including life, health, accident, automobile, fire, or workers' compensation organizations. Most actuaries specialize either as casualty actuaries, dealing with property and liability insurance, or as life actuaries, working with life and health insurance. In addition, actuaries may concentrate on pension plan programs sponsored and administered by various levels of government, private business, or fraternal or benevolent associations.

Actuaries work in many departments in insurance companies, including underwriting, group insurance, investment, pension,

Questions and Answers about U.S. Bills

Q. How long do bills stay in circulation?

A. The amount of time a bill circulates depends on its denomination.
$1: 22 months
$5: 2 years
$10: 3 years
$20: 4 years
$50: 9 years
$100: 9 years

Q. How many bills are produced a day?

A. The Bureau of Engraving and Printing, an agency under the U.S. Treasury Department, produces 37 million notes a day, a total face value of approximately $696 million. Almost half of all notes produced are $1 bills.

Q. Have bills always represented amounts of only a dollar or more?

A. During the Civil War, people hoarded coins that were made of precious metals for their value. To battle the coin shortage, the U.S Treasury printed paper notes valuing 3 cents, 5 cents, 10 cents, 25 cents, and 50 cents.

Q. Does a $10 bill weigh more than a $1 bill?

A. All bank notes, regardless of their value, weigh one gram.

Q. What are bills made of?

A. All bank notes are 25 percent linen and 75 percent cotton. Red and blue synthetic fibers are woven into the bills. Before World War I, these fibers were made of real silk.

Source: The U.S. Treasury Bureau of Engraving and Printing http://www.moneyfactory.com

sales, and service. In addition to their own company's business, they analyze characteristics of the insurance business as a whole. They study general economic and social trends as well as legislative, health, and other developments, all of which may affect insurance practices. With this broad knowledge, some actuaries reach executive positions, where they can influence and help determine company policy and develop new lines of business. *Actuary executives* may communicate with government officials, company executives, policyholders, or the public to explain complex technical matters. They may testify before public agencies regarding proposed legislation that has a bearing on the insurance business, for example, or they may explain proposed changes in premium rates or contract provisions.

Actuaries may also work with a consulting firm, providing advice to clients including insurance companies, corporations, hospitals, labor unions, and government agencies. They develop employee benefits, calculating future benefits and employer contributions, and set up pension and welfare plans. *Consulting actuaries* also advise health care and financial services firms, and they may work with small insurance companies lacking an actuarial department.

Since the government regulates the insurance industry and administers laws on pensions, it also requires the services of actuaries to determine whether companies are complying with the law. A small number of actuaries are employed by the federal government and deal with Social Security, Medicare, disability and life insurance, and pension plans for veterans, members of the armed forces, and federal employees. Those in state governments may supervise and regulate insurance companies, oversee the operations of state retirement or pension systems, and manage problems related to unemployment insurance and workers' compensation.

REQUIREMENTS

High School

If you are interested in this field, you should pursue a traditional college preparatory curriculum including mathematical and computer science classes and also take advantage of advanced courses such as calculus. Introductory business, economics, accounting, and finance courses are important, as is English to develop your oral and written skills.

Postsecondary Training

A bachelor's degree with a major in mathematics or statistics is highly recommended for entry into the industry, and course work in elementary and advanced algebra, differential and integral calculus, descriptive and analytical statistics, principles of mathematical statistics, probability, and numerical analysis are all important. Computer science is also a vital part of actuarial training. Approximately 100 universities and colleges offer degrees in actuarial science. Employers, however, are increasingly hiring graduates with majors in economics, business, and engineering who have a strong math background. College students should broaden their education to include business, economics, and finance as well as English and communications. Because actuarial work revolves around social and political issues, course work in the humanities and social sciences will also prove useful.

Certification or Licensing

Full professional status in an actuarial specialty is based on completing a series of 10 examinations. Success is based on both formal and on-the-job training. Actuaries can become associate members of the Society of Actuaries after successfully completing seven of the 10 examinations for the life and health insurance, finance, and pension fields. Similarly, they can reach associate status in the Casualty Actuarial Society after successfully completing seven out of 10 exams in the property and liability field. Most actuaries achieve associateship in three to five years. Actuaries who successfully complete the entire series of exams for either organization are granted full membership and become fellows.

The American Society of Pension Actuaries also offers several different designations (both actuarial and nonactuarial) to individuals who pass the required examinations in the pension field and have the appropriate work experience.

Consulting pension actuaries who service private pension plans must be enrolled and licensed by the Joint Board for the Enrollment of Actuaries (http://www.irs.gov/taxpros/actuaries), a U.S. government agency. Only these actuaries can work with pension plans set up under the Employee Retirement Income Security Act. To be accepted, applicants must meet certain professional and educational requirements stipulated by the Joint Board.

Completion of the entire series of exams may take from five to 10 years. Because the first exams offered by these various boards and societies cover core material (such as calculus, linear algebra, probability and statistics, risk theory, and actuarial math), students generally wait to commit to a specialty until they have taken the initial tests. Students pursuing a career as an actuary should complete the first two or three preliminary examinations while still in college, since these tests cover subjects usually taught in school; the more advanced examinations cover aspects of the profession itself.

Employers prefer to hire individuals who have already passed the first two exams. Once employed, companies generally give employees time during the workday to study. They may also pay exam fees, provide study materials, and award raises upon an employee's successful completion of an exam.

Other Requirements

An aptitude in mathematics, statistics, and computer science is a must to become a successful actuary, as are sound analytical and problem-solving skills. Solid oral and written communication skills are also required in order to be able to explain and interpret complex work to the client.

Prospective actuaries should also have an inquisitive mind with an interest in historical, social, and political issues and trends. You should have a general feel for the business world and be able to assimilate a wide range of complex information in order to see the "big picture" when planning policies. Actuaries like to solve problems; they are strategists who enjoy and excel at games such as chess. Actuaries need to be motivated and self-disciplined to concentrate on detailed work, especially under stress, and to undertake the rigorous study for licensing examinations.

EXPLORING

If you think you are interested in the actuarial field, try pursuing extracurricular opportunities that allow you to practice strategic thinking and problem-solving skills; these may include chess, math, or investment clubs at your school. Other activities that foster leadership and management, such as student council positions, will also be beneficial. Any kind of business or research-oriented summer or part-time experience will be valuable, especially with an accounting or law firm.

There are more than 45 local actuarial clubs and regional affiliates throughout the United States that offer opportunities for informal discussion and networking. Talk with people in the field to better understand the nature of the work, and use the association's resources to learn more about the field. The Society of Actuaries offers free educational publications.

College undergraduates can take advantage of summer internships and employment in insurance companies and consulting firms. Students will have the chance to rotate among jobs to learn various actuarial operations and different phases of insurance work.

EMPLOYERS

There are approximately 14,000 actuaries employed in the United States. About 70 percent of this number are employed in the insurance industry. Other actuaries work for financial service-providing firms including commercial banks, investment banks, and retirement funds. Others are employed by actuarial consulting services and in academia. Some actuaries are self-employed.

STARTING OUT

The best way to enter this field is by taking the necessary beginning examinations while still in college. Once students have graduated and passed these exams, they are in a very good position to apply for entry-level jobs in the field and can command higher starting salaries. Some college students organize interviews and find jobs through their college placement office, while others interview with firms recruiting on campus. Many firms offer summer and year-round actuarial training programs or internships that may result in a full-time job.

Beginning actuaries may prepare calculations for actuarial tables or work with policy settlements or funds. With experience, they may prepare correspondence, reports, and research. Beginners who have already passed the preliminary exams often start with more responsibility and higher pay.

ADVANCEMENT

Advancement within the profession to assistant, associate, or chief actuary greatly depends on the individual's on-the-job performance, competence on the actuarial examinations, and leadership capabilities.

Some actuaries qualify for administrative positions in underwriting, accounting, or investment because of their broad business knowledge and specific insurance experience. Because their judgment is so valuable, actuaries may advance to administrative or executive positions, such as head of a department, vice-president or president of a company, manager of an insurance rating bureau, partner in a consulting firm, or, possibly, state insurance commissioner. Actuaries with management skills and a strong business background may move into other areas such as marketing, advertising, and planning.

EARNINGS

Starting salaries for actuaries with bachelor's degrees in actuarial science averaged $43,580 in Summer 2003, according to a survey conducted by the National Association of Colleges and Employers.

New college graduates who have not passed any actuarial examinations earn slightly less. Insurance companies and consulting firms offer merit increases or bonuses to those who pass examinations. According to a 2001 survey done by the Life Office Management Association, entry-level actuaries with the largest U.S. companies earned approximately $44,546. Associate actuaries with such companies earned approximately $91,000. Experienced actuaries in large companies earned approximately $109,000.

The U.S. Department of Labor reports that actuaries earned a median annual salary of $68,120 in 2001. Ten percent earned less than $38,180, while the top 10 percent earned more than $132,630. Actuaries receive paid vacations, health and life insurance, pension plans, and other fringe benefits.

WORK ENVIRONMENT

Actuaries spend much of their 40-hour workweek behind a desk poring over facts and figures, although some travel to various units of the organization or to other businesses. This is especially true of the consulting actuary, who will most likely work longer hours. Consulting actuaries tend to have more diverse work and more personal interaction in working with a variety of clients. Though the work can be stressful and demands intense concentration and attention to detail, actuaries find their jobs to be rewarding and satisfying and feel that they make a direct and positive impact on people's lives.

OUTLOOK

The U.S. Department of Labor predicts slower than average growth for the actuary field through the next decade. Growth of the insurance industry—traditionally the leading employer of actuaries—has slowed, and many firms are downsizing and even merging to reduce expenditures. Competition for entry-level jobs will remain stiff, as favorable publicity about the profession has drawn a large number of new workers.

Consulting actuaries should enjoy a stronger employment outlook than their counterparts in the insurance industry, as many large corporations increasingly rely on consultants to handle actuarial work that was formerly done in-house.

The insurance industry continues to evolve, and actuaries will be in demand to establish rates in several new areas of coverage, including prepaid legal, dental, and kidnapping insurance. In many cases, actuarial data that used to be supplied by state rating bureaus are now being developed in actuarial departments of private companies, which were affected by states' new competitive rating laws. Other new areas of insurance coverage that will involve actuaries include product and pollution liability insurance as well as greater workers' compensation and medical malpractice coverage. Insurers will call on actuaries to help them respond to new state and federal regulations while cutting costs, especially in the areas of pension reform and no-fault automobile insurance. In the future, actuaries will also be employed by noninsurance businesses or will work in business- and investment-related fields. Some are already working in banking and finance.

Actuaries will be needed to assess the financial impact of health problems such as AIDS and the changing health care system. As demographics change, people live and work longer, and as medicine advances, actuaries will need to reexamine the probabilities of death, sickness, and retirement.

Casualty actuaries will find more work as companies find themselves held responsible for product liability. In the wake of recent environmental disasters, there will also be a growing need to evaluate environmental risk.

As business goes global, it presents a whole new set of risks and problems as economies develop and new markets emerge. As private enterprise expands in the former Soviet Union, how does a company determine the risk of opening, say, a department store in Moscow?

Actuaries are no longer just mathematical experts. With their unique combination of analytical and business skills, their role is expanding as they become broad-based business professionals solving social as well as financial problems.

FOR MORE INFORMATION

For general information about actuary careers, contact

American Academy of Actuaries
1100 17th Street, NW, Seventh Floor
Washington, DC 20036
Tel: 202-223-8196
http://www.actuary.org

For information about continuing education and professional designations, contact

American Society of Pension Actuaries
4245 North Fairfax Drive, Suite 750
Arlington, VA 22203

Tel: 703-516-9300
Email: aspa@aspa.org
http://www.aspa.org

The Be An Actuary *section of the CAS website offers comprehensive information on the career of actuary.*

Casualty Actuarial Society (CAS)
1100 North Glebe Road, Suite 600
Arlington, VA 22201
Tel: 703-276-3100
Email: office@casact.org
http://www.casact.org

For information about continuing education and professional designations, contact

Society of Actuaries
475 North Martingale Road, Suite 600
Schaumburg, IL 60173
Tel: 847-706-3500
http://www.soa.org

ADVERTISING AND MARKETING MANAGERS

QUICK FACTS

School Subjects
Business
Computer science

Personal Skills
Helping/teaching
Leadership/management

Work Environment
Primarily indoors
One location with some travel

Minimum Education Level
Bachelor's degree

Salary Range
$29,210 to $55,940 to $125,880 (advertising managers)
$37,740 to $74,370 to $138,540 (marketing managers)

Certification or Licensing
None available

Outlook
Faster than the average

DOT
164

GOE
11.05.02, 11.09.01

NOC
0611

O*NET-SOC
11-2011.00, 11-2021.00

OVERVIEW

Advertising and marketing managers plan, organize, direct, and coordinate the operations of advertising and marketing firms. They may oversee an entire company, a geographical territory of a company's operations, or a specific department within a company. There are approximately 290,000 advertising and marketing managers employed in the United States.

HISTORY

The advertising industry formally emerged in the 1840s, when newspaper-advertising solicitors began representing groups of newspapers. In 1865, a new system was introduced: buying newspaper space and dividing and selling it to advertisers at higher prices. Other forms of advertising also came onto the scene. By the early 1900s, for example, outdoor posters developed into the billboard form, and the merchants who used them were the principal advertisers. In 1922, radio station WEAF in New York City offered program time to advertisers. The use of television advertising began just before the end of World War II. Today, the Internet is catapulting the world of advertising into a whole new realm, allowing vendors not only to target and reach customers but to interact with them as well.

The business discipline of marketing began to take shape as sellers realized that if a group of potential buyers could be found for a product, the product could be better designed to suit the needs of those buyers. Sellers also discovered the importance of identifying a group of buyers before starting an advertising campaign. By doing so, the producer could style the campaign to target that specific group, thereby increasing the chances of a product's success. Marketing, therefore, provided a service for both sellers and buyers.

As the need for advertising and marketing grew, companies specializing in product promotion and specialization were born. It is no surprise that the increasingly complex responsibilities involved in advertising and marketing products and services require managers to organize and run day-to-day office activities.

THE JOB

Advertising and marketing managers formulate policies and administer the advertising and marketing firm's operations. Managers may oversee the operations of an entire company, a geographical territory of a company's operations, or a specific department. Managers direct a company's or a department's daily activities within the context of the organization's overall plan. They implement organizational policies and goals. This may involve developing sales or promotional materials, analyzing the department's budgetary requirements, and hiring, training, and supervising staff. Advertising and marketing managers are often responsible for long-range planning for their company or department. This involves setting goals for the organization and developing a workable plan for meeting those goals.

Advertising and marketing managers work to coordinate their department's activities with other departments. If the firm is privately owned, the owner may be the manager. In a large corporation, however, there will be a management structure above the advertising and marketing manager.

In companies that have several different locations, advertising and marketing managers may be assigned to oversee specific geographic areas. For example, a large ad firm with facilities all across the nation is likely to have a number of managers in charge of various territories. There might be a Midwest manager, a Southwest manager, a Southeast manager, a Northeast manager, and a Northwest manager. These managers are often called *regional* or *area managers*. Some advertising and marketing firms break their management territories up into even smaller sections, such as a single state or a part of a state. Managers overseeing these smaller segments are often called *district managers,* and typically report directly to an area or regional manager.

Advertising managers are responsible for coordinating the work of researchers, copywriters, artists, telemarketers, space buyers, time buyers, other specialists. One type of advertising manager is the *account manager,* who represents the agency to its clients.

Managers working at large advertising agencies usually handle a variety of accounts, while those working at smaller agencies usually only handle certain types of clients. For example, smaller firms may handle only financial accounts, hotels, book publishers, or industrial clients. Some managers work for agencies that are known for promoting package goods. Others work in retail and department store promotion.

In contrast, marketing managers work with their staff and other advertising professionals to determine how ads should look, where they should be placed, and when the advertising should begin. Managers must keep staff focused on a target audience when working on the promotion of a particular product or service. Managers must also carefully time the release of an ad. For example, launching an advertising campaign too early may create interest well before the product is available. In such cases, by the time the product is released, the public may no longer be interested.

The marketing manager must also oversee his or her department in developing a distribution plan for products. If a product is expected to sell well to a certain group, for example, then marketing professionals must decide how to deliver to members of that group based on when and where they shop.

Once markets are evaluated and merchandise is designed, the actual production begins. The job of the manager is not yet done, however. Along with the public relations department, marketing managers contact members of the press with the aim of getting product information out to the public.

Because research studies show how a product looks on the shelf can often affect sales, managers work with *designers* to explore new color combinations, more appealing shapes, interesting patterns, and new materials.

Marketing managers use a scientific and statistical approach in answering a client's questions about selling a product to the public. The advertising aspect of a marketing campaign must get attention, arouse interest, secure belief, create desire, and stir action. Beauty, comfort, convenience, and quality are the promises that sell all kinds of products, from consumables to cars.

REQUIREMENTS

High School

The educational background of advertising and marketing managers varies as widely as the nature of their diverse responsibilities. If you are interested in a managerial career, you should start preparing in high school by taking college preparatory classes. Because communication is important, take as many English classes as possible. Speech classes are another way to improve your communication skills. Courses in mathematics, business, economics, and computer science are also excellent choices to help you prepare for this career.

Postsecondary Training

Most advertising and marketing managers have a bachelor's degree in advertising, marketing, or business administration. However, degrees in English, journalism, speech communications, economics, or the fine arts are also applicable. Useful college classes include those in psychology, sociology, business, economics, and any art medium. Graduate and professional degrees are common at the managerial level.

Because managers coordinate the efforts of their whole departments, most have worked in other lower level advertising and marketing jobs. Candidates for managerial positions who have extensive experience and developed portfolios will have a competitive edge.

Other Requirements

There are a number of personal characteristics that advertising and marketing managers must possess to succeed in their work. You will need good communication and interpersonal skills and the ability to delegate work to other members of your staff. Because advertising and marketing campaigns are often run under strict deadlines, the ability to think on your feet and work well under pressure is critical.

Other important traits for advertising and marketing managers are intelligence, decisiveness, intuition, creativity, honesty, loyalty, a sense of responsibility, and planning and abilities.

EXPLORING

To get experience in this line of work, try developing your own ad campaign. Take a product you enjoy, for example, a brand of soda you drink, and try to organize a written ad campaign. Consider the type of customers that you should target and what wording and images would work best to attract this audience.

You can also explore this career by developing your managerial skills in general. Whether you're involved in drama, sports, school publications, or a part-time job, there are managerial duties associated with any organized activity. These can involve planning, scheduling, managing other workers or volunteers, fund-raising, or budgeting.

EMPLOYERS

There are approximately 100,000 advertising and promotions managers and 190,000 marketing managers employed in the United States. Half of all advertising managers and nearly two-thirds of marketing managers work in the services and manufacturing industries.

Virtually every business in the United States has some form of advertising and marketing position. Obviously, the larger the company is, the more managerial positions it is likely to have. Another factor is the geographical territory covered by the business. It is safe to say that companies doing business in larger geographical territories are likely to have more managerial positions than those with smaller territories.

STARTING OUT

You will first need experience in lower level advertising and marketing jobs before advancing to a managerial position. To break into an advertising or marketing firm, use your college placement office for assistance. In addition, a number of firms advertise job listings in newspapers and Internet job boards.

Your first few jobs in advertising and marketing should give you experience in working with clients, studying the market, and following up on client service. This work will give you a good sense of the rhythm of the job and the type of work required.

ADVANCEMENT

Most advertising and marketing management and top executive positions are filled by experienced lower level workers who have displayed valuable skills, such as leadership, self-confidence, creativity, motivation, decisiveness, and flexibility. In smaller firms, advancement to a management position may come slowly, while promotions may occur more quickly in larger firms.

Advancement may be accelerated by participating in advanced training programs sponsored by industry and trade associations or by enrolling in continued education programs at local universities. These programs are sometimes paid for by the firm. Managers committed to improving their knowledge of the field and of related disciplines—especially computer information systems—will have the best opportunities for advancement.

EARNINGS

According to 2001 data from the U.S. Bureau of Labor Statistics, the median annual earnings for advertising and promotions managers were $55,940. The lowest 10 percent earned $29,210 or less, while the highest 10 percent earned $125,880 or more. The median salary for marketing managers was $74,370. The lowest 10 percent earned $37,740 or less, while the highest 10 percent earned $138,540 or more.

Salary levels vary substantially, depending upon the level of responsibility, length of service, and type, size, and location of the advertising and marketing firm. Top-level managers in large firms can earn much more than their counterparts in small firms. Also, salaries in large metropolitan areas, such as New York City, are higher than those in smaller cities.

Benefit and compensation packages for managers are usually excellent and may even include such things as bonuses, stock awards, and company-paid insurance premiums.

WORK ENVIRONMENT

Advertising and marketing managers are provided with comfortable offices near the departments they direct. Higher level managers may have spacious, lavish offices and may enjoy such privileges as executive dining rooms, company cars, country club memberships, and liberal expense accounts.

Managers often work long hours under intense pressure to meet advertising and marketing goals. Workweeks consisting of 55–60 hours at the office are not uncommon—in fact, some higher level managers spend up to 80 hours working each week. These long hours limit time available for family and leisure activities.

Advertising and marketing firms are usually highly charged with energy and are both physically and psychologically exciting places to work. Managers work with others as a team in a creative environment where a lot of ideas are exchanged among colleagues. As deadlines are critical in marketing and advertising campaigns, it is important that the manager possesses the ability to handle pressure and stress effectively. Patience and flexibility are also essential, as are organization and time-management skills.

OUTLOOK

Overall, employment of advertising and marketing managers and executives is expected to grow faster than the average through the next decade, according to the U.S. Bureau of Labor Statistics. Many job openings will be the result of managers being promoted to better positions, retiring, or leaving their positions to start their own businesses. Even so, the compensation and prestige of these positions make them highly sought after, and competition to fill openings will be intense. College graduates with experience, a high level of creativity, and strong communication skills should have the best job opportunities.

The outlook for the advertising and marketing industries is closely tied to the overall economy. When the economy is good, business expands both in terms of the firm's output and the number of people it employs, which creates a need for more managers. In economic downturns, firms often lay off employees and cut back on production, which lessens the need for managers.

FOR MORE INFORMATION

The AAF combines the mutual interests of corporate advertisers, agencies, media companies, suppliers, and academia. Visit its website to learn more about internships, scholarships, student chapters, and awards.

American Advertising Federation (AAF)
1101 Vermont Avenue, NW, Suite 500
Washington, DC 20005-6306
Tel: 202-898-0089
Email: aaf@aaf.org
http://www.aaf.org

For industry information, contact

American Association of Advertising Agencies
405 Lexington Avenue, 18th Floor
New York, NY 10174-1801
Tel: 212-682-2500
http://www.aaaa.org

For information on the practice, study, and teaching of marketing, contact

American Marketing Association
311 South Wacker Drive, Suite 5800
Chicago, IL 60606
Tel: 800-AMA-1150
http://www.marketingpower.com

For a brochure on a career in management, contact

National Management Association
2210 Arbor Boulevard
Dayton, OH 45439
Tel: 937-294-0421
Email: nma@nma1.org
http://nma1.org

AGRICULTURAL CONSULTANTS

QUICK FACTS

School Subjects	Certification or Licensing
School Subjects Agriculture Business Economics	**Certification or Licensing** None available
Personal Skills Helping/teaching Leadership/management	**Outlook** Decline
Work Environment Indoors and outdoors Primarily multiple locations	**DOT** 096
Minimum Education Level Bachelor's degree	**GOE** 11.02.03
Salary Range $23,442 to $35,519 to $94,098	**NOC** 2123
	O*NET-SOC 25-9021.00

OVERVIEW

Agricultural consultants, sometimes known as *agricultural extension service workers,* live in rural communities and act as resources for farmers on a range of topics from agricultural technology to the issues facing the modern rural family. They are employed by either the U.S. Department of Agriculture (USDA) or by the Department of Agriculture and the agricultural colleges in that state. Agricultural consultants advise farmers on improved methods of agriculture and agricultural work such as farm management, crop rotation, soil conservation, livestock breeding and feeding, use of new machinery, and marketing. They assist individuals wishing to start their own farms, provide the most current agricultural advancements to the community, and speak to the community or local government groups on agricultural issues. They also supervise the work of family and community educators and young people's clubs such as 4-H. This government-sponsored program is called the Cooperative State Research, Education and Extension Service (CSREES).

HISTORY

In the late 18th century, President George Washington decided to establish an educational agency of the federal government dedicated to assisting the nation's farmers. Washington's proposal eventually developed into what is now the USDA.

In 1862, President Abraham Lincoln promoted the Morrill Act, which established land grant colleges. Under this act, each state was given 30,000 acres of land for each senator and representative in Congress. The state was to sell the land and use the proceeds to build colleges that would specialize in education for agriculture and engineering.

Once established, the state agricultural colleges were faced with the task of compiling enough data to develop an agricultural curriculum that would be of use to the American farmer. Under the Hatch Act of 1887, experimental stations were created. These agricultural laboratory settings were devoted to gathering information regarding soils, crops, livestock, fruits, and machinery. They became sources of information for both agricultural colleges and farmers.

Land-grant colleges became important resources for agricultural data and education. However, it soon became clear that sending into the field educated people who were familiar with farmers' work was more effective than expecting farmers to leave their work or come from remote areas to attend college classes. Thus, the role of the agricultural consultant came into being.

The Cooperative Extension Service was developed and placed in operation in 1914 on a federal basis by the passage of the Smith-Lever Act. The service was opened to any state that wished to join the educational project on a cooperative basis, and most states accepted the opportunity. Because of this, every state agricultural college in the nation today has an extension service as one of its major departmental classifications.

In 1994, the USDA's Reorganization Act created CSREES, which expands the research and higher education functions of the former cooperative State Research Service and the education and outreach functions of the former Extension Service.

THE JOB

Agricultural consultants teach agricultural subjects at places other than college campuses. The aim of these educational programs is to teach agricultural workers to analyze and solve agricultural problems. The programs cover such topics as soil and crop improvement, livestock, farm machinery, fertilizers, new methods of planting, and any other subjects that may be of assistance to the farmer. Rather than working in classrooms, consultants work on site, possibly while the farmer is engaged in planting or harvesting, or in small evening meetings of five or six farmers. Occasionally classes are offered in more formal settings, during which the consultant speaks before larger groups and makes presentations.

County agricultural agents work closely with federal agricultural agents to gather information to be presented to the farmers. Information on agronomy (the theory and practice of soil management and crop production), livestock, marketing, agricultural and home economics, horticulture, and entomology (the study of insects) may come either from the state agricultural college or from the CSREES. The county agricultural worker's job is to review the new information, decide what is most pertinent to local operations, and then present it as effectively as possible to the farmers in that particular area. The county or federal extension service agent's work is primarily educational in nature and is aimed at increasing the efficiency of agricultural production and marketing and the development of new and different markets for agricultural products.

County agricultural agents also work closely with *family and community educators* (FCEs), who assist and instruct families on ways to improve their home life. This work ranges from offering advice and suggestions on preserving fruits and vegetables to improving health care and nutrition, assisting in balancing family budgets, and handling family stress. The FCE is responsible for keeping current in every area relating to the rural home and for sharing this information with families in a particular county or group of counties.

4-H Club agents organize and direct the educational projects and activities of the 4-H Club, the largest out-of-school youth program in the United States. Nearly 7 million young people participate in 4-H Clubs in rural and urban settings. 4-H educational programs focus on building lifelong learning skills that develop youth potential. An extensive set of programs engages youth in healthy learning experiences, increasing self-esteem, and developing problem-solving skills. Programs address stress management, self-protection, parent-teen communication, personal development, careers, and global understanding. Youth are encouraged to explore science, technology, and citizenship. 4-H Club agents analyze the needs of individuals and the community, develop teaching materials, train volunteers, and organize exhibits at state and county fairs. They also introduce children and adolescents to techniques in raising animals and plants, including breeding, husbandry, and nutrition.

Due to technological advancements in electronic communication, there are interesting opportunities for careers in communications with the USDA Extension Service. There is a degree of specialization involved, especially at the federal level. Federal agricultural consultants often become program leaders who are responsible for developing and maintaining relationships with various land-grant colleges, universities, government agencies, and private agencies involved in agriculture. In some cases, they also become *educational research and training specialists* responsible for developing research programs in all phases of consulting work. The results of these programs are shared with the various state agencies.

Subject matter specialists develop programs through which new information can be presented effectively to the farmers. *Educational media specialists* condense information and distribute it as it becomes available to the states for use in their local extension programs. These consultants may be designated *extension service specialists*. An extension service worker who is in charge of programs for a group of counties is known as a *district extension service agent.*

REQUIREMENTS

High School

You should follow your high school's college preparatory program and take courses in English, government, foreign language, and history. Also, be sure to take courses in mathematics and the sciences, particularly biology and physics. Computer courses will also be beneficial. Take any economics courses available, along with accounting and business classes, as agricultural consultants are actively involved in farm management.

Postsecondary Training

To do this work, you'll need a bachelor's degree with a major in agriculture or economics. If you hope to join the on-campus staff at your state's agricultural college, you'll need at least a master's degree.

College courses usually required for this work are English, history, chemistry, biology, economics, education, sociology, and speech, as well as animal science, crop production, horticulture, soils, and farm management. A number of colleges have developed regular agricultural extension curriculums to be followed by those hoping to enter the field.

After finishing college, county agents are kept up to date on the latest programs, policies, and teaching techniques through in-service training programs run by state agricultural colleges and the state Department of Agriculture.

Other Requirements

You'll need a background of practical farming experience and a thorough knowledge of problems confronting farmers, members of rural communities, and their families. Farmers naturally feel more comfortable seeking advice from people whom they feel have a complete understanding of their work.

You must be a good teacher and should enjoy working with people. You must also be assertive yet diplomatic and have an affinity for farmers and their problems. In addition, you will be expected to organize group projects, meetings, and broad educational programs that both adults and young people involved in agriculture will find stimulating and useful. You'll need the professional interest and enthusiasm that will enable you to keep up with the huge amount of new agricultural information constantly being released. You must be willing to learn and use the latest teaching techniques to disseminate current agricultural practices and knowledge to local residents.

EXPLORING

To get a sense of the job, you can read the pamphlets and occupational information brochures the USDA publishes about this field, and you can request meetings with your local agricultural agent. Any of the state agricultural colleges will send materials or release the name of the local agent for interested students.

Another way to prepare to explore this field is to join groups such as 4-H, National FFA Organization (formerly Future Farmers of America), and the Boy or Girl Scouts. You may also volunteer to work at an extension office. It may be possible to visit with farmers or others engaged in agriculture to hear their impressions of the work carried on by the agricultural consultants in your particular county.

EMPLOYERS

Federal agricultural consultants work for the USDA in Washington, D.C., to assist county extension officers and supervisors in planning, developing, and coordinating national, regional, and state extension programs. County agricultural agents may be employed jointly by the Department of Agriculture and the agricultural college in each state.

County agents may also specialize, especially in those counties employing more than two or three agents. Many counties with diverse agricultural businesses and farms will often have five or more agents. A single county may employ specialists in fruit and grain production, dairy, poultry production, farm machinery, pest control, soils, nursery management, conservation, and livestock.

STARTING OUT

Although your college's placement service may be of some help in finding a job, you will need to apply to the director of the extension service at the agricultural college in the state in which you hope to work. If there is a job vacancy, the director of the extension service will screen the qualifications of the various applicants and submit the names to a board or council responsible for making the final selection.

ADVANCEMENT

Competent consultants, as a rule, are promoted fairly rapidly and early in their careers. The promotions may be in the form of positions of higher responsibility within the same county, reassignment to a different county within the state, or an increase in salary. Many agents, after moving through a succession of more demanding extension jobs, join the staff at the state agricultural college. Many directors of extension services began their careers in this way.

It is also possible to branch out to other areas. Agricultural consultants often go into related jobs, especially those in industries that specialize in agricultural products. The training they have received and their background in agriculture makes them excellent candidates for many jobs in the agricultural industry.

EARNINGS

The earnings of agricultural consultants vary from state to state and from county to county. Most USDA professionals start out at the GS-5 level (government pay grade), which in 2003 ranged between $23,442 and $30,471 annually, depending on education and experience. Agricultural consultants then move up through the government pay grades, earning more. GS-9 level, for example, had a starting base pay of $35,519 in 2003. With some years of experience with the USDA, and with additional education, consultants can advance to GS-14, which in 2003 paid between $72,381 and $94,098 a year. Most consultants are eligible for other benefits such as paid vacations and sick days, health insurance, and pension plans.

WORK ENVIRONMENT

This work is often both mentally and physically taxing. Agricultural consultants face numerous problems that demand their presence in the field for long periods of time. They may be in their office handling routine matters every day for a month and then not work in the office for the next six weeks. (Consultants usually have a private office where they can speak in confidence with those who seek assistance.) As a rule, agricultural consultants spend about half of their time in the field working with farmers on specific problems, scheduling or conducting group meetings, or simply distributing new updated information. They usually drive from 500 to 1,500 miles per month while on the job. The work may be hard on the consultant's family, since evening meetings are required, and the agent is often invited to weekend events as well. For example, agents may conduct small informal meetings on Monday and Tuesday nights to discuss particular problems that a small group of county farmers faces. They may be home on Wednesday, work with a student's 4-H Club on Thursday, conduct another meeting on Friday, and then judge a livestock show at the county fair on Saturday.

Hours for consultants are not regular, and the pay is not particularly high considering the number of hours agents are required to work. But this work can be very rewarding. There is great satisfaction in working with people who genuinely appreciate the time, advice, and assistance the agent brings.

OUTLOOK

The work of agricultural consultants is heavily dependent on the employment of farmers and farm managers, and the U.S. Department of Labor predicts a decline in employment for these workers through the next decade. As farms consolidate and there are fewer farm families, the need for agricultural consultants may also decline. However, consultants may find opportunities working with rural nonfarming families and various suburban residents who are interested in specialty areas such as urban horticulture and gardening.

As the farming industry is becoming more complex, those consultants with the most thorough education and training will have the best job prospects. The idea of agricultural consulting programs is spreading to many foreign countries. Job opportunities may come from a need for U.S. county and federal agents to assist their counterparts in other countries in setting up and operating agricultural consulting programs.

FOR MORE INFORMATION

To learn about CSREES and to access a list of land-grant universities, contact

U.S. Department of Agriculture
Cooperative State Research, Education, and Extension Service
1400 Independence Avenue, SW, Room 4008, Waterfront Centre
Washington, DC 20250-2216
Tel: 202-720-2047
http://www.reeusda.gov

For more information on opportunities and education in the agricultural field, contact the following organizations:

4-H
Families, 4-H, and Nutrition
CSREES/USDA
1400 Independence Avenue, SW
Washington DC 20250-2225
http://www.4h-usa.org

National FFA Organization
National FFA Center
PO Box 68960
Indianapolis, IN 46268-0960
Tel: 317-802-6060
http://www.ffa.org

BUSINESS MANAGERS

QUICK FACTS

School Subjects
Business
Computer science
Economics

Personal Skills
Helping/teaching
Leadership/management

Work Environment
Primarily indoors
One location with some travel

Minimum Education Level
Bachelor's degree

Salary Range
$38,710 to $61,160 to $136,760+

Certification or Licensing
None available

Outlook
About as fast as the average

DOT
189

GOE
11.05.01

NOC
0611

O*NET-SOC
11-1011.00, 11-1011.02, 11-1021.00, 11-3031.01

OVERVIEW

Business managers plan, organize, direct, and coordinate the operations of firms in business and industry. They may oversee an entire company, a geographical territory of a company's operations, or a specific department within a company. Of the approximately 3 million managerial jobs in the United States, about 60 percent are found in retail, services, and manufacturing industries.

HISTORY

Everyone has some experience in management. For example, if you schedule your day so that you can get up, get to school on time, go to soccer practice after school, have the time to do your homework, and get to bed at a reasonable hour, you are practicing management skills. Running a household, paying bills, balancing a checkbook, and keeping track of appointments, meetings, and social activities are also examples of managerial activities. Essentially, the term "manage" means to handle, direct, or control.

Management is a necessary part of any enterprise in which a person or group of people are trying to accomplish a specific goal. In fact, civilization could not have grown to its present level of complexity without the planning and organizing involved in effective management. Some of the earliest examples of written documents had to do with the management of business and commerce. As societies and individuals accumulated property and wealth, they needed effective record keeping of taxes, trade agreements, laws, and rights of ownership.

The technological advances of the industrial revolution brought about the need for a distinct class of managers. As complex factory systems developed, skilled and trained managers were needed to organize and operate them. Workers became specialized in a limited number of tasks, which required managers to coordinate and oversee production.

As businesses began to diversify their production, industries became so complex that their management had to be divided among several different managers. With the expanded scope of managers and the trend toward decentralized management, the transition to the professional manager took place. In the 1920s, large corporations began to organize with decentralized administration and centralized policy control.

Managers provided a forum for the exchange and evaluation of creative ideas and technical innovations. Eventually these management concepts spread from manufacturing and production to office, personnel, marketing, and financial functions. Today, management is more concerned with results than activities, taking into account individual differences in styles of working.

THE JOB

Management is found in every industry, including food, clothing, banking, education, health care, and business services. All types of businesses have managers to formulate policies and administer the firm's operations. Managers may oversee the operations of an entire company, a geographical territory of a company's operations, or a specific department, such as sales and marketing.

Business managers direct a company's or a department's daily activities within the context of the organization's overall plan. They implement organizational policies and goals. This may involve developing sales or promotional materials, analyzing the department's budgetary requirements, and hiring, training, and supervising staff. Business managers are often responsible for long-range planning for their company or department. This involves setting goals for the organization and developing a workable plan for meeting those goals.

A manager responsible for a single department might work to coordinate his or her department's activities with other departments. A manager responsible for an entire company or organization might work with the managers of various departments or locations to oversee and coordinate the activities of all departments. If the business is privately owned, the owner may be the manager. In a large corporation, however, there will be a management structure above the business manager.

Jeff Bowe is the Midwest General Manager for Disc Graphics, a large printing company headquartered in New York. Bowe oversees all aspects of the company's Indianapolis plant, which employs about 50 people. When asked what he is responsible for, Bowe answers, "Everything that happens in this facility." Specifically, that includes sales, production, customer service, capital expenditure planning, hiring and training employees, firing or downsizing, and personnel management.

The hierarchy of managers includes top executives, such as the *president*, who establishes an organization's goals and policies along with others, such as the chief executive officer, chief financial officer, chief information officer, executive vice president, and the board of directors. Top executives plan business objectives and develop policies to coordinate operations between divisions and departments and establish procedures for attaining objectives. Activity reports and financial statements are reviewed to determine progress and revise operations as needed. The president also directs and formulates funding for new and existing programs within the organization. Public relations plays a big part in the lives of executives as they deal with executives and leaders from other countries or organizations, and with customers, employees, and various special interest groups.

The top-level managers for Bowe's company are located in the company's New York headquarters. Bowe is responsible for reporting certain information about the Indianapolis facility to them. He may also have to work collaboratively with them on certain projects or plans. "I have a conversation with people at headquarters about every two to three days." he says. "I get corporate input on very large projects. I would also work closely with them if we had some type of corporate-wide program we were working on—something where I would be the contact person for this facility."

Although the president or chief executive officer retains ultimate authority and responsibility, Bowe is responsible for overseeing the day-to-day operations of the Indianapolis location. A manager in this position is sometimes called a *chief operating officer* or *COO*. Other duties of a COO may include serving as chairman of committees, such as management, executive, engineering, or sales.

Some companies have an *executive vice president*, who directs and coordinates the activities of one or more departments, depending on the size of the organization. In very large organizations, the duties of executive vice presidents may be highly specialized. For example, they may oversee the activities of business managers of marketing, sales promotion, purchasing, finance, personnel training, industrial relations, administrative services, data processing, property management, transportation, or legal services. In smaller organizations, an executive vice president might be responsible for a number of these departments. Executive vice presidents also assist the chief executive officer in formulating and administering the organization's policies and developing its long-range goals. Executive vice presidents may serve as members of management committees on special studies.

Companies may also have a *chief financial officer* or *CFO*. In small firms, the CFO is usually responsible for all financial management tasks, such as budgeting, capital expenditure planning, cash flow, and various financial reviews and reports. In larger companies, the CFO may oversee financial management departments to help other managers develop financial and economic policy and oversee the implementation of these policies.

Chief information officers or *CIOs* are responsible for all aspects of their company's information technology. They use their knowledge of technology and business to determine how to best use information technology to meet company goals. This may include researching, purchasing, and overseeing the set up and use of technology systems, such as Intranet, Internet, and computer networks. These managers sometimes take a role in implementing a company's website.

In companies that have several different locations, managers may oversee specific geographic areas. For example, a large retailer with facilities all across the nation is likely to have a number of managers in charge of various territories. There might be a Midwest manager, a Southwest manager, a Southeast manager, a Northeast manager, and a Northwest manager. These managers are often called *regional* or *area managers*. Some companies break their management territories up into even smaller sections, such as a single state or a part of a state. Managers overseeing these smaller segments are often called *district managers*, and typically report directly to an area or regional manager.

REQUIREMENTS

High School

Many business managers have a bachelor's degree in liberal arts or business administration. According to Jeff Bowe, the best way to prepare academically for a career in business management is to get a well-rounded education. Because communication is important, take as many English and speech classes as possible. Courses in mathematics, business, and computer science are also excellent choices to help you prepare for this career. Finally, Bowe recommends taking a foreign language. "Today speaking a foreign language is more and more important," he says. "Which language is not so important. Any of the global languages are something you could very well use, depending upon where you end up."

Postsecondary Training

Business managers often have a college degree in a subject that pertains to the department they direct or the organization they administer; for example, a business manager of finance might have a degree in accounting or economics, whereas a director of research and development might have a degree in engineering or science. As computers are an invaluable part of most workplaces, many managers must have experience with the information technology that applies to their field.

Graduate and professional degrees are common among business managers. Bowe, along with many managers in administrative, marketing, financial, and manufacturing activities, has a master's degree in business administration. Managers in highly technical manufacturing and research activities often have a master's degree or doctorate in a technical or scientific discipline. A law degree is mandatory for business managers of corporate legal departments, and hospital managers generally have a master's degree in health services administration or business administration. In some industries, such as retail trade or the food and beverage industry, competent individuals without a college degree may become business managers.

Other Requirements

There are a number of personal characteristics that can help one be a successful business manager, depending upon the specific responsibilities of the position. A manager who oversees other employees should have good communication and interpersonal skills. The ability to delegate work is another important personality trait of a good manager. According to Bowe, the ability to think on your feet is often key in business management. "You have to be able to think extremely quickly and not in a reactionary manner," he says. Bowe also says that a certain degree of organization is important, since managers are often managing several different things simultaneously. Traits considered important for top executives are intelligence, decisiveness, intuition, creativity, honesty, loyalty, a sense of responsibility, and planning and abilities. Finally, the successful manager should be flexible and interested in staying abreast of new developments in his or her industry. "In general, you need to be open to change because your customers change, your market changes, your technology changes," he says. "If you won't try something new, you really have no business being in management."

EXPLORING

To get experience as a manager, start by focusing on your own interests. There are managerial duties associated with any organized activity, whether you're involved in drama, sports, school publications, or a part-time job. These duties can involve planning, scheduling, managing other workers or volunteers, fundraising, or budgeting. Local businesses also have job opportunities through which you can get firsthand knowledge and experience of management structure. If you can't get an actual job, at least try to schedule a meeting with a business manager to talk with him or her about the career. Some schools or community organizations arrange job shadowing, where you can spend part of a day "shadowing" a selected employee to see what his or her job is like. Joining Junior Achievement is another excellent way to get involved with local businesses and learn about how they work (see the end of this article for contact information). Finally, take every opportunity to work with computers, since computer skills are vital to today's business world.

EMPLOYERS

There are approximately 3 million general managers and executives employed in the United States. These jobs are found in every industry. However, approximately 60 percent are in the manufacturing, retail, and service industries. In a 1998 survey of members of the American Management Association, 42.6 percent of the 4,585 participants worked in manufacturing. Approximately 32 percent worked in the for-profit services industry.

Virtually every business in the United States has some form of managerial positions. Obviously, the larger the company is, the more managerial positions it is likely to have. Another factor is the geographical territory covered by the business. It is safe to say that companies doing business in larger geographical territories are likely to have more managerial positions than those with smaller territories.

STARTING OUT

Generally you will need a college degree for this type of career, although many retail stores, grocery stores, and restaurants hire promising applicants who have only a high school diploma. Job seekers usually apply directly to the manager of such places. Your college placement office is often the best place to start looking for these positions. A number of listings can also be found in newspaper help wanted ads.

Many organizations have management trainee programs that college graduates can enter. Such programs are advertised at college career fairs or through college job placement services. Often, however, these management trainee positions in business and government are filled by employees who are already working for the organization and who demonstrate management potential. Jeff Bowe suggests researching the industry you are interested in to find out what might be the best point of entry for that field. "I came into the printing company through customer service, which is a good point of entry because it's one of the easiest things to learn," he says. "Although it requires more technical know-how now than it did then, customer service is still not a bad entry point for this industry."

ADVANCEMENT

Most business management and top executive positions are filled by experienced lower level managers and executives who display valuable managerial traits, such as leadership, self-confidence, creativity, motivation, decisiveness, and flexibility. In small firms advancement to a higher management position may come slowly, while promotions may occur more quickly in larger firms.

Advancement may be accelerated by participating in different kinds of educational programs available for managers. These are often paid for by the organization. Company training programs broaden knowledge of company policy and operations. Training programs sponsored by industry and trade associations and continuing education courses in colleges and universities can familiarize managers with the latest developments in management techniques. In recent years, large numbers of middle managers were laid off as companies streamlined operations. Competition for jobs is keen, and business managers committed to improving their knowledge of the field and of related disciplines—especially computer information systems—will have the best opportunities for advancement.

Business managers may advance to executive or administrative vice president. Vice presidents may advance to peak corporate positions such as president or chief executive officer. Presidents and chief executive officers, upon retirement, may become members of the board of directors of one or more firms. Sometimes business managers establish their own firms.

EARNINGS

Salary levels for business managers vary substantially, depending upon the level of responsibility, length of service, and type, size, and location of the organization. Top-level managers in large firms can earn much more than their counterparts in small firms. Also, salaries in large metropolitan areas, such as New York City, are higher than those in smaller cities.

According to the U.S. Department of Labor, general managers had a median yearly income of $61,160 in 2000. To show the range of earnings for general managers, however, the Department notes that those in the computer and data processing industry had an annual median of $101,340; those in public relations, $84,610; and those at eating and drinking establishments, $38,710.

Chief executives earned a median of $113,810 annually in 2000. And again, salaries varied by industry. For example, the median yearly salary for those in management and public relations was $136,760, while those at commercial banks earned a median of $120,840. A survey by Abbott, Langer, & Associates found that chief executives working for nonprofits had a median yearly salary of

$75,000 in 2000. Some executives, however, earn hundreds of thousands of dollars more than this annually.

Benefit and compensation packages for business managers are usually excellent and may even include such things as bonuses, stock awards, company-paid insurance premiums, use of company cars, paid country club memberships, expense accounts, and generous retirement benefits.

WORK ENVIRONMENT

Business managers are provided with comfortable offices near the departments they direct. Top executives may have spacious, lavish offices and may enjoy such privileges as executive dining rooms, company cars, country club memberships, and liberal expense accounts.

Managers often travel between national, regional, and local offices. Top executives may travel to meet with executives in other corporations, both within the United States and abroad. Meetings and conferences sponsored by industries and associations occur regularly and provide invaluable opportunities to meet with peers and keep up with the latest developments. In large corporations, job transfers between the parent company and its local offices or subsidiaries are common.

Business managers often work long hours under intense pressure to meet, for example, production and marketing goals. Jeff Bowe's average workweek consists of 55–60 hours at the office. This is not uncommon—in fact, some executives spend up to 80 hours working each week. These long hours limit time available for family and leisure activities.

OUTLOOK

Overall, employment of business managers and executives is expected to grow about as fast as the average through the next decade, according to the U.S. Bureau of Labor Statistics. Many job openings will be the result of managers being promoted to better positions, retiring, or leaving their positions to start their own businesses. Even so, the compensation and prestige of these positions make them highly sought after, and competition to fill openings will be intense.

Projected employment growth varies by industry. For example, employment in the service industry, particularly business services, should increase faster than the average, while employment in some manufacturing industries is expected to decline.

The outlook for business managers is closely tied to the overall economy. When the economy is good, businesses expand both in terms of their output and the number of people they employ, which creates a need for more managers. In economic downturns, businesses often lay off employees and cut back on production, which lessens the need for managers.

FOR MORE INFORMATION

For news about management trends, resources on career information and finding a job, and an online job bank, contact

American Management Association
1601 Broadway
New York, NY 10019-7420
Tel: 800-262-9699
http://www.amanet.org

For brochures on careers in management for women, contact

Association for Women in Management
927 15th Street, NW, Suite 1000
Washington, DC 20005
Tel: 202-659-6364
Email: awm@benefits.net
http://www.womens.org

For information about programs for students in kindergarten through high school, and information on local chapters, contact

Junior Achievement
One Education Way
Colorado Springs, CO 80906
Tel: 719-540-8000
Email: newmedia@ja.org
http://www.ja.org

For a brochure on management as a career, contact

National Management Association
2210 Arbor Boulevard
Dayton, OH 45439
Tel: 937-294-0421
Email: nma@nma1.org
http://nma1.org

BUYERS

QUICK FACTS

School Subjects	Certification or Licensing
Business Economics Mathematics	Voluntary
Personal Skills Helping/teaching Leadership/management	**Outlook** Decline
Work Environment Primarily indoors One location with some travel	**DOT** 162
Minimum Education Level High school diploma	**GOE** 08.01.03
Salary Range $22,500 to $38,590 to $73,740+	**NOC** 6233
	O*NET-SOC 11-3061.00, 13-1021.00, 13-1022.00

OVERVIEW

There are two main types of *buyers*. *Wholesale buyers* purchase merchandise directly from manufacturers and resell it to retail firms, commercial establishments, and other institutions. *Retail buyers* purchase goods from wholesalers (and occasionally from manufacturers) for resale to the general public. In either case, buyers must understand their customers' needs and be able to purchase goods at an appropriate price and in sufficient quantity. Sometimes a buyer is referred to by the type of merchandise purchased—for example, jewelry buyer or toy buyer. *Government buyers* have similar responsibilities but need to be especially sensitive to concerns of fairness and ethics since they use public money to make their purchases. There are approximately 536,000 buyers and related workers currently working in the United States.

HISTORY

The job of the buyer has been influenced by a variety of historical changes, including the growth of large retail stores in the 20th century. In the past, store owners typically performed almost all of the business activities, including the purchase of merchandise. Large stores, in contrast, had immensely more complicated operations, requiring large numbers of specialized workers, such as sales clerks, receiving and shipping clerks, advertising managers, personnel officers, and buyers. The introduction of mass production systems at factories required more complicated planning, ordering, and scheduling of purchases. A wider range of available merchandise also called for more astute selection and purchasing techniques.

THE JOB

Wholesale and retail buyers are part of a complex system of production, distribution, and merchandising. Both are concerned with recognizing and satisfying the huge variety of consumer needs and desires. Most specialize in acquiring one or two lines of merchandise.

Retail buyers work for retail stores. They generally can be divided into two types: The first, working directly under a merchandise manager, not only purchases goods but directly supervises salespeople. When a new product appears on the shelves, for example, buyers may work with salespeople to point out its distinctive features. This type of retail buyer thus takes responsibility for the products' marketing. The second type of retail buyer is concerned only with purchasing and has no supervisory responsibilities. These buyers cooperate with the sales staff to promote maximum sales.

All retail buyers must understand the basic merchandising policies of their stores. Purchases are affected by the size of the buyer's annual budget, the kind of merchandise needed in each buying season, and trends in the market. Success in buying is directly related to the profit or loss shown by particular departments. Buyers often work with *assistant buyers,* who spend much of their time maintaining sales and inventory records.

All buyers must be experts in the merchandise that they purchase. They order goods months ahead of their expected sale, and they must be able to predetermine marketability based upon cost, style, and competitive items. Buyers must also be well acquainted with the best sources of supply for each product they purchase.

Depending upon the location, size, and type of store, a retail buyer may deal directly with traveling salespeople (ordering from samples or catalogs), order by mail or by telephone directly from the manufacturer or wholesaler, or travel to key cities to visit merchandise showrooms and manufacturing establishments. Most use a combination of these approaches.

Buying trips to such cities as New York, Chicago, and San Francisco are an important part of the work for buyers at a larger store. For specialized products, such as glassware, china, liquors, and gloves, some buyers make yearly trips to major European production centers. Sometimes manufacturers of similar items organize trade shows to attract a number of buyers. Buying trips are difficult; a buyer may visit six to eight suppliers in a single day. The buyer must make decisions on the spot about the opportunity for profitable sale of merchandise. The important element is not how much the buyer personally likes the merchandise but about customers' taste. Most buyers operate under an annual purchasing budget for the departments they represent.

Mergers between stores and expansion of individual department stores into chains of stores have created central buying positions. *Central buyers* order in unusually large quantities. As a result, they have the power to develop their own set of specifications for a particular item and ask manufacturers to bid on the right to provide it. Goods purchased by central buyers may be marketed under the manufacturer's label (as is normally done) or ordered with the store's label or a chain brand name.

To meet this competition, independent stores often work with *resident buyers,* who purchase merchandise for a large number of stores. By purchasing large quantities of the same product, resident buyers can obtain the same types of discounts enjoyed by large chain stores and then pass along the savings to their customers.

Because they work with public funds and must avoid any appearance of favoritism or corruption, *government buyers* sometimes purchase merchandise through open bids. The buyer may establish a set of specifications for a product and invite private firms to bid on the job. Some government buyers are required to accept the lowest bid. Each purchase must be well documented for public scrutiny. Like other types of buyers, government buyers must be well acquainted with the products they purchase, and they must try to find the best quality products for the lowest price.

REQUIREMENTS

High School

A high school diploma generally is required for entering the field of buying. Useful high school courses include mathematics, business, English, and economics.

Postsecondary Training

A college degree may not be a requirement for becoming a buyer, but it is becoming increasingly important, especially for advancement. A majority of buyers have attended college, many majoring in business, engineering, or economics. Some colleges and universities also offer majors in purchasing or materials management. Regardless of the major, useful courses in preparation for a career in buying include accounting, economics, commercial law, finance, marketing, and various business classes, such as business communications, business organization and management, and computer applications in business.

Retailing experience is helpful to gain a sense of customer tastes and witness the supply and demand process. Additional training is available through trade associations, such as the National Association of Purchasing Management, which sponsors conferences, seminars, and workshops.

Certification or Licensing

Certification, although not required, is becoming increasingly important. Various levels of certification are available through the American Purchasing Society, the National Association of Purchasing Management, and the National Institute of Government Purchasing. To earn most certifications you must have work experience, meet education requirements, and pass written and oral exams.

Other Requirements

If you are interested in becoming a buyer, you should be organized and have excellent decision-making skills. Predicting consumer tastes and keeping stores and wholesalers appropriately stocked requires resourcefulness, good judgment, and confidence. You should also have skills in marketing to identify and promote products that will sell. Finally, leadership skills are needed to supervise assistant buyers and deal with manufacturers' representatives and store executives.

EXPLORING

One way to explore the retailing field is through part-time or summer employment in a store. A good time to look for such work is during the Christmas holiday season. Door-to-door selling is another way to gain retailing experience. Occasionally, experience in a retail store can be found through special high school programs.

EMPLOYERS

Buyers work for a wide variety of businesses, both wholesale and retail, as well as for government agencies. Employers range from small stores, where buying may be only one function of a manager's job, to multinational corporations, where a buyer may specialize in one type of item and buy in enormous quantity.

Of the approximately 536,000 purchasing managers, buyers, and purchasing agents employed throughout the country, more than 50 percent work in wholesale trade and manufacturing. Approximately 17 percent work in retail trade, such as for grocery stores and department stores. Others work in businesses that provide services and in government agencies.

STARTING OUT

Most buyers find their first job by applying to the personnel office of a retail establishment or wholesaler. Because knowledge of retailing is important, buyers may be required to have work experience in a store.

Most buyers begin their careers as retail sales workers. The next step may be *head of stock*. The head of stock maintains stock inventory records and keeps the merchandise in a neat and well-organized fashion both to protect its value and to permit easy access. He or she usually supervises the work of several employees. This person also works in an intermediate position between the salespeople on the floor and the buyer who provides the merchandise. The next step to becoming a buyer may be assistant buyer. For many department stores, promotion to full buyer requires this background.

Large department stores or chains operate executive training programs for college graduates who seek buying and other retail executive positions. A typical program consists of 16 successive weeks of work in a variety of departments. This on-the-job experience is supplemented by formal classroom work that most often is conducted by senior executives and training department personnel. Following this orientation, trainees are placed in junior management positions for an additional period of supervised experience and training.

ADVANCEMENT

Buyers are key employees of the stores or companies that employ them. One way they advance is through increased responsibility, such as more authority to make commitments for merchandise and more complicated buying assignments.

Buyers are sometimes promoted to *merchandise manager,* a position in which they supervise other buyers, help develop the store's merchandising policies, and coordinate buying and selling activities with related departments. Other buyers may become vice presidents in charge of merchandising, or even store presidents. Because buyers learn much about retailing in their job, they are in a position to advance to top executive positions. Some buyers use their knowledge of retailing and the contacts they have developed with suppliers to set up their own businesses.

EARNINGS

How much a buyer earns depends on various factors, including the employer's sales volume. Mass merchandisers, such as discount or chain department stores, pay among the highest salaries.

The U.S. Department of Labor reports the median annual income for wholesale and retail buyers was $38,590 in 2001. The lowest paid 10 percent of these buyers made less than $22,500 yearly, and at the other end of the pay range, the highest paid 10 percent earned more than $73,740 annually. The Department of Labor also reports that buyers working for the federal government had median annual earnings of $53,010 in 2000.

Most buyers receive the usual benefits, such as vacation, sick leave, life and health insurance, and pension plans. Retail buyers may receive cash bonuses for their work and may also receive discounts on merchandise they purchase from their employer.

WORK ENVIRONMENT

Buyers work in a dynamic and sometimes stressful atmosphere. They must make important decisions on an hourly basis. The results of their work, both successes and failures, show up quickly on the profit and loss statement.

Buyers frequently work long or irregular hours. Evening and weekend hours are common, especially during the holiday season, when the retail field is at its busiest. Extra hours may be required to bring records up to date, for example, or to review stock and to become familiar with the store's overall marketing design for the coming season. Travel may also be a regular part of a buyer's job, possibly requiring several days away from home each month.

Although buyers must sometimes work under pressure, they usually work in pleasant, well-lit environments. They also benefit from having a diverse set of responsibilities.

OUTLOOK

According to the U.S. Department of Labor, employment of wholesale and retail buyers is projected to decline through the next decade. Reasons for this decrease include the large number of business mergers and acquisitions, which results in the blending of buying departments and the elimination of redundant jobs. In addition, the use of computers, which increases efficiency, and the trend of some large retail companies to centralize their operations will both contribute to fewer new jobs for buyers. Some job openings will result from the need to hire replacement workers for those who leave the field.

FOR MORE INFORMATION

For career information and job listings, contact

American Purchasing Society
8 East Galena Boulevard, Suite 203
Aurora, IL 60506
Tel: 630-859-0250
http://www.american-purchasing.com

For information on the magazine, Your Future Purchasing Career, lists of colleges with purchasing programs, and interviews with people in the field, contact the ISM.

Institute for Supply Management (ISM)
PO Box 22160
Tempe, AZ 85285-2160
Tel: 800-888-6276
http://www.ism.ws

For information on purchasing careers in the government and certification, contact

National Institute of Government Purchasing
151 Spring Street
Herndon, VA 20170-5223
Tel: 800-367-6447
http://www.nigp.org

COLLEGE ADMINISTRATORS

QUICK FACTS

School Subjects
Business
English
Speech

Personal Skills
Helping/teaching
Leadership/management

Work Environment
Primarily indoors
Primarily one location

Minimum Education Level
Bachelor's degree

Salary Range
$33,640 to $61,700 to $272,200+

Certification or Licensing
None available

Outlook
About as fast as the average

DOT
090

GOE
11.05.02

NOC
0312

O*NET-SOC
11-9033.00

OVERVIEW

College administrators coordinate and oversee programs such as admissions and financial aid in public and private colleges and universities. They frequently work with teams of people to develop and manage student services. Administrators also oversee specific academic divisions of colleges and universities.

HISTORY

Before the Civil War, most U.S. colleges and universities managed their administration with a president, a treasurer, and a part-time librarian. Members of the faculty often were responsible for the administrative tasks of the day, and there was no uniformity in college admissions requirements.

By 1860, the average number of administrative officers in U.S. colleges was still only four. However, as the job of running an institution expanded in scope in response to ever-increasing student enrollment, the responsibilities of administration began to splinter. After creating positions for registrar, secretary of faculty, chief business officer, and a number of departmental deans, most schools next hired a director of admissions to oversee the application and acceptance of students. In addition, several eastern schools and a few prominent college presidents, Charles Eliot of Harvard and Nicholas Butler of Columbia among them, saw the need to establish organizations whose purpose would be to put an end to the chaos. The College Entrance Examination Board was formed to create standardized college entrance requirements. By 1910, there were 25 leading eastern colleges using the Board's exams. Today, most colleges require that a student submit standardized test scores, such as the SAT or ACT, when applying.

After World War II, returning veterans entered America's colleges and universities by the thousands. With this great influx of students, college administrators were needed to better organize the university system. During this time, financial aid administration also became a major program. Today, as the costs of a college education continue to rise dramatically, college financial aid administrators are needed to help students and parents find loans, grants, scholarships, and work-study programs.

THE JOB

A college administrator's work is demanding and diverse. An administrator is responsible for a wide range of tasks in areas such as counseling services, admissions, alumni affairs, financial aid, academics, and business. The following are some of the different types of college administrators, but keep in mind that this is only a partial list. It takes many administrators in many different departments to run a college.

Many college and university administrators are known as *deans.* Deans are the administrative heads of specific divisions or groups within the university and are in charge of overseeing the activities and policies of that division. One type of dean is an *academic dean.* Academic deans are concerned with such issues as the requirements for a major, the courses offered, and the faculty hired within a specific academic department or division. The field of academic deanship includes such titles as dean of the college of humanities, dean of social and behavioral sciences, and dean of the graduate school, just to name a few. The *dean of students* is responsible for the student-affairs program, often including such areas as student housing, organizations, clubs, and activities.

Registrars prepare class schedules and final exam schedules. They maintain computer records of student data, such as grades and degree requirements. They prepare school catalogs and student handbooks. *Associate registrars* assist in running the school registrar's office.

Recruiters visit high school campuses and college fairs to provide information about their school and to interest students in applying for admission. They develop relationships with high school administrators and arrange to meet with counselors, students, and parents.

Financial aid administrators direct the scholarship, grant, and loan programs that provide financial assistance to students and help them meet the costs of tuition, fees, books, and other living expenses. The administrator keeps students informed of the financial assistance available to them and helps answer student and parent questions and concerns. At smaller colleges, this work might be done by a single person, the *financial aid officer.* At larger colleges and universities, the staff might be bigger, and the financial aid officer will head a department and direct the activities of *financial aid counselors,* who handle most of the personal contact with students.

Other college administrators include *college admissions counselors,* who review records, interview prospective students, and process applications for admission. *Alumni directors* oversee the alumni associations of colleges and universities. An alumni director maintains relationships with the graduates of the college primarily for fundraising purposes.

Such jobs as university *president, vice president,* and *provost* are among the highest ranking college and university administrative positions. Generally the president and vice president act as high-level managers, overseeing the rest of a college's administration. They handle business concerns, press relations, public image, and community involvement, and they listen to faculty and administration concerns, often casting the final vote on issues such as compensation, advancement, and tenure. At most schools, the provost is in charge of the many collegiate deans. Working through the authority of the deans, the provost manages the college faculty. The provost also oversees budgets, the academic schedule, event planning, and participates in faculty hiring and promotion decisions.

REQUIREMENTS

High School

A good, well-rounded education is important for anyone pursuing some of the top administrative positions. To prepare for a job in college administration, take accounting and math courses, as you may be dealing with financial records and student statistics. To be a dean of a college, you must have good communication skills, so you should take courses in English literature and composition. Also, speech courses are important, as you'll be required to give presentations and represent your department at meetings and conferences. Follow your guidance counselor's college preparatory plan, which will likely include courses in science, economics, foreign language, history, and sociology.

Postsecondary Training

Education requirements for jobs in college administration depend on the size of the school and the job position. Some assistant positions may not require anything more than a few years of experience in an office. For most jobs in college administration, however, you'll need at least a bachelor's degree. For the top administrative positions, you'll need a master's or a doctorate. A bachelor's degree in any field is usually acceptable for pursuing this career. After you've received your bachelor's, you may choose to pursue a master's in student personnel, administration, or subjects such as economics, psychology, and sociology. Other important studies include education, counseling, information processing, business, and finance. In order to become a college dean, you'll need a doctorate degree and many years of experience with a college or university. Your degree may be in your area of study or in college administration.

Other Requirements

As a college administrator, you should be very organized and able to manage a busy office of assistants. Some offices require more organization than others; for example, a financial aid office handles the records and aid disbursement for the entire student body and requires a director with an eye for efficiency and the ability to keep track of all the various sources of student funding. As a dean, however, you'll work in a smaller office, concentrating more on issues concerning faculty and committees, and you'll rely on your diplomatic skills for maintaining an efficient and successful department. People skills are valuable for college deans, as you'll be representing your department both within the university and at national conferences.

Whatever the administrative position, it is important to have patience and tact to handle a wide range of personalities as well as an emotional steadiness when confronted with unusual and unexpected situations.

EXPLORING

To learn something about what the job of administrator entails, talk to your high school principal and superintendent. Also, interview administrators at colleges and universities. Many of their office phone numbers are listed in college directories. The email addresses of the administrators of many different departments, from deans to registrars, are often published on college websites. You should also discuss the career with the college recruiters who visit your high school. Familiarize yourself with all the various aspects of running a college and university by looking at college student handbooks and course catalogs. Most handbooks list all the offices and administrators and how they assist students and faculty.

EMPLOYERS

Administrators are needed all across the country to run colleges and universities. Job opportunities exist at public and private institutions, community colleges, and universities both large and small. In a smaller college, an administrator may run more than one department. There are more job openings for administrators in universities serving large student bodies.

STARTING OUT

There are several different types of entry-level positions available in the typical college administrative office. If you can gain part-time work or an internship in admissions or another office while you are still in school, you will have a great advantage when seeking work in this field after graduation. Any other experience in an administrative or managerial position, which involves working with people or with computerized data, is also helpful. Entry-level positions often involve filing, data processing, and updating records or charts. You might also move into a position as an administrator after working as a college professor. Deans in colleges and universities have usually worked many years as tenured professors.

The department of human resources in most colleges and universities maintains a listing of job openings at the institution and will often advertise the positions nationally. *The Chronicle of Higher Education* (http://www.chronicle.com) is a newspaper with national job listings. The College and University Professional Association for Human Resources (CUPA-HR) also maintains a job list at its website: http://www.cupahr.org.

ADVANCEMENT

Entry-level positions, which usually require only a bachelor's degree, include *admissions counselors,* who advise students regarding admissions requirements and decisions, and *evaluators,* who check high school transcripts and college transfer records to determine whether applying students may be admitted. Administrative assistants are hired for the offices of registrars, financial aid departments, and deans.

Advancement from any of these positions will depend on the manner in which an office is organized as well as how large it is. One may move up to assistant director or associate director, or, in a larger office, into any specialized divisions such as minority admissions, financial aid counseling, or disabled student services. Advancement also may come through transferring to other departments, schools, or systems.

Workshops and seminars are available through professional associations for those interested in staying informed and becoming more knowledgeable in the field, but it is highly unlikely that an office employee will gain the top administrative level without a graduate degree.

EARNINGS

Salaries for college administrators vary widely among two-year and four-year colleges and among public and private institutions, but they are generally comparable to those of college faculty. According to the U.S. Department of Labor's 2001 National Occupational Employment and Wage Estimates, the median salary for education administrators was $61,700. The lowest paid 10 percent of administrators earned $33,640 per year, while the highest paid made $112,620 annually.

According to findings by CUPA-HR, the following academic deans had these median annual salaries for 2000–01: dean of medicine, $272,200; dean of engineering, $146,938; dean of arts and sciences,

$94,666; and dean of mathematics, $69,449. The CUPA-HR also reports the median annual salary for registrars as $58,241, for dean of students as $67,000, and for director of student activities as $39,292.

According to a study done by the *Chronicle of Higher Education*, the average pay for college presidents was $207,000 a year in 2000. Though college presidents can earn high salaries, they are often not as high as earnings of other top administrators and even some college coaches. For example, competition can drive up the pay for highly sought after medical specialists, economics educators, or football coaches.

Most colleges and universities provide excellent benefits packages including health insurance, paid vacation, sick leave, and tuition remission. Higher level administrators such as presidents, deans, and provosts often receive such bonuses as access to special university clubs, tickets to sporting events, expense accounts for entertaining university guests, and other privileges.

WORK ENVIRONMENT

College and universities are usually pleasant places to work. Offices are often spacious and comfortable, and the campus can be a scenic, relaxing work setting.

Employment in most administrative positions is usually on a 12-month basis. Many of the positions, such as admissions director, financial aid counselor, and dean of students, require a great deal of direct contact with students, and so working hours may vary according to student needs. It is not unusual for college administrators to work long hours during peak enrollment periods, such as the beginning of each quarter or semester. During these periods, the office can be fast paced and stressful as administrators work to assist as many students as possible. Directors are sometimes required to work evenings and weekends to provide broader student access to administrative services. In addition, administrators are sometimes required to travel to other colleges, career fairs, high schools, and professional conferences to provide information about the school for which they work.

OUTLOOK

The U.S. Department of Labor predicts that overall employment for education administrators will grow about as fast as the average through the next decade. Competition for these prestigious positions, however, will be stiff. Many faculty at institutions of higher learning have the educational and experience requirements for these jobs. Candidates may face less competition for positions in nonacademic areas, such as admissions or fund-raising. Those who are already working within a department seeking an administrator and those willing to relocate will have the best chances of getting administrative positions.

FOR MORE INFORMATION

For information about publications, current legislation, and membership, contact

American Association of University Administrators
PO Box 261363
Plano, TX 75026-1363
http://www.aaua.org

For job listings and information about membership, contact

College and University Professional Association for Human Resources
Tyson Place
2607 Kingston Pike, Suite 250
Knoxville, Tennessee 37919
Tel: 865-637-7673
http://www.cupahr.org

COMMODITIES BROKERS

QUICK FACTS

School Subjects Business Mathematics	**Certification or Licensing** Required
Personal Skills Communication/ideas Leadership/management	**Outlook** Faster than the average
Work Environment Primarily indoors Primarily one location	**DOT** 162
Minimum Education Level High school diploma	**GOE** 11.06.03
Salary Range $25,990 to $56,690 to $1,000,000+	**NOC** 1113
	O*NET-SOC 41-3031.00, 41-3031.01

OVERVIEW

Commodities brokers, also known as *futures commission merchants,* act as agents in carrying out purchases and sales of commodities for customers or traders. Commodities are primary goods that are either raw or partially refined. Such goods are produced by farmers (corn, wheat, or cattle) or are mined (gold, copper, or silver). Brokers, who may work at a brokerage house, on the floor of a commodities exchange, or independently, are paid a fee or commission for acting as the middlemen to conduct and complete the trade.

HISTORY

In medieval Europe, business was transacted at local market fairs, and commodities, primarily agricultural, were traded at scheduled times and places. As market fairs grew, "fair letters" were set up as a currency representing a future cash settlement for a transaction. With these letters, merchants could travel from one fair to another.

This was the precursor to the Japanese system, in which landowners used "certificates of receipt" for their rice crops. As the certificates made their way into the economy, the Dojima Rice Market was established and became the first place where traders bought and sold contracts for the future delivery of rice.

"Forward contracts" entered the U.S. marketplace in the early 19th century. Farmers, swept up in the boom of industrial growth, transportation, and commerce, began to arrange for the future sale of their crops. Traders entered the market along with the development of these contracts. However, there were no regulations to oversee that the commodity was actually delivered or that it was of an acceptable quality. Furthermore, each transaction was an individual business deal because the terms of each contract were variable. To address these issues, the Chicago Board of Trade was formed in 1848, and by 1865 it had set up standards and rules for trading "to arrive" contracts, now known as commodity futures contracts.

THE JOB

A futures contract is an agreement to deliver a particular commodity, such as wheat, pork bellies, or coffee, at a specific date, time, and place. For example, a farmer might sell his oats before they are sown (known as hedging) because he can't predict what kind of price he'll be able to demand later on. If the weather is favorable and crops are good, he'll have competition, which will drive prices down. If there is a flood or drought, oats will be scarce, driving the price up. He wants to ensure a fair price for his product to protect his business and limit his risk, since he can't predict what will happen.

On the other side of the equation is the user of the oats, perhaps a cereal manufacturer, who purchases these contracts for a delivery of oats at some future date. Producers and users do not correspond to a one-to-one ratio, and the broker is a middleman who does the buying and selling of contracts between the two groups. Brokers may place orders to buy or sell contracts for themselves, for individual clients, or for companies, all of whom hope to make a profit by correctly anticipating the direction of a commodity's price. Brokers are licensed to represent clients, and brokers' first responsibility is to take care of their clients' orders before doing trading for themselves. *Traders* also buy and sell contracts for themselves. Unlike brokers, however, they are not licensed (and thus not allowed) to do this work for clients.

When placing a trade for others, brokers are paid a fee or a commission for acting as the agent in making the sale. There are two broad categories of brokers, though they are becoming less distinct. *Full service brokers* provide considerable research to clients, offer price quotes, give trading advice, and assist the customer in making trading decisions. *Discount brokers* simply fill the orders as directed by clients. Some brokers offer intermediate levels of optional services on a sliding scale of commission, such as market research and strategic advice.

In general, brokers are responsible for taking and carrying out all commodity orders and being available on call to do so; reporting back to the client upon fulfilling the order request; keeping the client abreast of breaking news; maintaining account balances and other financial data; and obtaining market information when needed and informing the client about important changes in the marketplace.

Brokers can work on the floor of a commodity futures exchange—the place where contracts are bought and sold—for a brokerage house or independently. The exchange has a trading floor where brokers transact their business in the trading pit. There are 11 domestic exchanges, with the main ones in Chicago, Kansas City, New York, and Minneapolis. To be allowed to work on the floor, a broker must have a membership (also known as a "seat") in the exchange or must be employed by a company with a seat in the exchange, which is a private organization. Memberships are limited to a specific number, and seats may be rented or purchased. Although seat prices vary due to factors such as the health of the overall economy and the type of seat being purchased, they are all extremely expensive. As an example, consider seats at the Chicago Mercantile Exchange (CME). The CME has several divisions with seats for each. Full CME seats give the member the right to trade in any division of the exchange, from futures in broiler chickens to interest rates on Treasury bills; other seats give the member the right to trade only in a certain area. An International Monetary Market seat, for example, allows the member to trade only on currency and interest rate futures. Seat prices at the CME can range from tens of thousands of dollars to hundreds of thousands of dollars (full CME seats have been known to sell for $700,000 and more). Naturally, this expense alone limits the number of individuals who can become members. In addition to being able to afford a seat, candidates for membership to any exchange must undergo thorough investigations of their credit standings, financial backgrounds, characters, and understanding of trading.

Most brokers do not have seats but work for brokerage houses that deal in futures. Examples of these houses include Merrill Lynch or Dean Witter, which deal in stocks, bonds, commodities, and other investments, and smaller houses, such as R. J. O'Brien, that handle only commodities.

Companies can also have a seat on the exchange, and they have their own *floor brokers* in the pit to carry out trades for the brokerage house. Brokers in the company take orders from the public for buying or selling a contract and promptly pass it on to the floor broker in the pit of the exchange. Brokers also have the choice of running their own business. Known as *introducing brokers,* they handle their own clients and trades and use brokerage houses to place their orders. Introducing brokers earn a fee by soliciting business trades, but they don't directly handle the customer's funds.

REQUIREMENTS

High School

Although there are no formal educational requirements for becoming a broker, a high school diploma and a college degree are strongly recommended. Commodities brokers need to have a wide range of knowledge, covering such areas as economics, world politics, and sometimes even the weather. To begin to develop this broad base of knowledge, start in high school by taking history, math, science, and business classes. Since commodities brokers are constantly working with people to make a sale, take English classes to enhance your communication skills. In addition to this course work, you might also consider getting a part-time job working in a sales position. Such a job will also give you the chance to hone your communication and sales skills.

Postsecondary Training

The vast majority of brokers have a college degree. While there is no "commodities broker major," you can improve your chances of obtaining a job in this field by studying economics, finance, or business administration while in college. Keep in mind that you should continue to develop your understanding of politics and technologies, so government and computer classes will also be useful.

Brokerage firms look for employees who have sales ability, strong communication skills, and self-confidence. Commodities is often a second career for many people who have demonstrated these qualities in other positions.

Certification or Licensing

To become a commodities broker, it is necessary to pass the National Commodities Futures Examination (the Series 3 exam) to become eligible to satisfy the registration requirements of federal, state, and industry regulatory agencies. The test covers market and trading knowledge as well as rules and regulations and is composed of true/false and multiple choice questions. Registration for the exam is through the National Association of Securities

Top 25 Economics Graduate Schools

U.S. News & World Report prepares annual ranking lists for graduate school programs. The following lists show the top ranked economics schools.

Massachusetts Institute of Technology
http://econ-www.mit.edu
Harvard University (Mass.)
http://www.economics.harvard.edu
Princeton University (N.J.)
http://www.econ.princeton.edu
Stanford University (Calif.)
http://www-econ.stanford.edu
University of Chicago
http://economics.uchicago.edu
University of California-Berkeley
http://emlab.berkeley.edu/econ
Yale University (Conn.)
http://www.econ.yale.edu
Northwestern University (Ill.)
http://www.econ.northwestern.edu
University of Pennsylvania
http://www.econ.upenn.edu
University of Wisconsin-Madison
http://www.ssc.wisc.edu/econ
University of California-Los Angeles
http://econweb.sscnet.ucla.edu
University of Michigan-Ann Arbor
http://www.econ.lsa.umich.edu

(continues)

Top 25 Economics Graduate Schools

(continued)

University of Minnesota-Twin Cities
http://www.econ.umn.edu
California Institute of Technology
http://www.hss.caltech.edu/ss/phd/overview
Columbia University (N.Y.)
http://www.columbia.edu/cu/economics
University of Rochester (N.Y.)
http://www.econ.rochester.edu
Cornell University (N.Y.)
http://www.arts.cornell.edu/econ
University of California-San Diego
http://www.econ.ucsd.edu
Carnegie Mellon University (Pa.)
http://littlehurt.gsia.cmu.edu/gsiadoc/contents.asp
New York University
http://www.econ.nyu.edu
Brown University (R.I.)
http://www.econ.brown.edu
Duke University (N.C.)
http://www.econ.duke.edu
University of Texas-Austin
http://www.eco.utexas.edu
Johns Hopkins University (Md.)
http://www.econ.jhu.edu
University of Maryland-College Park
http://www.bsos.umd.edu/econ

Source: *U.S. News & World Report* (ranked in 2001)

Dealers Regulation. Preparation materials are available through a number of sources, such as the Institute for Financial Markets (http://www.theifm.org). Brokers must also register with the National Futures Association.

Other Requirements

To be a successful broker, you must possess a combination of research and money-management skills. You need to be attentive to detail and have a knack for analyzing data. Strong communications and sales skills are important as well, as brokers make money by convincing people to let them place their trades. An interest in and awareness of the world around you will also be a contributing factor to your success in this field, as commodities are influenced by everything from political decisions and international news to social and fashion trends.

You must also be emotionally stable to work in such a volatile environment. You need to be persistent, aggressive, and comfortable taking risks and dealing with failure. Strong, consistent, and independent judgment is also key. You must be a disciplined and diligent worker, able to comb through reams of market reports and charts to gain a thorough understanding of a particular commodity and the mechanics of the marketplace. You also need to be outspoken and assertive and able to yell out prices loudly and energetically on the trading floor and to command attention.

EXPLORING

Students interested in commodities trading should visit one of the futures exchanges. All of them offer public tours, and you'll get to see up close just how the markets work and the roles of the players involved. All the exchanges offer educational programs and publications, and most have a website (See "For More Information" at the end of this article). The CME publishes *The Merc at Work,* the full text of which is also available at its website, as well as many other educational handbooks and pamphlets. There are hundreds of industry newsletters and magazines available (such as *Futures* magazine), and many offer free samples of publications or products. Read what trading advisers have to say and how they say it. Learn their lingo and gain an understanding of the marketplace. If you have any contacts in the industry, arrange to spend a day with a broker. Watch and learn as he or she enters, processes, and reports orders.

Do your own research. Adopt a commodity, chart its prices, test some of your own ideas, and analyze the marketplace. There are also a variety of inexpensive software programs, as well as websites, that simulate trading.

Finally, consider a job as a *runner* during the summer before your freshman year in college. Runners transport the order, or "paper," from the phone clerk to the broker in the pit and relay information to and from members on the floor. This is the single best way to get hands-on experience in the industry.

EMPLOYERS

Commodities brokers work on the floor of a commodity futures exchange, for brokerage houses, or independently.

STARTING OUT

College graduates can start working with a brokerage house as an associate and begin handling stocks. After several years they can take the certification exam and move into futures. Another option is to start as support staff, either at the exchange or the brokerage house. Sales personnel try to get customers to open accounts, and account executives develop and service customers for the brokerage firm. At the exchange, phone clerks receive incoming orders and communicate the information to the runners. Working in the back as an accountant, money manager, or member of the research staff is another route to becoming a broker. School placement offices may be able to assist graduates in finding jobs with brokerage houses. You can also apply directly to brokerage houses.

Many successful brokers and traders began their careers as runners, and each exchange has its own training program. Though the pay is low, runners learn the business very quickly with a hands-on experience not available in an academic classroom. Contact one of the commodities exchanges for information on becoming a runner.

ADVANCEMENT

A broker who simply executes trades can advance to become a full-service broker. Through research and analysis and the accumulation of experience and knowledge about the industry, a broker can advance from an order filler and become a commodity trading adviser. A broker can also become a money manager and make all trading decisions for clients.

Within the exchange, a broker can become a *floor manager,* overseeing the processes of order taking and information exchange. To make more money, a broker can also begin to place his or her own trades for his or her own private account, though the broker's first responsibility is to the customers.

EARNINGS

This is an entrepreneurial business. A broker's commission is based on the number of clients he or she recruits, the amount of money they invest, and the profit they make. The sky's the limit. In recent years, the most successful broker made $25 million. A typical salary for a newly hired employee in a brokerage might average $1,500 per month plus a 30 percent commission on sales. Smaller firms are likely to pay a smaller commission. The U.S. Department of Labor reports that the median annual earnings for securities, commodities, and financial services sales representatives (a group including commodities brokers) were $59,690 in 2001. The lowest paid 10 percent earned less than $25,990; the highest paid 25 percent earned more than $113,460 annually.

Benefits vary but are usually very good at large employers. For example, those working at the Chicago Board of Trade, one of the world's leading futures exchanges, enjoy numerous benefits. Employees are eligible for vacation six months after employment and receive three weeks after three years. Employees are also paid for sick days, personal days, and eight holidays. During the summer months various departments offer flex time, allowing employees to take Fridays off by working longer hours during the week. Employees also receive numerous forms of insurance, including medical, life, and disability. Full tuition reimbursement is available, as is a company-matched savings plan, a tax-deferred savings plan, and a pension program. Other large exchanges and brokerage houses offer similar combinations of benefits.

WORK ENVIRONMENT

The trading floor is noisy and chaotic, as trading is done using an "open outcry" system. Every broker must be an auctioneer, yelling out his own price bids for purchases and sales. The highest bid wins and silences all the others. When a broker's primal scream is not heard, bids and offers can also be communicated with hand signals.

Brokers stand for most of the day, often in the same place, so that traders interested in their commodity can locate them easily. Each broker wears a distinctly colored jacket with a prominent identification badge. The letter on the badge identifies the broker and appears on the paperwork relating to the trade. Members of the exchange and employees of member firms wear red jackets. Some brokers and traders also have uniquely patterned jackets to further increase their visibility in the pit.

Brokers and traders do not have a nine-to-five job. While commodities trading on the exchange generally takes place from 9:00 A.M. to 1:00 P.M., international trading runs from 2:45 P.M. to 6:50 A.M.

In the rough and tumble world of the futures exchange, emotions run high as people often win or lose six-figure amounts within hours. Tension is fierce, the pace is frantic, and angry verbal—and sometimes physical—exchanges are not uncommon.

OUTLOOK

The U.S. Bureau of Labor Statistics predicts employment for securities, commodities, and financial services sales agents to grow faster than the average throughout the next decade. Growth will result from people expecting high returns on their investments (leading them to increasingly invest in markets), the growing number and increasing complexity of investment options, and the new commodities available for investment due to the increasingly globalized marketplace. Additionally, as people and companies become more interested in and sophisticated about investing, they are entering futures markets and need the services provided by brokers.

New computer and information technology is rapidly influencing and advancing the industry. A growing number of exchanges now use electronic systems to automate trades, and many use them exclusively. Many systems have unique features designed specifically to meet customers' needs. New technology, such as electronic order entry, hookups to overseas exchanges, and night trading, is rapidly evolving, offering brokers new ways to manage risk and provide price information.

Because many people are attracted to this work by the possibility of earning large incomes, competition for jobs is particularly keen. However, job turnover is also fairly high due to the stress of the work and the fact that many beginning brokers are not able to establish a large enough clientele to be profitable. Small brokerage firms may offer the best opportunities for those just starting out in this work.

FOR MORE INFORMATION

This center provides information on workshops, home study courses, educational materials, and publications for futures and securities professionals.

Center for Futures Education
PO Box 309
Grove City, PA 16127
Tel: 724-458-5860
Email: info@thectr.com
http://www.thectr.com

For a history of CBOT, and information on tours and educational programs, contact

Chicago Board of Trade (CBOT)
141 West Jackson Boulevard
Chicago, IL 60604-2994
Tel: 312-435-3500
http://www.cbot.com

For a general overview of options, visit the Learning Center *section of the CBOE website*

Chicago Board Options Exchange (CBOE)
400 South LaSalle Street
Chicago, IL 60605
Tel: 888-OPTIONS
Email: help@cboe.com
http://www.cboe.com

The CME offers a wide variety of educational programs and materials, and general information on commodities careers through the Education link of its website.

Chicago Mercantile Exchange (CME)
30 South Wacker Drive
Chicago, IL 60606
Tel: 312-930-6937
Email: info@cme.com
http://www.cme.com

For information on careers and education, contact

National Association of Securities Dealers
1735 K Street, NW
Washington, DC 20006-1500
Tel: 202-728-8000
http://www.nasd.com

For information on membership, training, and registration, contact

National Futures Association
200 West Madison Street, Suite 1600
Chicago, IL 60606-3447
Tel: 800-621-3570
Email: information@nfa.futures.org
http://www.nfa.futures.org

The educational section of the Philadelphia Stock Exchange website provides a glossary of terms, suggested reading, and an overview of the financial industry.

Philadelphia Stock Exchange
1900 Market Street
Philadelphia, PA 19103-3584
Tel: 800-THE-PHLX
Email: info@phlx.com
http://www.phlx.com

Visit the websites or contact the following exchanges for general background information about the field:

Minneapolis Grain Exchange
http://www.mgex.com

New York Board of Trade
http://www.nybot.com

New York Mercantile Exchange
http://www.nymex.com

COST ESTIMATORS

QUICK FACTS

School Subjects Business Economics Mathematics	**Certification or Licensing** Recommended
Personal Skills Leadership/management Technical/scientific	**Outlook** About as fast as the average
Work Environment Indoors and outdoors Primarily multiple locations	**DOT** 160
Minimum Education Level Some postsecondary training	**GOE** 11.06.01
Salary Range $27,710 to $45,800 to $75,460+	**NOC** 2234
	O*NET-SOC 13-1051.00

OVERVIEW

Cost estimators use standard estimating techniques to calculate the cost of a construction or manufacturing project. They help contractors, owners, and project planners determine how much a project or product will cost to decide if it is economically viable. There are approximately 211,000 cost estimators employed in the United States.

HISTORY

Cost estimators collect and analyze information on various factors influencing costs, such as the labor, materials, and machinery needed for a particular project. Cost estimating became a profession as production techniques became more complex. Weighing the many costs involved in a construction or manufacturing project soon required specialized knowledge beyond the skills and training of the average builder or contractor. Today, cost estimators work in many industries but are predominantly employed in construction and manufacturing.

THE JOB

In the construction industry, the nature of the work is largely determined by the type and size of the project being estimated. For a large building project, for example, the estimator reviews architectural drawings and other bidding documents before any construction begins. The estimator then visits the potential construction site to collect information that may affect the way the structure is built, such as the site's access to transportation, water, electricity, and other needed resources. While out in the field, the estimator also analyzes the topography of the land, taking note of its general characteristics, such as drainage areas and the location of trees and other vegetation. After compiling thorough research, the estimator writes a quantity survey, or takeoff. This is an itemized report of the quantity of materials and labor a firm will need for the proposed project.

Large projects often require several estimators, all specialists in a given area. For example, one estimator may assess the electrical costs of a project, while another concentrates on the transportation or insurance costs. In this case, it is the responsibility of a *chief estimator* to combine the reports and submit one development proposal.

In manufacturing, estimators work with engineers to review blueprints and other designs. They develop a list of the materials and labor needed for production. Aiming to control costs but maintain quality, estimators must weigh the option of producing parts in-house or purchasing them from other vendors. After this research, they write a report on the overall costs of manufacturing, taking into consideration influences such as improved employee learning curves, material waste, overhead, and the need to correct problems as manufacturing goes along.

To write their reports, estimators must know current prices for labor and materials and other factors that influence costs. They obtain this data through commercial price books, catalogs, and the Internet or by calling vendors directly to obtain quotes.

Estimators should also be able to compute and understand accounting and mathematical formulas in order to make their cost reports. Computer programs are frequently used to do the routine calculations, producing more accurate results and leaving the estimator more time to analyze data.

REQUIREMENTS

High School

To prepare for a job in cost estimating, you should take courses in accounting, business, economics, and mathematics. Because a large part of this job involves comparing calculations, it is essential that you are comfortable with and confident in your math skills. English courses with a heavy concentration in writing will help to develop your communication skills. Cost estimators must be able to write clear and accurate reports of their analyses. Finally, drafting and shop courses are also useful since estimators must be able to review and understand blueprints and other design plans.

Postsecondary Training

Though not required for the job, most employers of cost estimators in both construction and manufacturing prefer applicants with formal education. In construction, cost estimators generally have associate's or bachelor's degrees in construction management, construction science, engineering, or architecture. Those employed with manufacturers often have degrees in physical science, business, mathematics, operations research, statistics, engineering, economics, finance, or accounting.

Many colleges and universities offer courses in cost estimating as part of the curriculum for an associate's, bachelor's, or master's degree. These courses cover subjects such as cost estimating, cost control, project planning and management, and computer applications. The Association for the Advancement of Cost Engineering International offers a list of education programs related to cost engineering. Check out the association's website at http://www.aacei.org for more information.

Certification or Licensing

Although it is not required, many cost estimators find it helpful to become certified to improve their standing within the professional community. Obtaining certification proves that the estimator has obtained adequate job training and education. Information on certification procedures is available from organizations such as the American Society of Professional Estimators, the Association for the Advancement of Cost Engineering International, and the Society of Cost Estimating and Analysis.

Other Requirements

To be a cost estimator, you should have sharp mathematical and analytical skills. Cost estimators must work well with others and be confident and assertive when presenting findings to engineers, business owners, and design professionals. To work as a cost estimator in the construction industry, you will likely need some experience before you start, which can be gained through an internship or cooperative education program.

EXPLORING

Practical work experience is necessary to become a cost estimator. Consider taking a part-time position with a construction crew or manufacturing firm during your summer vacations. Because of more favorable working conditions, construction companies are the busiest during the summer months and may be looking for additional assistance. Join any business or manufacturing clubs that your school may offer.

Another way to discover more about career opportunities is simply by talking to a professional cost estimator. Ask your school counselor to help arrange an interview with an estimator to ask questions about his or her job demands, work environment, and personal opinion of the job.

EMPLOYERS

Approximately 211,000 cost estimators are employed in the United States: 50 percent by the construction industry and 20 percent by manufacturing companies. Other employers include engineering and architecture firms, business services, and the government.

Estimators are employed throughout the country, but the largest concentrations are found in cities or rapidly growing suburban areas. More job opportunities exist in or near large commercial or government centers.

STARTING OUT

Cost estimators often start out working in the industry as laborers, such as construction workers. After gaining experience and taking the necessary training courses, a worker may move into the more specialized role of estimator. Another possible route into cost estimating is through a formal training program, either through a professional organization that sponsors educational programs or through technical schools, community colleges, or universities.

School placement counselors can be good sources of employment leads for recent graduates. Applying directly to manufacturers, construction firms, and government agencies is another way to find your first job.

Whether employed in construction or manufacturing, most cost estimators are provided with intensive on-the-job training. Generally, new hires work with experienced estimators to become familiar with the work involved. They develop skills in blueprint reading and learn construction specifications before accompanying estimators to the construction site. In time, new hires learn how to determine quantities and specifications from project designs and report appropriate material and labor costs.

ADVANCEMENT

Promotions for cost estimators are dependent on skill and experience. Advancement usually comes in the form of more responsibility and higher wages. A skilled cost estimator at a large construction company may become a chief estimator. Some experienced cost estimators go into consulting work, offering their services to government, construction, and manufacturing firms.

EARNINGS

Salaries vary according to the size of the construction or manufacturing firm and the experience and education of the worker. According to the *Occupational Outlook Handbook,* the median annual salary for cost estimators was $45,800 in 2000. The lowest paid 10 percent earned less than $27,710 and the highest paid 10 percent earned over $75,460. By industry, the median annual earnings were as follows: residential building construction, $46,360; miscellaneous special trade contractors, $45,740; plumbing, heating, and air-conditioning, $47,680; electrical work, $49,630; and commercial building construction, $50,930. Starting salaries for graduates of engineering or construction management programs were higher than those with degrees in other fields.

WORK ENVIRONMENT

Much of the cost estimator's work takes place in a typical office setting with access to accounting records and other information. However, estimators must also visit construction sites or manufacturing facilities to inspect production procedures. These sites may be dirty, noisy, and potentially hazardous if the cost estimator is not equipped with proper protective gear such as hard hats or earplugs. During a site visit, cost estimators consult with engineers, work supervisors, and other professionals involved in the production or manufacturing process.

Estimators usually work a 40-hour week, although longer hours may be required if a project faces a deadline. For construction estimators, overtime hours almost always occur in the summer when most projects are in full force.

OUTLOOK

Employment for cost estimators is expected to increase about as fast as the average through the next decade, according to the U.S. Department of Labor. As in most industries, highly trained college graduates and those with the most experience have the best job prospects.

Many jobs will arise from the need to replace workers leaving the industry, either to retire or change jobs. In addition, growth within the residential and commercial construction industry is a large cause for much of the employment demand for estimators. The fastest growing areas in construction are in special trade and government projects, including the building and repairing of highways, streets, bridges, subway systems, airports, waterways, and electrical plants.

In manufacturing, employment is predicted to remain stable. Estimators will be in demand because employers will continue to need their services to control operating costs.

FOR MORE INFORMATION

For information on certification and educational programs, contact

American Society of Professional Estimators
11141 Georgia Avenue, Suite 412
Wheaton, MD 20902
Tel: 301-929-8848
Email: info@aspenational.com
http://www.aspenational.com

For information on certification, educational programs, and scholarships, contact

Association for the Advancement of Cost Engineering International
209 Prairie Avenue, Suite 100
Morgantown, WV 26501

Tel: 800-858-2678
Email: info@aacei.org
http://www.aacei.org

For information on certification, job listings, and a glossary of cost estimating terms, visit the SCEA website.

Society of Cost Estimating and Analysis (SCEA)
101 South Whiting Street, Suite 201
Alexandria, VA 22304
Tel: 703-751-8069
Email: scea@sceaonline.net
http://www.sceaonline.net

DEMOGRAPHERS

QUICK FACTS

School Subjects Computer science Mathematics Sociology	**Certification or Licensing** None available
Personal Skills Communication/ideas Technical/scientific	**Outlook** About as fast as the average
Work Environment Primarily indoors One location with some travel	**DOT** 054
Minimum Education Level Bachelor's degree	**GOE** 11.03.02
Salary Range $21,900 to $48,330 to $76,530	**NOC** 2161
	O*NET-SOC 15-2041.00, 19-3093.00

OVERVIEW

Demographers are population specialists who collect and analyze vital statistics related to human population changes, such as births, marriages, and deaths. They plan and conduct research surveys to study population trends and assess the effects of population movements. Demographers work for government organizations as well as at private companies across the country.

HISTORY

Throughout history, people have conducted population studies of one kind or another for various reasons. As early as the mid-1600s, for example, the English were the first to systematically record and register all births and deaths. Over the years, recording techniques were refined and expanded to conduct more sophisticated population surveys so that governments could collect information, such as number of people and extent of property holdings, to measure wealth and levy taxes.

In recent years, census taking has become much more comprehensive, and the scientific methods of collecting and interpreting demographic information have also improved extensively. Demographers now have a leading role in developing detailed population studies that are designed to reveal the essential characteristics of a society, such as the availability of health care or average income levels.

THE JOB

Demography is the statistical study of human populations. A demographer works to establish ways in which numbers may be organized to produce new and useful information. For example, demographers may study data collected on the frequency of disease in a certain area, develop graphs and charts to plot the spread of that disease, and then forecast the probability that the medical problem may spread.

Many demographers work on the basis of a "sampling" technique in which the characteristics of the whole population are judged by taking a sample of a part of it. For example, demographers may collect data on the educational level of residents living in various locations throughout a community. They can use this information to make a projection of the average educational level of the community as a whole. In this way, demographers conduct research and forecast trends on various social and economic patterns throughout an area.

Demographers not only conduct their own surveys but often work with statistics gathered from government sources, private surveys, and public opinion polls. They may compare different statistical information, such as an area's average income level and its population, and use it to forecast the community's future educational and medical needs. They may tabulate the average age, income, educational levels, crime rate, and poverty rate of a farming community and compare the results with the same statistics of an urban environment.

Computers have radically changed the role of the demographer. Now, much greater amounts of data can be collected and analyzed. In the U.S. Census Bureau, for example, demographers work with material that has been compiled from the nationwide census conducted every 10 years. Millions of pieces of demographic information, such as age, gender, occupation, educational level, and country of origin, are collected from people around the country. A demographer may take this statistical information, analyze it, and then use it to forecast population growth or economic trends.

Demographers investigate and analyze a variety of social science questions for the government, such as rates of illness, availability of police services, and other issues that define a community. Private companies, such as retail chains, may use the information to make marketing decisions, such as where to open a new store and how to best reach possible customers.

Demographers may work on long-range planning. Population trends are especially important in such areas as educational and economic planning, and a demographer's analysis is often used to help set policy on health care issues and a host of other social science concerns. Local, state, and national government agencies all use the demographer's statistical forecasts in an attempt to accurately provide transportation, education, and other services.

Demographers may teach demographic research techniques to students. They also work as consultants to private businesses. Much of their time is spent doing library research, analyzing demographic information of various population groups.

An *applied statistician*, a specialized type of demographer, uses accepted theories and known statistical formulas to collect and analyze data in a specific area, such as the availability of health care in a specified location.

REQUIREMENTS

High School

Since you will need at least a bachelor's degree to find work as a demographer, you should take college preparatory courses, such as social studies, English, and mathematics (algebra and geometry) while in high school. In addition, take any statistics classes that your school offers. Training in computer science is also advantageous because computers are used extensively for research and statistical analysis.

Postsecondary Training

College course work should include classes in social research methods, economics, public policy, public health, statistics, and computer applications. Keep in mind that while you can get some starting jobs in the field with a bachelor's degree, most social scientists go on to attain advanced degrees. Many demographers get a doctorate in statistics, sociology, or demography. Approximately 110 universities offer master's programs in statistics, and about 60 have statistics departments offering doctorate programs.

Other Requirements

To work as a demographer, you should enjoy using logic to solve problems and have an aptitude for mathematics. You should also enjoy detailed work and must like to study and learn. Research experience is helpful. Other qualities that are helpful include intellectual curiosity and creativity, good written and oral communication skills, objectivity, and systematic work habits.

EXPLORING

A part-time or summer job at a company with a statistical research department is a good way of gaining insight into the career of demographer. Discussions with professional demographers are another way of learning about the rewards and responsibilities in this field. While in high school, ask your mathematics teachers to give you some simple statistical problems related to population changes to practice the kinds of statistical techniques that demographers use. Exploring statistical surveys and information from the Gallup Organization on the Internet (http://www.gallup.com) is another way to learn about this career. Additionally, undertaking your own demographic survey of an organization or group, such as your school or after-school club, is a project worth considering.

EMPLOYERS

Federal agencies such as the U.S. Census Bureau and the Bureau of Labor Statistics employ a large number of demographers, as do local and state government agencies. Private industry uses the services of demographers, as do universities, colleges, and foundations. Some demographers work as independent consultants rather than full-time employees for any one organization.

STARTING OUT

The usual method of entering the profession is through completion of an undergraduate or graduate degree in sociology or public health with an emphasis in demographic methods. However, according to Cary Davis, former vice president of the Population Reference Bureau in Washington, D.C., most entry-level positions require a graduate degree. "In fact," says Davis, "no one on my staff knows of any demographer who has less than a master's degree. Focus on an area that interests you, such as births and deaths or public health."

Qualified applicants can apply directly to private research firms or other companies that do population studies. University placement offices can help identify such organizations. Government jobs are listed with the Civil Service Commission.

ADVANCEMENT

According to Cary Davis, demographers who narrow their focus and become specialized in an area of interest are most likely to advance. Those with the highest degree of education are also most likely to be promoted.

EARNINGS

Earnings vary widely according to education, training, and place of employment. Social scientists (including sociologists who specialize in demography) earned a median annual salary of approximately $48,330 in 2000, according to the U.S. Department of Labor. Those with a bachelor's degree who started to work for the federal government began in the $21,900–$27,200 range in 2001. Social scientists with a master's degree working for the federal government started at about $33,300, while those with a doctorate started at about $40,200.

In 2001, statisticians working for the federal government (often including demographers) averaged an annual salary of $68,900. Those working in mathematical positions averaged $76,530.

Vacation days and other benefits, such as sick leave, group insurance, and a retirement plan, are typically offered to demographers working full time for any large organization.

WORK ENVIRONMENT

Most demographers work in offices or classrooms during a regular 40-hour week. Depending on the project and deadlines, however, overtime may be required. Those engaged in research may work with other demographers assembling related information. Most of the work revolves around analyzing population data or interpreting computer information. A demographer is also usually responsible for writing a report detailing the findings. Some travel may be required, such as to attend a conference or complete limited field research.

OUTLOOK

According to the U.S. Department of Labor, the social science field is expected to grow about as fast as the average over the next several years. However, there will be keen competition in many areas. Those with the most training and greatest amount of education, preferably a Ph.D., should find the best job prospects. Employment opportunities should be greatest in and around large metropolitan areas, where many colleges, universities, research facilities, and federal agencies are located. Individuals with statistical training will have an advantage.

FOR MORE INFORMATION

For career publications, lists of accredited schools, and job information, contact

American Sociological Association
1307 New York Avenue, NW, Suite 700
Washington, DC 20005
Tel: 202-383-9005
Email: executive.office@asanet.org
http://www.asanet.org

This organization includes demographers, sociologists, economists, public health professionals, and other individuals interested in research and education in the population field. For information on job opportunities, publications, and annual conferences and workshops, contact

Population Association of America
8630 Fenton Street, Suite 722
Silver Spring, MD 20910-3812
Tel: 301-565-6710
Email: info@popassoc.org
http://www.popassoc.org

ECONOMISTS

QUICK FACTS

School Subjects Business Economics Mathematics	**Certification or Licensing** None available
Personal Skills Helping/teaching Technical/scientific	**Outlook** About as fast as the average
Work Environment Primarily indoors Primarily one location	**DOT** 050
Minimum Education Level Master's degree	**GOE** 11.03.05
Salary Range $21,900 to $67,080 to $114,580+	**NOC** 4162
	O*NET-SOC 19-3011.00

OVERVIEW

Economists are concerned with how society uses scarce resources such as land, labor, raw materials, and machinery to produce goods and services for current consumption and future production. Economists study how economic systems address three basic questions: "What shall we produce?" "How shall we produce it?" and "For whom shall we produce it?" The economist then compiles, processes, and interprets the answers to these questions. There are about 134,000 economists and market and survey researchers employed in the United States.

HISTORY

Economics deals with the struggle to divide up a finite amount of goods and services to satisfy an unlimited amount of human needs and desires. No society, no matter how rich and successful, is able to produce everything needed or wanted by individuals. This reality was evident to people throughout history. In ancient Greece, the philosopher Plato discussed economic topics in his work, *The Republic,* saying the division of labor among people was the only way to supply a larger need. Individuals, he said, are not naturally self-sufficient and thus they need to adopt cooperative efforts in the exchange of goods and services.

It was not until 1776 that the theory of economics was given a name. Adam Smith, in his work *Wealth of Nations,* described that individuals, given the opportunity to trade freely, will not create chaos. Instead, free trade results in an orderly, logical system. His belief in this free trade system became what is now called laissez-faire capitalism, which discourages government trade restrictions.

The importance of economics is evidenced by its status as the only social science in which a Nobel Prize is awarded. In the last century, economics has come to be used in making a broad array of decisions within businesses, government agencies, and many other kinds of organizations.

THE JOB

Economists grapple with many issues relating to the supply and demand of goods and services and the means by which they are produced, traded, and consumed. While most economists either teach at the university level or perform research for government agencies, many work for individual for-profit or not-for-profit organizations.

Economics professors teach basic macro- and microeconomics courses as well as courses on advanced topics such as economic history and labor economics. (Macroeconomics deals with the "big picture" of economics, and microeconomics deals with individual companies and persons.) They also perform research, write papers and books, and give lectures, thereby contributing their knowledge to the advancement of the discipline.

Government economists study national economic trends and problems; their analyses often suggest possible changes in government policy to address such issues.

For-profit and not-for-profit companies both employ economists to assess connections of organizational policy to larger business conditions and economic trends. Management often will rely on this research to make financial and other kinds of decisions that affect the company.

In their education, economists usually specialize in a particular area of interest. While the specialties of university economists range across the entire discipline, other economists' expertise generally falls into one of several categories. *Financial economists* examine the relationships among money, credit, and purchasing power to develop monetary policy and forecast financial activity. *International economists* analyze foreign trade to bring about favorable trade balances and establish trade policies. *Labor economists* attempt to forecast labor trends and recommend labor policies for businesses and government entities. *Industrial economists* study the way businesses are internally organized and suggest ways to make maximum use of assets. *Environmental economists* study the relationships between economic issues and the allocation and management of natural resources. *Agricultural economists* study food production, development in rural areas, and the allocation of natural resources.

REQUIREMENTS

High School

A strong college preparatory program is necessary in high school if you wish to enter this field. Courses in other social sciences, economics, mathematics, and English are extremely important to a would-be economist, since analyzing, interpreting, and expressing one's informed opinions about many different kinds of data are the main tasks of someone employed in this field. Also, take computer classes so that you will be able to use this research tool in college and later on. Finally, since you will be heading off to college and probably postgraduate studies, consider taking a foreign language to round out your educational background.

Postsecondary Training

A bachelor's degree with a major in economics is the minimum requirement for an entry-level position such as research assistant. A master's degree, or even a Ph.D., is more commonly required for most positions as an economist.

Typically, an economics major takes at least 10 courses on various economic topics, plus two or more mathematics courses, such as statistics and calculus or algebra. The federal government requires candidates for entry-level economist positions to have a minimum of 21 semester hours of economics and three hours of statistics, accounting, or calculus. Graduate-level courses include such specialties as advanced economic theory, econometrics, international economics, and labor economics.

Other Requirements

Economists' work is detail oriented. They do extensive research and enjoy working in the abstract with theories. Their research work must be precise and well documented. In addition, economists must be able to clearly explain their ideas to a range of people, including other economic experts, political leaders, and even students in a classroom.

EXPLORING

You can augment your interest in economics by taking related courses in social science and mathematics and by becoming informed about business and economic trends through reading business-related publications such as newspaper business sections and business magazines. In addition to economics course work, college students can participate in specific programs and extracurricular activities sponsored by the university's business school, such as internships with government agencies and businesses and business-related clubs and organizations.

EMPLOYERS

Many economists teach at colleges and universities. Others work as researchers at government agencies, such as the U.S. Department of Labor, or international organizations, such as the United Nations. Still others find employment at not-for-profit or for-profit organizations, helping these organizations determine how to use their resources or grow in profitability. Most economics-related positions are concentrated in large cities, such as New York, Chicago, Los Angeles, and Washington, D.C., although academic positions are spread throughout the United States.

STARTING OUT

The bulletins of the various professional economic associations are good sources of job opportunities for beginning economists. Your school placement office should also assist you in locating internships and in setting up interviews with potential employers.

ADVANCEMENT

An economist's advancement depends on his or her training, experience, personal interests, and ambition. All specialized areas provide opportunities for promotion to jobs requiring more skill and competence. Such jobs are characterized by more administrative, research, or advisory responsibilities. Consequently, promotions are governed to a great extent by job performance in the beginning fields of work. In university-level academic positions, publishing papers and books about one's research is necessary to become tenured.

EARNINGS

Economists are among the highest paid social scientists. According to the Bureau of Labor Statistics, the median salary for economists was $67,080 in 2001. The lowest paid 10 percent made less than $37,700 and the highest paid 10 percent earned more than $114,580.

The U.S. Department of Labor reports that economists employed by the federal government earned average annual salaries of $74,090 in 2001. Starting salaries for federal government economists vary by degree attained. Economists with bachelor's degrees earned between $21,900 and $27,200; economists with master's degrees earned approximately $33,300; and those with Ph.D.'s earned between $40,200 and $48,200.

A survey by the Center for Business and Economic Research reports the following mean salary offers in 2002–03 for college economics educators by academic rank: associate and full professors, $110,738; senior assistant professors, $71,213.

Private-industry economists' salaries can be much higher—into the six figures. Notably, in a study published in *Money* magazine, economists' salaries tended to be 3.1 times higher at mid-career than their starting salaries. According to the survey, this is a higher increase than in any other profession; lawyers made 2.77 times more and accountants 2.21 times more in their mid-careers than at the start. Benefits such as vacation and insurance are comparable to those of workers in other organizations.

WORK ENVIRONMENT

Economists generally work in offices or classrooms. The average workweek is 40 hours, although academic and business economists' schedules often can be less predictable. Economists in nonteaching positions often work alone writing reports, preparing statistical charts, and using computers, but they may also be part of a research team. Most economists work under deadline pressure and sometimes must work overtime. Regular travel may be necessary to collect data or to attend conferences or meetings.

OUTLOOK

The employment of economists is expected to grow as fast as the average for all occupations over the next decade, according to the U.S. Department of Labor. Most openings will occur as economists retire, transfer to other job fields, or leave the profession for other reasons. Economists employed by private industry—especially in testing, research, and consulting—will enjoy the best prospects. In the academic arena, economists with master's and doctorate degrees will face strong competition for desirable teaching jobs. The demand for secondary school economics teachers is expected to grow. Economics majors with only bachelor's degrees will experience the greatest employment difficulty, although their analytical skills can lead to positions in related fields such as management and sales. Those who meet state certification requirements may wish to become secondary school economics teachers, as demand for teachers in this specialty is expected to increase.

FOR MORE INFORMATION

For information on agricultural economics and a list of colleges that offer programs in the field, contact

American Agricultural Economics Association
415 South Duff Avenue, Suite C
Ames, IA 50010-6600
Tel: 515-233-3202
http://www.aaea.org

For information on job listings and resources of interest to economists, contact

American Economic Association
2014 Broadway, Suite 305
Nashville, TN 37203
Tel: 615-322-2595
Email: info@econlit.org
http://www.aeaweb.org

For information on graduate programs in environmental and resource economics, contact

Association of Environmental and Resource Economists
1616 P Street, NW, Suite 410, Room 400
Washington, DC 20036
Tel: 202-328-5077
http://www.aere.org

For the publication, Careers in Business Economics, *contact or check out the following website:*

National Association for Business Economics
1233 20th Street, NW, Suite 505
Washington, DC 20036
Tel: 202-463-6223
Email: nabe@nabe.com
http://www.nabe.com

The NCEE promotes the economic education of students from kindergarten through 12th grade and offers teacher training courses and materials. For more information, contact

National Council on Economic Education (NCEE)
1140 Avenue of the Americas
New York, NY 10036
Tel: 800-338-1192
Email: info@ncee.net
http://www.ncee.net

EDITORS

QUICK FACTS

School Subjects English Journalism	**Certification or Licensing** None available
Personal Interests Communication/ideas Helping/teaching	**Outlook** Faster than the average
Work Environment Primarily indoors Primarily one location	**DOT** 132
Minimum Education Level Bachelor's degree	**GOE** 01.01.01
Salary Range $20,000 to $40,000 to $150,000+	**NOC** 5122
	O*NET-SOC 27-3041.00

OVERVIEW

Editors perform a wide range of functions, but their primary responsibility is to ensure that text provided by writers is suitable in content, format, and style for the intended audiences. Readers are an editor's first priority. Among the employers of editors are book publishers, magazines, newspapers, newsletters, corporations of all kinds, advertising agencies, radio stations, television stations, and Internet sites. The U.S. Department of Labor estimates that there are about 122,000 editors employed in the United States.

HISTORY

The history of book editing is tied closely to the history of the book and bookmaking and the history of the printing process. The 15th-century invention of the printing press by German goldsmith Johannes Gutenberg and the introduction of movable type in the West revolutionized the craft of bookmaking by enabling the mass production of books. Making changes to copy before a book was put into production also became more feasible. Printing had been invented hundreds of years earlier in Asia, but books did not proliferate there as quickly as they did in the West, which saw millions of copies in print by 1500.

In the early days of publishing, authors worked directly with the printer, and the printer was often the publisher and seller of the author's work. Eventually, however, booksellers began to work directly with the authors and eventually took over the role of publisher. The publisher then became the middleman between author and printer.

The publisher worked closely with the author and sometimes acted as the editor. The word *editor* derives from the Latin word *edere* or *editum* and means supervising or directing the preparation of text. Eventually, specialists were hired to perform the editing function. These editors, who were also called advisers or literary advisers in the 19th century, became an integral part of the publishing business.

The editor, also called the *sponsor* in some houses, sought out the best authors, worked with them, and became their advocate in the publishing house. Some editors became so important that their very presence in a publishing house could determine the quality of author that might be published there. Some author-editor collaborations have become legendary. The field has grown through the 20th and 21st century, with computers greatly speeding up the process by which editors move copy to the printer.

THE JOB

Editors work for many kinds of publishers, publications, and corporations. Editors' titles vary widely, not only from one area of publishing to another but also within each area.

Although some editors write for the organizations that employ them, most editors work with materials that others provide. For this reason, one of the most important steps in the editing process is acquiring the work of writers. In the fields of book and journal publishing, that work is usually performed by *acquisitions editors,* who are often called *acquiring editors.* Acquisitions editors may either generate their own ideas or use ideas provided by their publishers or other staff members. If they begin with an idea, they look for writers who can create an effective book or article based on that idea. One benefit of that method is that such ideas are ones that the editors believe are likely to be commercially successful or intellectually successful or both. Often, however, editors use ideas that they receive from writers in the form of proposals.

In some cases, the acquisitions editor will receive a complete manuscript from an author instead of a proposal. However, most of the time the writer will submit a query letter that asks whether the editor is interested in a particular idea. If the editor believes that the idea has potential and is suitable for the publishing house, the editor will discuss the idea further with the writer. Unless the writer is well known or is known and trusted by the editor, the editor usually asks the writer for a sample chapter or section. If the editor likes the sample chapter and believes that the author can complete an acceptable manuscript, the publishing house will enter into a contract with the writer. In some cases, the editor will prepare that contract; in others, the publisher or someone else at the publishing house will prepare the contract. The contract specifies when the manuscript is due, how much the author will be paid, how long the manuscript must be, and what will happen if the author cannot deliver a manuscript that the editor believes is suitable for publication, among other things.

After the contract has been signed, the writer will begin work. The acquisitions editor must keep track of the author's progress. Publishing budgets must be prepared in advance so that vendors can be paid and books can be advertised, so it is important that the manuscript be delivered by the due date. Some authors work well on their own and complete their work efficiently and effectively. In many cases, however, authors have problems. They may need advice from the editor regarding content, style, or organization of information. Often the editor will want to see parts of the manuscript as they are completed. That way, any problems in the writer's work can be identified and solved as soon as possible.

Some typical problems are statements the writer makes that may leave the publisher open to charges of libel or plagiarism. If this problem arises, the editor will require the writer to revise the manuscript. If the writer uses materials that were created by other people (such as long quotations, tables, or artwork), it may be necessary to request permission to use those materials. If permission is required but is not given, the materials cannot be used. It is usually the author's job to obtain permission, but sometimes the editor performs that task. In any case, the editor must make sure that necessary permissions are obtained. When an acceptable manuscript has been delivered, the acquisition editor's job is usually complete.

Some publishing houses have editors who specialize in working with authors. These *developmental editors* do not acquire manuscripts. Instead, they make sure the author stays on schedule and does a good job of organizing material and writing.

Once an acceptable manuscript has been delivered to the publishing house, it is turned over to a *copy editor*. This editor's job is to read the manuscript carefully and make sure that it is sufficiently well written, factually correct (sometimes this job is done by a *researcher* or *fact checker*), grammatically correct, and appropriate in tone and style for its intended readers. If a book is not well written, it is not likely to be well received by readers. If it is not factually correct, it will not be taken seriously by those who spot its errors. If it is not grammatically correct, it will not be understood. If it is not appropriate for its audience, it will be utterly useless. Any errors or problems in a printed piece reflect badly not only on the author but also on the publishing house.

The copy editor must be an expert in the English language, have a keen eye for detail, and know how to identify problems. The editor will simply correct some kinds of errors, but in some cases—especially when the piece deals with specialized material—the editor may need to ask, or query, the author about certain points. An editor must never change something that he or she does not understand, since one of the worst errors an editor can make is to change something that is correct to something that is incorrect.

After the manuscript has been edited by the copy editor, it may be (but is not always) sent to the author for review. When the editor and author have agreed on the final copy, the editor or another specialist will use various kinds of coding to mark the manuscript for typesetting. The codes, which usually correlate to information provided by a *graphic designer*, tell the *typesetter* which typefaces to use, how large to make the type, what the layout of the finished pages will look like, and where illustrations or other visual materials will be placed on the pages, among other things.

After the manuscript has been typeset and turned into galley proofs, or typeset copy that has not been divided into pages, the galleys are usually sent to the author to be checked. If the author finds errors or requests that changes be made, the copy editor or the *production editor* will oversee the process, determining which changes will be made.

Managing the editorial staff is the job of the *managing editor*, who draws up budgets for projects, oversees schedules, assigns projects to other editors, and ensures that the editorial staff is working efficiently. The managing editor's boss is the *editor in chief, editorial director*, or *executive editor*. This editor works closely with the publisher, determining the kinds of materials the house will publish and ensuring that the editorial staff carries out the wishes of the publisher. The editor in chief and managing editor also work closely with the heads of other departments, such as marketing, sales, and production.

The basic functions performed by *magazine and newspaper editors* are much like those performed by book editors, but a significant amount of the writing that appears in magazines and newspapers, or periodicals, is done by *staff writers*. Periodicals often use editors who specialize in specific areas, such as *city editors*, who oversee the work of *reporters* who specialize in local news, and *department editors*. Department editors specialize in areas such as business, economics, fashion, sports, and features, to name only a few. These departments are determined by the interests of the audience that the periodical intends to reach. Like book houses, periodicals use copy editors, researchers, and fact checkers, but at small periodicals, one or a few

Money Men

We see it every day, we handle it everyday, but many of us cannot remember who is on what bill. Here's a handy list from the U.S. Treasury that summarizes the faces on U.S. currency.

$1: George Washington, 1st U.S. President
$2: Thomas Jefferson, 3rd U.S. President
$5: Abraham Lincoln, 16th U.S. President
$10: Alexander Hamilton, 1st Secretary of State
$20: Andrew Jackson, 7th U.S. President
$50: Ulysses Grant, 18th U.S. President
$100: Ben Franklin, U.S. Statesman
*$500: William McKinley, 25th U.S. President
*$1000: Grover Cleveland, 22nd and 24th U.S. President
*$5000: James Madison, 4th U.S. President
*$10,000: Salmon Chase, U.S. Treasury Secretary under Lincoln
*$100,000: Woodrow Wilson, 28th U.S. President

*Currency no longer in print or circulation.

editors may be responsible for tasks that would be performed by many people at a larger publication.

REQUIREMENTS

High School

Editors must be expert communicators, so you should excel in English if you wish to be an editor. You must learn to write extremely well, since you will be correcting and even rewriting the work of others. If elective classes in writing are available in your school, take them. Study journalism and take communications courses. Work as a writer or editor for the school paper. Take a photography class. Since virtually all editors use computers, take computer courses. You absolutely must learn to type. If you cannot type accurately and rapidly, you will be at an extreme disadvantage. Don't forget, however, that a successful editor must have a wide range of knowledge. The more you know about many areas, the more likely you will be to do well as an editor. Don't hesitate to explore areas that you find interesting. Do everything you can to satisfy your intellectual curiosity. As far as most editors are concerned, there is no useless information.

Postsecondary Training

An editor must have a bachelor's degree, and advanced degrees are highly recommended for book editors and magazine editors. Most editors have degrees in English or journalism, but it is not unheard of for editors to major in one of the other liberal arts. If you know that you want to specialize in a field such as economics or scientific editing, you may wish to major in that area while taking a minor in English, writing, or journalism. There are many opportunities for editors in technical fields, since most of those who go into editing are interested primarily in the liberal arts. Many colleges offer courses in book editing, magazine design, general editing, and writing. Some colleges, such as New York University, the University of Chicago, and Stanford University, offer programs in publishing, and many magazines and newspapers offer internships to students. Take advantage of these opportunities. It is extremely important that you gain some practical experience while you are in school. Work on the school paper or find a part-time job with a newspaper or magazine. Don't hesitate to work for a publication in a noneditorial position. The more you know about the publishing business, the better off you will be.

Other Requirements

Good editors are fanatics for the written word. Their passion for good writing comes close to the point of obsession. They are analytical people who know how to think clearly and communicate what they are thinking. They read widely. They not only recognize good English when they see it but also know what makes it good. If they read something they don't understand, they analyze it until they do understand it. If they see a word they don't know, they look it up. When they are curious about something, they take action and research the subject. They are not satisfied with not knowing things.

You must be detail oriented to succeed as an editor. You must also be patient, since you may have to spend hours turning a few pages of near-gibberish into powerful, elegant English. If you are the kind of person who can't sit still, you probably will not succeed as an editor. To be a good editor, you must be a self-starter who is not afraid to make decisions. You must be good not only at identifying problems but also at solving them, so you must be creative. If you are both creative and a perfectionist, editing may be the line of work for you.

EXPLORING

One of the best ways to explore the field of editing is to work on a school newspaper or other publication. The experience you gain will definitely be helpful, even if your duties are not strictly editorial. Being involved in writing, reporting, typesetting, proofreading, printing, or any other task will help you to understand editing and how it relates to the entire field of publishing.

If you cannot work for the school paper, try to land a part-time job with a local newspaper or newsletter. If that doesn't work, you might want to publish your own newsletter. There is nothing like trying to put together a small publication to make you understand how publishing works. You may try combining another interest with your interest in editing. For example, if you are interested in environmental issues, you might want to start a newsletter that deals with environmental problems and solutions in your community.

Another useful project is keeping a journal. In fact, any writing project will be helpful, since editing and writing are inextricably linked. Write something every day. Try to rework your writing until it is as good as you can make it. Try different kinds of writing, such as letters to the editor, short stories, poetry, essays, comedic prose, and plays.

EMPLOYERS

One of the best things about the field of editing is the variety of opportunities it offers. The most obvious employers for editors are book publishers, magazines, and newspapers. There are many varieties of all three of these types of publishers. There are small and large publishers, general and specialized publishers, local and national publishers. If you have a strong interest in a particular field, you will undoubtedly find various publishers that specialize in it.

Another excellent source of employment is business. Almost all businesses of any size need writers and editors on a full-time or part-time basis. Corporations often publish newsletters for their employees or produce publications that talk about how they do business. Large companies produce annual reports that must be written and edited. In addition, advertising is a major source of work for editors, proofreaders, and writers. Advertising agencies use editors, proofreaders, and quality-control people, as do typesetting and printing companies (in many cases, proofreaders edit as well as proofread). Keep in mind that somebody has to work on all the printed material you see every day, from books and magazines to menus and matchbooks.

STARTING OUT

There is tremendous competition for editorial jobs, so it is important for a beginner who wishes to break into the business to be as well prepared as possible. College students who have gained experience as interns, have worked for publications during the summers, or have attended special programs in publishing will be at an advantage. In addition, applicants for any editorial position must be extremely careful when preparing cover letters and resumes. Even a single error in spelling or usage will disqualify an applicant. Applicants for editorial or proofreading positions must also expect to take and pass tests that are designed to determine their language skills.

Many editors enter the field as editorial assistants or proofreaders. Some editorial assistants perform only clerical tasks, whereas others may also proofread or perform basic editorial tasks. Typically, an editorial assistant who performs well will be given the opportunity to take on more and more editorial duties as time passes. Proofreaders have the advantage of being able to look at the work of editors, so they can learn while they do their own work.

Good sources of information about job openings are school placement offices, classified ads in newspapers and trade journals, specialized publications such as *Publishers Weekly* (http://publishersweekly.

com), and Internet sites. One way to proceed is to identify local publishers through the Yellow Pages. Many publishers have websites that list job openings, and large publishers often have telephone job lines that serve the same purpose.

ADVANCEMENT

In book houses, employees who start as *editorial assistants* or *proofreaders* and show promise generally become copy editors. After gaining skill in that position, they may be given a wider range of duties while retaining the same title. The next step may be a position as a *senior copy editor*, which involves overseeing the work of *junior copy editors*, or as a *project editor*. The project editor performs a wide variety of tasks, including copyediting, coordinating the work of in-house and freelance copy editors, and managing the schedule of a particular project. From this position, an editor may move up to become first assistant editor, then managing editor, then editor-in-chief. These positions involve more management and decision making than is usually found in the positions described previously. The editor-in-chief works with the publisher to ensure that a suitable editorial policy is being followed, while the managing editor is responsible for all aspects of the editorial department. The assistant editor provides support to the managing editor.

Newspaper editors generally begin working on the copy desk, where they progress from less significant stories and projects to major news and feature stories. A common route to advancement is for copy editors to be promoted to a particular department, where they may move up the ranks to management positions. An editor with a proven success record may become a city editor, who is responsible for news, or a managing editor, who runs the entire editorial operation of a newspaper.

Magazine editors advance in much the same way that book editors do. After they become copy editors, they work their way up to become senior editors, managing editors, and editors in chief. In many cases, magazine editors advance by moving from a position on one magazine to the same position with a larger or more prestigious magazine. Such moves often bring significant increases in both pay and status.

EARNINGS

Although a small percentage of editors are paid extremely well, the average editor is not well paid. Competition for editing jobs is fierce, and there is no shortage of people who wish to enter the field. For that reason, companies that employ editors generally pay relatively low wages.

A *Publishers Weekly* salary survey reported that editorial salaries in 2002 ranged from $152,750 for top editorial personnel at large publishing houses to just below $30,000 for editorial assistants at smaller companies. Beginning salaries of $20,000 or less are still common in many areas. The salaries of magazine editors are roughly comparable to those of book editors.

According to 2001 data from the U.S. Department of Labor, median annual earnings for editors were $39,960. The lowest 10 percent earned less than $23,090 and the highest 10 percent earned more than $73,460. In 2000, the median annual earnings for editors in computer and data processing services were $45,800; in periodicals, $42,560; in newspapers, $37,560; and in book publishing, $37,550.

Technical editors usually earn higher salaries than newspaper, magazine, or book editors. According to a 2001 salary survey conducted by the Society for Technical Communication, the average salary for technical writers and editors is $55,360.

WORK ENVIRONMENT

Editors' work environments vary widely. For the most part, publishers realize that a quiet atmosphere is conducive to work that requires tremendous concentration. It takes an unusual ability to focus and edit in a noisy place. Most editors work in private offices or cubicles. Book editors often work in quieter surroundings than do newspaper editors or quality-control people in advertising agencies, who sometimes work in rather loud and hectic situations.

Even in relatively quiet surroundings, however, editors often have many distractions. A project editor who is trying to do some copyediting or review the editing of others may, for example, have to deal with phone calls from authors, questions from junior editors, meetings with members of the editorial and production staff, and questions from freelancers, among many other distractions. In many cases, editors have computers that are exclusively for their own use, but in others, editors must share computers that are located in a common area.

Deadlines are an important issue for virtually all editors. Newspaper and magazine editors work in a much more pressurized atmosphere than book editors because they face daily or weekly deadlines, whereas book production usually takes place over several months.

In almost all cases, editors must work long hours during certain phases of the editing process. Some newspaper editors start work at

5:00 A.M., others work until 11:00 P.M. or even through the night. Feature editors, columnists, and editorial page editors usually can schedule their day in a more regular fashion, as can editors who work on weekly newspapers. Editors working on hard news, however, may receive an assignment that must be completed, even if work extends well into the next shift.

OUTLOOK

According to the *Occupational Outlook Handbook*, employment of editors will increase faster than the average over the next several years. At the same time, however, competition for those jobs will remain intense, since so many people want to enter the field. Book publishing will remain particularly competitive, since many people still view the field in a romantic light. Much of the expansion in publishing is expected to occur in small newspapers, radio stations, and television stations. In these organizations, pay is low even by the standards of the publishing business.

One of the major trends in publishing is specialization. More and more publishing ventures are targeting relatively narrow markets, which means that there are more opportunities for editors to combine their work and their personal interests. It is also true, however, that many of these specialty publications do not survive for long.

There will be increasing job opportunities for editors in Internet publishing as online publishing and services continue to grow. Advertising and public relations will also provide employment opportunities.

A fairly large number of positions—both full time and freelance—become available when experienced editors leave the business for other fields. Many editors make this decision because they find that they can make more money in other businesses than they can as editors.

FOR MORE INFORMATION

The ACES organizes educational seminars and maintains lists of internships. Its website is an excellent source of information about careers in editing.

American Copy Editors Society (ACES)
3 Healy Street
Huntington, NY 11743
http://www.copydesk.org

This organization of book publishers offers an extensive website to learn about the book business.

Association of American Publishers
71 Fifth Avenue, Second Floor
New York, NY 10003
Tel: 212-255-0200
http://www.publishers.org

This organization provides information about internships and about the newspaper business in general.

Dow Jones Newspaper Fund
PO Box 300
Princeton, NJ 08543-0300
Tel: 609-452-2820
Email: newsfund@wsj.dowjones.com
http://www.dowjones.com/newsfund

The EFA is an organization for freelance editors. Members receive a newsletter and a free listing in their directory.

Editorial Freelancers Association (EFA)
71 West 23rd Street, Suite 1910
New York, NY 10010-4102
Tel: 866-929-5400
Email: info@the-efa.org
http://www.the-efa.org

This organization is a good source of information on internships.

Magazine Publishers of America
919 Third Avenue
New York, NY 10022
Tel: 212-872-3700
http://www.magazine.org

This publication focuses on economics research and hires a large editorial staff. For sample articles, visit

The RAND Journal of Economics
1700 Main Street
Santa Monica, CA 90401
Tel: 310-393-0411
Email: RJE@rand.org
http://www.rje.org

The Slot is a website founded and maintained by Bill Walsh, financial copy desk chief at the Washington Post. *Walsh offers tips on proper word usage, grammar lessons, and style guides.*

The Slot
http://www.theslot.com

For population statistics, as well as information on regional offices, jobs, and a calendar of events, contact

U.S. Census Bureau
Washington, DC 20233
Tel: 301-457-4608
Email: recruiter@census.gov
http://www.census.gov

EXPORT-IMPORT SPECIALISTS

QUICK FACTS

School Subjects
Business
Foreign language
Mathematics

Personal Skills
Helping/teaching
Leadership/management

Work Environment
Primarily indoors
Primarily multiple locations

Minimum Education Level
Bachelor's degree

Salary Range
$16,000 to $54,350 to $106,560+

Certification or Licensing
Required by all states

Outlook
About as fast as the average

DOT
184

GOE
11.05.02

NOC
1236

O*NET-SOC
41.4011.00, 41-4012.00

OVERVIEW

Export-import specialists plan and coordinate business transactions that involve importing goods from or exporting goods to foreign countries. They may work for the government, an international company, or as a representative of an individual client. Export-import specialists are involved in various aspects of foreign trade, from negotiating trade agreements to planning and supervising the actual delivery of goods.

HISTORY

Exporting and importing is more than the flow of goods among different countries. Taken as a whole, what a country exports and imports largely determines its economic health. Trade relations have also been a major force in determining whether two nations are allies or enemies.

The people who facilitate the actual trading of finished goods, raw materials, and services are a varied group. In colonial times, a trader was basically anyone with the means of transporting or receiving and distributing goods. Thus, the owner of a ship that made the long voyage between America and England was a trader. So was the owner of a general store in America who bought the clothes and dry goods from other countries and sold them in his store. As America grew, so did the volume of goods it produced for trade. The fertile new country produced enough crops to feed citizens and to trade with less fertile countries. Traders moved huge barges of grain moved down the Mississippi River to the Gulf of Mexico.

America is a comparatively rich country and its consumers demand a huge variety of products that make large profits for today's importers. But before the 1940s, the United States had a largely protectionist approach to foreign trade, meaning that the government enforced high tariffs and rigorous import restrictions to protect home market producers from overseas competition. In the 1960s, the United States experienced a decline of its dominant position in world trade, and in most of the years after 1970 it has reported a negative trade balance (more imports than exports). During the past several years, the U.S. trade deficit reached an all-time high as economic crises in other countries caused exports of everything from soybeans to automobiles to decline. No other developed nation has had such a large difference between exports and imports. Canada, Japan, and the European Union have all experienced an export growth greater than import growth. Because of this imbalance, the United States is keenly interested in either expanding the export of American goods or controlling the import of foreign goods.

Today's economic climate is characterized by a push for free trade, whose proponents favor open markets and economic interdependence. In a move toward more free trade, President Clinton signed two trade agreements in 1993. The North American Free Trade Agreement (NAFTA) is a pact between the United States, Canada, and Mexico. Some of its provisions include the elimination of all tariffs over the next 15 years on goods produced and sold in North America, the barring of government impositions on special requirements for foreign investors, and the lifting of certain restrictions on services, such as banking, telecommunications, and transportation. The second pact, the General Agreement on Tariffs and Trade (GATT), was approved by the U.S.

Congress and the governments of 116 other participants. It reduces international trade barriers, including tariffs, import quotas, and export subsidies. NAFTA and a proposed Free Trade Area of the Americas (FTAA) agreement have come under fire from protesters, including labor, small farmers, and environmental concerns. They say the agreements allow large corporations to bypass environmental and worker protection laws and take business and jobs from average workers to concentrate power in the hands of a few corporate giants. Many countries fear that economic globalization will cause them to lose their economic independence as well as their social and cultural identities.

Experts cannot agree on whether such open trade policies have helped or hurt the United States. Familiar terms such as *trade deficit* or *balance of trade* are reported daily in the news. The U.S. trade deficit continues to grow, but at the same time, U.S. exports account for more than one-third of U.S. economic growth, according to the National Association of Manufacturers. The growth of foreign business and its importance to the national economy has created a need for specialists who can handle the complex problems of international business.

THE JOB

A variety of professionals are involved in the export-import industry. Some are involved only with the importing of raw materials or finished goods, while others are only involved with exporting. Many specialists, however, are involved in both the importing and exporting of foreign trade. All specialists must understand international law and be aware of export-import regulations, such as duty fees, but specific responsibilities vary according to the area of specialization.

Export managers direct foreign sales activities, including negotiating sales and distribution contracts and arranging payment for exported goods. They handle details involved in the transportation of goods, including licensing agreements, customs declarations, and packing and shipping. Export managers work with foreign buyers, federal agents, and company executives to coordinate shipping, air freight, and other transportation methods. They also supervise clerical staff in preparing foreign correspondence and other foreign language material, such as sales literature and bid requests, meant to expedite foreign trade.

Customs brokers act as intermediaries between importers and the customs service. They prepare entry papers for goods arriving from abroad. They file appropriate documents to allow delivery of foreign goods and to assess import duties and taxes. Customs brokers must be familiar with more than 500 pages of customs regulations and thousands of tariff items. They must determine proper classifications of dutiable value and know which goods are subject to quotas. They may also help importers find the best routes for shipment. Customs brokers act as troubleshooters between importers and the federal government, counseling importers on relevant rules and regulations, working out any last-minute problems, and arranging for storage of goods in warehouses, if necessary. They may be in regular contact with more than 40 government agencies, such as the U.S. Department of Agriculture regarding meat-import questions or the Consumer Product Safety Commission regarding product safety.

Import-export agents are independent contractors who usually work for several clients. They manage activities of import-export firms, coordinating settlements between foreign and domestic buyers and sellers. They plan delivery of goods and supervise workers in the shipping and receiving departments. Import-export agents act as trade representatives throughout the freight-handling process. They oversee the assessment of import and export taxes and the granting of entry permits. They also resolve any concerns on the part of customs officials or foreign or domestic business people.

Freight forwarders act as agents for exporters in moving cargo to overseas destinations. They are familiar with the import rules and regulations of foreign countries, methods of shipping, U.S. government export regulations, special packaging or handling restrictions, hazardous materials rules, and the documents connected with foreign trade. Freight forwarders advise clients on freight costs, port charges, consular fees, cost of special documentation, and insurance costs. Forwarders find the most appropriate services so that products are moved by the most timely and cost-effective methods, making arrangements for storage, pick-and-pack operations, consolidations or full-container movements, as well as inland transportation. They also assist with initial quotations, prepare invoices, and bank clients' documents for collection.

REQUIREMENTS

High School

To prepare for this career take college-preparatory classes, such as English, social studies, geography, and mathematics. Developing a fluency in a foreign language, especially one that is widely used in international trade, such as Japanese, Russian, or German, is very important.

Postsecondary Training

A college degree is becoming more important in the export-import field. Undergraduate degrees in business management, political science, or economics are good foundations for this type of career. Course work should include classes in international trade, marketing, business administration, communications, computer applications, and statistics. Many people who want management positions in the export-import field are now deciding to get a master's in business administration (M.B.A.), with an emphasis in international trade.

Certification or Licensing

Customs brokers must be licensed by the U.S. Customs Service, which is now part of the Customs and Border Protection Agency. The licensing process requires passing a written examination that covers export-import rules and regulations. Specifics on the licensing procedures are available from the U.S. Customs Service. Ocean freight forwarders are licensed by the Federal Maritime Commission, and International Air Cargo Agents are accredited by the International Air Transportation Association. Exporters of military equipment, nuclear fissionable materials, and some other items must have a license from the U.S. Department of Commerce.

The National Customs Brokers & Forwarders Association of America (NCBFAA) offers professional-level certification for ocean freight forwarders. To become certified, a candidate must have a minimum of three years forwarding experience and pass an eight-hour exam. Candidates who meet these criteria may use the Certified Ocean Forwarder (COF) designation.

The NCBFAA also offers the following technical-level certifications to workers in the export-import industry: cargo transportation basics, regulation of U.S. exports, U.S. export clearance, export/import transactions, ocean and through intermodal transportation, cargo security and insurance, and ocean freight forwarding. These certifications break down the diverse body of knowledge in the COF program into more specialized segments.

Other Requirements

To be a successful export-import specialists, you should be able to quickly analyze purchasing decisions and evaluate products being shipped in. You should have good verbal and written communications skills and be able to work well with other people. The ability to speak one or more foreign languages will help you to communicate far more effectively with trading partners and other foreign representatives.

EXPLORING

You may be able to find part-time or summer employment in a large store or other retail establishment, which will provide helpful insight into a merchandising career. After graduating from high school, an internship with an international company will give you valuable exposure to the export-import field. Discussions with professionals already working in the field are an excellent way to learn about career opportunities. Freight forwarders are among the best sources of information and assistance on U.S. export regulations and documentation, shipping methods, and foreign import regulations. In addition, to familiarize yourself with the field, pay attention to news reports on the U.S. trade balance, trade policies, and export and import levels of major goods, such as automobiles.

EMPLOYERS

The largest employers of export-import specialists are oil companies, manufacturers, trading companies, shipping firms, worldwide freight forwarders, airlines, warehouse firms, trucking firms, banks, agricultural-product producers, and department store chains. Major trade cities are New York, Miami, Boston, New Orleans, Chicago, Houston, Philadelphia, Seattle, Tacoma, San Francisco, Oakland, and Los Angeles.

STARTING OUT

The vast majority of entry-level positions are now reserved for college graduates, most of whom secure their first position by applying directly to the U.S. Customs Service, individual seaports and airports, international trading companies, and other organizations that hire export-import specialists. Public and private employment services may also refer qualified applicants to suitable entry positions. People with a master's in business administration and a fluency in one or more foreign languages will have the best opportunities in this field.

ADVANCEMENT

Those in the export-import field usually have constant contact with other international firms and government agencies and therefore have frequent opportunities to switch employers. Specific advancement opportunities depend to some extent on the specialty within the field and vary greatly depending on the skill and drive of the individual.

An experienced export manager may become the marketing manager or vice president in charge of coordinating overseas distribution. Customs brokers may become export managers or may be promoted to other positions within the export-import department of a company. After developing contacts and sales expertise, wholesalers may also become management consultants or start their own export-import firm. Import-export agents may become sales representatives for other export-import firms or go into business for themselves.

EARNINGS

Earnings vary widely depending on specific job responsibilities and the size of the export-import firm. According to the U.S. Department of Labor, in 2001 the median annual earnings of sales representatives of wholesale and manufacturing, technical and scientific products were $54,350, including commission. Salaries ranged from less than $28,070 to more than $106,560 a year. Some companies adjust salaries to reflect total volume of sales. Other companies pay straight commission (usually about 10 percent of total sales), while others pay a combination of salary, commission, and benefits. While wholesalers can make huge amounts of money, a slow period could adversely affect their earning potential. Purchasers and buyers, the professionals who seek the best deal on raw materials and finished products for their employers, earned a median income of $38,590 in 2001, according to the U.S. Department of Labor. Salaries ranged from less than $22,500 to more than $73,740 a year.

Customs brokers and freight forwarders are paid according to the amount of foreign trade they handle. Beginning brokers can expect to earn $19,000–$24,000 per year, and experienced brokers earn over $35,000 per year. Beginning agents earn between $16,000 and $20,000 per year, and experienced agents earn between $23,000 and $35,000.

WORK ENVIRONMENT

Export-import specialists usually work in comfortable offices or customs buildings. They generally work a 40-hour week, although long hours may be required to negotiate a trade agreement or to plan and coordinate delivery of goods. Evening and weekend work may be necessary at times.

There may be a lot of travel, especially for wholesalers and those stationed overseas. These employees must adapt to the living and working conditions of the host country and should be aware of, and sensitive to, cultural differences in these countries. Some specialists, however, stay in one city and never travel abroad.

OUTLOOK

Opportunities in the export-import field should grow at an average rate over the next 10 years. Employment stability in this field is largely dependent on general economic conditions, and job prospects will vary from industry to industry and firm to firm. For example, it may be harder to find work as a textile wholesaler representing a U.S. firm than as a computer wholesaler.

Since the United States is already the largest trading nation in the world, the agreements enacted in the 1990s to encourage a free-trade policy should help create even more work in the field. The U.S. trade deficit, however, continues to widen and imports are rising at a faster rate than the Gross Domestic Product.

FOR MORE INFORMATION

For industry information and job listings, contact

American Association of Exporters and Importers
PO Box 7813
Washington, DC 20044-7813
Tel: 202-661-2181
Email: hq@aaei.org
http://www.aaei.org

For statistics on U.S. trade, contact

International Trade Administration
U.S. Department of Commerce
1401 Constitution Avenue, NW
Washington, DC 20230
http://www.ita.doc.gov

For information on membership and certification, contact

National Customs Brokers & Forwarders Association of America, Inc.
1200 18th Street, NW, Suite 901
Washington, DC 20036
Tel: 202-466-0222
Email: staff@ncbfaa.org
http://www.ncbfaa.org

FEDERAL AND STATE OFFICIALS

QUICK FACTS

School Subjects
Economics
Government
History

Personal Skills
Communication/ideas
Leadership/management

Work Environment
Primarily indoors
One location with some travel

Minimum Education Level
Bachelor's degree

Salary Range
$10,000 to $40,000 to $400,000+

Certification or Licensing
None available

Outlook
About as fast as the average

DOT
188

GOE
11.05.03

NOC
0011

O*NET-SOC
11-1031.00

OVERVIEW

Federal and state officials hold positions in the legislative, executive, and judicial branches of government at the state and national levels. They include governors, judges, senators, representatives, and the president and vice president of the country. Government officials are responsible for preserving the government against external and domestic threats, supervising and resolving conflicts between private and public interest, regulating the economy, protecting political and social rights of the citizens, and providing goods and services. Officials may, among other things, pass laws, set up social service programs, and allocate the taxpayers' money on goods and services.

HISTORY

In ancient states, the scope of government was almost without limitation. As Aristotle put it, "What was not commanded by the government was forbidden." Government functions were challenged by Christianity during the Roman Empire, when the enforcement of religious sanctions became the focus of political authority. It was not until the 18th century that the modern concept of government as separate from the church came into being.

The Roman Republic had a great deal of influence on those who framed the U.S. Constitution. The supreme council of state in ancient Rome was called the Senate. Even the name Capitol Hill is derived from Capitoline Hill of Rome. The Congress of the United States was modeled after British Parliament and assumed the powers that London held before American independence. Limiting the powers of the individual states, the U.S. Congress was empowered to levy taxes, engage in foreign diplomacy, and regulate Native American affairs.

THE JOB

Think about the last time you cast a vote, whether in a school, local, state, or federal election. How did you make your decision? Was it based on the personal qualities of the candidate? The political positions of the candidate? Certain issues of importance to you? Or do you always vote for the same political party? As voters, we choose carefully and consider many factors when electing a government. Whether you're electing a new governor and lieutenant governor for the state, a president and vice president for the country, or senators and representatives for the state legislature or the U.S. Congress, you're choosing people to act on behalf of your interests. The decisions of state and federal lawmakers affect your daily life and your future. State and federal officials pass laws concerning the arts, education, taxes, employment, health care, and other areas in efforts to change and improve communities and standards of living.

Besides the *president* and *vice president* of the United States, the executive branch of the national government consists of the president's cabinet, including, among others, the secretaries of state, treasury, defense, interior, agriculture, homeland security, and health and human services. These officials are appointed by the president and approved by the Senate. The members of the Office of Management and Budget, the Council of Economic Advisers, and the National Security Council are also executive officers of the national government.

Nearly every state's governing body resembles that of the federal government. Just as the U.S. Congress is composed of the Senate and the House of Representatives, so does each state (with one exception, Nebraska) have a senate and a house. The executive branch of the U.S. government is headed by the president and vice president, while states elect governors and lieutenant governors. The *governor* is the chief executive officer of a state. In all states, a large government administration handles a variety of functions related to agriculture, highway and motor vehicle supervision, public safety and corrections, regulation of intrastate business and industry, and some aspects of education, public health, and welfare. The governor's job is to manage this administration. Some states also have a *lieutenant governor,* who serves as the presiding officer of the state's senate. Other elected officials commonly include a secretary of state, state treasurer, state auditor, attorney general, and superintendent of public instruction.

State senators and *state representatives* are the legislators elected to represent the districts and regions of cities and counties within the state. The number of members of a state's legislature varies from state to state. In the U.S. Congress, there are 100 senators (as established by the Constitution—two senators from each state) and 435 representatives. The number of representatives each state is allowed to send to the U.S. Congress varies based on the state's population as determined by the national census. Based on results from Census 2000, California is the most populous state and sends the most representatives (53). The primary function of all legislators, on both the state and national levels, is to make laws. With a staff of aides, senators and representatives attempt to learn as much as they can about the bills being considered. They research legislation, prepare reports, meet with constituents and interest groups, speak to the press, and discuss and debate legislation on the floor of the House or Senate. Legislators also may be involved in selecting other members of the government, supervising the government administration, appropriating funds, impeaching executive and judicial officials, and determining election procedures, among other activities. A state legislator may be involved in examining such situations as the state's relationship to Native American tribes, the level of school violence, and welfare reform.

"Time in each day goes by so quickly," says Don Preister, who serves on the state legislature in Nebraska, "there's no time to read up on all legislation and all the information the constituents send in." When the state senate is in session, Preister commits many hours to discussing and debating issues with other state senators and gathering information on proposed legislation. In addition to senate sessions, Preister attends committee hearings. His committees include Natural Resources and Urban Affairs. "A hearing lasts from 20 minutes to three or four hours," he says, "depending on the intensity of the issues." Despite having to devote about 60 hours a week to the job when the Senate is in session, Preister finds his work a wonderful opportunity to be of service to the community and to improve lives. "I take a lot of personal satisfaction from being a voice for people whose voices aren't often heard in government."

REQUIREMENTS

High School

Courses in government, civics, and history will give you an understanding of the structure of state and federal governments. English courses are important because you need good writing skills for communicating with constituents and other government officials. Math, accounting, and economics help you to develop the analytical skills needed for examining statistics and demographics. You should take science courses because you'll be making decisions concerning health, medicine, and technological advances. Journalism classes will teach you about the print and broadcast media and the role they play in politics.

Postsecondary Training

State and federal legislators come from all walks of life. Some hold master's degrees and doctorates, while others have only a high school education. Although a majority of government officials hold law degrees, others have undergraduate or graduate degrees in such areas as journalism, economics, political science, history, and English. Regardless of your major as an undergraduate, it is important to take classes in English literature, statistics, foreign language, Western civilization, and economics. Graduate studies can focus more on one area of study; some prospective government officials pursue master's degrees in public administration or international affairs. Consider participating in an internship program that will involve you with local and state officials. Contact the offices of your state legislators and of your state's members of Congress to apply for internships directly.

Other Requirements

"You should have concern for people," Don Preister says. "You should have an ability to listen and understand people and their concerns." This attention to the needs of communities should be of foremost importance to anyone pursuing a government office. Although historically some politicians have had questionable purposes in their campaigns for office, most successful politicians are devoted to making positive changes and improvements. Good people skills will help you make connections, get elected, and make things happen once in office. You should also enjoy argument, debate, and opposition, which are all things officials must face as they try to pass laws. A good temperament in such situations will earn you the respect of your colleagues. Strong character and a good background will help you to avoid the personal attacks that can accompany government office.

EXPLORING

If you are 16 or older, you can gain experience in a legislature. The U.S. Congress and possibly your state legislature offer opportunities for young adults who have demonstrated a commitment to government study to work as *pages*. Congressional pages run messages across Capitol Hill and have the opportunity to see senators and representatives debating and discussing bills. The length of a page's service can be for one summer or up to one year. Contact your state's senator or representative for an application.

You can also explore government careers by becoming involved with local elections. Many candidates for local and state offices welcome young people to assist with campaigns. You might be asked to make calls, post signs, or hand out information about the candidate. Not only will you get to see the politician at work, but you will also meet others with an interest in government.

Another great way to learn about government is to become involved in an issue of interest to you. Participate with a grassroots advocacy group or read about the bills up for vote in the state legislature and U.S. Congress. When you feel strongly about an issue and are well educated on the subject, contact the offices of state legislators and members of Congress to express your views. Visit the websites of the House and Senate and of your state legislature to read about bills, schedules, and the legislators. The National Conference of State Legislators (NCSL) also hosts a website (http://www.ncsl.org) that features legislative news and links to state legislatures.

EMPLOYERS

State legislators work for the state government, but many hold other jobs as well. Because of the part-time nature of some legislative offices, state legislators may hold part-time jobs or own their own businesses. Federal officials work full time for the Senate, the House, or the executive branch.

STARTING OUT

There is no direct career path for state and federal officials. Some enter into their positions after some success with political activism on the grassroots level. Others work their way up from local government positions to state legislature and into federal office. Those who serve as U.S. Congress members have worked in the military, journalism, academics, business, and many other fields.

Many politicians get their start assisting someone else's campaign or advocating for an issue. Don Preister's beginnings with the Nebraska state legislature are particularly inspiring. Because of his involvement in a grassroots campaign to improve his neighborhood, he was encouraged by friends and neighbors to run for senator of the district. However, others believed he'd never get elected running against a man who'd had a lot of political success, as well as great finances to back his campaign. "I didn't have any money," Preister says, "or any experience in campaigning. So I went door to door to meet the people of the district. I went to every house and apartment in the district." He won that election in 1992 and again in 1996 and 2000.

ADVANCEMENT

Initiative is one key to success in politics. Advancement can be rapid for someone who is a fast learner and is independently motivated, but a career in politics most often takes a long time to establish. Most state and federal officials start by pursuing training and work experience in their particular field, while getting involved in politics at the local level. Many people progress from local politics to state politics. It is not uncommon for a state legislator to eventually run for a seat in Congress. Appointees to the president's cabinet and presidential and vice presidential candidates frequently have held positions in Congress.

EARNINGS

In general, salaries for government officials tend to be lower than what the official could make working in the private sector. In the case of state legislators, the pay can be very much lower.

The Bureau of Labor Statistics reports that the median annual earnings of government legislators was $14,650 in 2001. Salaries generally ranged from less than $11,830 to more than $64,890, although some officials earn nothing at all.

According to the NCSL, state legislators make from $10,000 to $47,000 a year. A few states, however, don't pay state legislators anything but an expense allowance. But a state's executive officials are paid better: *The Book of the States* lists salaries of state governors as ranging from $60,000 in Arkansas to a high of $130,000 in New York.

In 2003, U.S. senators and representatives earned $154,700; the vice president was paid $198,600; and the president earned $400,000.

Congressional leaders such as the Speaker of the House and the Senate majority leader receive higher salaries than other Congress members. The Speaker of the House makes $186,300 a year. U.S. Congress members receive excellent insurance, vacation, and other benefits.

WORK ENVIRONMENT

Most government officials work in a typical office setting. Some may work a regular 40-hour week, while others will typically work long hours and weekends. One potential drawback to political life, particularly for the candidate running for office, is that there is no real off-duty time. One is continually under observation by the press and public, and the personal lives of candidates and officeholders are discussed frequently in the media.

Because these officials must be appointed or elected in order to keep their jobs, the ability to determine long-range job objectives is slim. There may be extended periods of unemployment, when living off of savings or working at other jobs may be necessary.

Frequent travel is involved in campaigning and in holding office, so some people with children may find the lifestyle demanding on their families.

OUTLOOK

The U.S. Department of Labor predicts that employment of federal and state officials will grow about as fast as the average through the next decade. To attract more candidates to run for legislative offices, states may consider salary increases and better benefits for state senators and representatives. But changes in pay and benefits for federal officials are unlikely. An increase in the number of representatives is possible as the U.S. population grows, but this would require additional office space and other costly expansions. For the most part, the structures of state and federal legislatures will remain unchanged, although the topic of term limits for representatives often arises in election years.

The federal government has made efforts to shift costs to the states; if this continues, it could change the way state legislatures and executive officers operate with regard to public funding. Already, welfare reform has resulted in state governments looking for financial aid in handling welfare cases and job programs. Arts funding may also become the sole responsibility of the states as the National Endowment for the Arts loses support from Congress.

With the government's commitment to developing a place on the Internet, contacting your state and federal representatives, learning about legislation, and organizing grassroots advocacy have become much easier than in the past. This leads to increased voter awareness of candidates, public policy issues, and legislation and may affect how future representatives make decisions. Look for government programming to be part of cable television's expansion into digital broadcasting. New modes of communication will allow constituents to become even more involved in the actions of their representatives.

FOR MORE INFORMATION

Visit the Senate and House websites for extensive information about Congress, government history, current legislation, and links to state legislature sites. To inquire about internship opportunities with your Congress member, contact

U.S. Senate
Office of Senator (Name)
United States Senate
Washington, DC 20510
Tel: 202-224-3121
http://www.senate.gov

U.S. House of Representatives
Office of the Honorable (Name)
Washington, DC 20515
Tel: 202-224-3121
http://www.house.gov

To read about state legislatures, policy issues, legislative news, and other related information, visit the NCSL's website.

National Conference of State Legislatures (NCSL)
444 North Capitol Street, NW, Suite 515
Washington, DC 20001
Tel: 202-624-5400
Email: info@ncsl.org
http://www.ncsl.org

FINANCIAL ANALYSTS

QUICK FACTS

School Subjects
Business
Computer science
Mathematics

Personal Skills
Communication/ideas
Leadership/management

Work Environment
Primarily indoors
Primarily one location

Minimum Education Level
Bachelor's degree

Salary Range
$29,499 to $55,130 to $107,720+

Certification or Licensing
Recommended

Outlook
Faster than the average

DOT
N/A

GOE
N/A

NOC
1112

O*NET-SOC
13-2051.00

OVERVIEW

Financial analysts analyze the financial situation of companies and recommend ways for those companies to manage, spend, and invest their money. The goal of financial analysts is to help their employer or clients make informed financial decisions with lucrative results. They assemble and evaluate the company's financial data and assess investment opportunities. They look at the company's financial history, the direction the company wants to take in the future, the company's place in the industry, and the company's current and projected economic conditions. Financial analysts also conduct similar research on companies that might present investment opportunities. They write reports and compile spreadsheets that show the benefits of certain investments or selling certain securities.

Among the businesses employing financial analysts are banks, brokerage firms, government agencies, mutual funds, and insurance and investment companies. There are approximately 239,000 financial analysts and *personal financial advisers* employed in the United States, and about six out of 10 are financial analysts.

HISTORY

U.S. securities markets date back to the early years of the nation. The first U.S. stock exchanges were created in the 1790s. The New York Stock Exchange (which did not get its present name until 1863) was one of these. It started as a group of men who did their trading under a tree at 68 Wall Street. The markets grew as the country's industries developed. The unregulated U.S. securities markets flourished just following World War I. According to the U.S. Securities and Exchange Commission (SEC), some 20 million people "took advantage of post-war prosperity and set out to make their fortunes in the stock market." The stock market crash of 1929, however, wiped out the savings of many investors. Consumers became wary of the markets and hesitated to invest again. Congress created the SEC in 1934 to keep watch over the markets and institute rules and regulations in the industry. The goal was to ensure that companies and stockbrokers divulged truthful information about their businesses, the investments offered, and the potential risk involved.

The Financial Analysts Federation (FAF), a group for investment professionals, was created in 1947. The FAF brought some prestige and respect to the profession. Then in 1959 the Institute of Chartered Financial Analysts (ICFA) was developed. Financial analysts who successfully completed the ICFA examination received the designation of chartered financial analyst (CFA). In June 1963, 268 analysts became the first group of CFA charterholders. The FAF and ICFA went on to merge in 1990, creating the Association for Investment Management and Research (AIMR).

Deregulations in the 1970s and 1980s brought about greater competition in the industry and more crossover between finance and banking. Knowledgeable professionals like financial analysts were in greater demand to help businesses keep up with the growing number and complexity of investment options. Financial analysts who forecast the rapid rise of technology stocks in the late-1990s were hailed in the industry and the media. But the steep decline of many of those same stocks by 2000–01 led to questions and concerns about the truthfulness of the information reported by certain financial analysts. In late 2000 the SEC instituted the Regulation Fair Disclosure rule, calling for fuller and more honest public disclosure of investment information.

Changes in technology itself have also affected the business conducted by financial analysts. Spreadsheet and statistical software programs present many improved and sophisticated options to compile and present data.

THE JOB

Financial analysts are sometimes called *investment analysts* or *security analysts.* The specific types, direction, and scope of analyses performed by financial analysts are many and varied, depending on the industry, the employer or client, and the analyst's training and years of experience. Financial analysts study their employer's or client's financial status and make financial and investment recommendations. To arrive at these recommendations, financial analysts examine the employer's or client's financial history and objectives, income and expenditures, risk tolerance, and current investments. Once they understand the employer's or client's financial standing and investment goals, financial analysts scout out potential investment opportunities. They research other companies, perhaps in a single industry, that their employer or client may want to invest in. This in-depth research consists of investigating the business of each company, including history, past and potential earnings, and products. Based on their findings, financial analysts may recommend that their employer or client buy stock in these companies. If the employer or client already holds stock in a particular company, financial analysts' research may indicate that stocks should be held or sold, or that more should be purchased.

Financial analysts work for companies in any number of industries, including banking, transportation, health care, technology, telecommunications, and energy. While investment options and concerns differ among these, financial analysts still apply the same basic analytic tools in devising investment strategies. They try to learn everything they can about the industry they're working in. They study the markets and make industry comparisons. They also research past performances and future trends of bonds and other investments.

Financial analysts compile many types of reports on their employer or client and on investment opportunities, such as profit-and-loss statements and quarterly outlook statements. They help develop budgets, analyze and oversee cash flow, and perform cost-benefit analyses. They conduct risk analyses to determine what the employer or client can risk at a given time and/or in future. Another responsibility is to ensure that their employer or client meets any relevant tax or regulatory requirements. Financial analysts compile their work using various software programs, often developing financial models, such as charts or graphs, to display their data.

Companies that want to go public (sell company shares to individual investors for the first time) often ask financial analysts to make projections of future earnings as well as presentations for potential investors. Financial analysts also make sure that all paperwork is in order and compliant with SEC rules and regulations.

Entry-level financial analysts, usually working under direct supervision, mainly conduct research and compile statistical data. After a few years of experience, they become more involved in presenting reports. While a financial analyst generally offers recommendations, a senior financial analyst often has the authority to actually decide purchases or sales. Senior financial analysts implement a company's business plan. In larger companies, they also assist different departments in conducting their own financial analyses and business planning. Those in senior positions become supervisors who train junior financial analysts.

Many specialties fall under the job title of financial analyst. These specialties vary from employer to employer, and duties overlap between different types of analysts. In smaller firms a financial analyst may have extensive responsibility, while at larger firms a financial analyst may specialize in one of any number of areas. *Budget analysts,* often known as *accountants* or *controllers,* look at the operating costs of a company or its individual departments and prepare budget reports. *Credit analysts* examine credit records to determine the potential risk in extending credit or lending money. *Investment analysts* evaluate investment data so they can make suitable investment recommendations. *Mergers and acquisitions analysts* conduct research and make recommendations relating to company mergers and acquisitions. *Money market analysts* assess financial data and investment opportunities, giving advice specifically in the area of money markets. *Ratings analysts* explore a company's financial situation to determine whether or not it will be able to repay debts. *Risk analysts* focus on evaluating the risks of investments. The intent is to identify and then minimize a company's risks and losses. *Security analysts* specialize in studying securities, such as stocks and bonds. *Tax analysts* prepare, file, and examine federal, state, and local tax payments and returns for their employer or client and perhaps also for local affiliates. They analyze tax issues and keep up with tax law changes. *Treasury analysts* manage their company's or client's daily cash position, prepare cash journal entries, initiate wire transfers, and perform bank reconciliations.

Analysts are considered either *buy-side analysts,* who usually work for money management firms, or *sell-side analysts,* sometimes called *sales analysts* or *Wall Street analysts,* who usually work for brokerage firms.

Personal financial advisers have many similar responsibilities (assessing finances, projecting income, recommending investments), but these are performed on behalf of individuals rather than companies.

REQUIREMENTS

High School

Since financial analysts work with numbers and compile data, you should take as many math classes as are available. Accounting, business, economics, and computer classes will be helpful as well. A good grasp of computer spreadsheet programs such as Excel is vital. Take extra care as you research and write reports in any subject matter or in public speaking: It will pay off later when you must conduct investment research and write and present investment recommendations.

Postsecondary Training

Most employers require that financial analysts hold a bachelor's degree in accounting, business administration, finance, or statistics. Other possible majors include communications, economics, international business, and public administration. Some companies will hire you if you hold a bachelor's degree in another discipline as long as you can demonstrate mathematical ability. In college, take business, economics, and statistics courses. Since computer technology plays such a big role in a financial analyst's work, computer classes can be helpful as well. English composition classes can prepare you for the writing you will need to do when preparing reports. Some employers require a writing sample prior to an interview.

Financial analysts generally continue to take courses to keep up with the ongoing changes in the world of finance, including international trade, state and federal laws and regulations, and computer technology. Proficiency in certain databases, presentation graphics, spreadsheets, and other software is expected. Some employers require their employees to have a master's degree.

Many top firms offer summer internship programs. Check company websites for the particulars, such as assignments and qualifications. An internship can provide you with helpful contacts and increase your chances of landing a job when you finish college.

Certification or Licensing

Financial analysts can earn the CFA title, which, while not required, is recommended. The CFA program, which is administered by AIMR, consists of three levels of examinations. These rigorous exams deal with such topics as economics, financial statement analysis, corporate finance, and portfolio management. AIMR states that a candidate may need to spend 250 hours studying to prepare for each level. The Motley Fool, a financial education company (http://www.fool.com), reported that about 50 percent of the candidates fail the first level. A candidate can take only one level per year, so a minimum of three years is required to become a CFA charterholder. If a candidate fails a level, it can be taken the next year. Candidates who do not successfully complete all three levels within seven years must reregister.

Before taking the exams, you must already have a bachelor's degree. There is no required course of study. Prior to earning the CFA charter, you must have spent three years in a related field working in the investment decision-making process and you must first apply to become a member of AIMR as well as a local society.

The CFA charter is recognized around the world as a standard in the finance industry. Many employers expect job seekers to be CFA charterholders. According to AIMR, more than 35,000 people have become CFA charterholders since the program was first administered in 1963.

For certain upper-level positions, some firms require that you have a certified public accountant (CPA) license.

Other Requirements

Research, organization, and communication skills are crucial for this job. Financial analysts conduct in-depth research, often looking for hard-to-find data. Organizational skills are important when it comes to compiling and presenting this data. Once you have explored a company's financial situation, you must communicate complicated ideas through presentations and/or written reports. You should be able to communicate clearly ideas both verbally when making presentations and on paper when writing reports.

The work requires strong analytic skills, so a knack for numbers and attention to detail are also helpful. An interest in solving problems will go a long way. It is important that a financial analyst be accurate and thorough in preparing financial statements.

You should enjoy reading and be able to retain what you read, since it is important to keep up with what's happening in the industry and take it into account when offering financial solutions to employers or clients. Since many financial analysts must travel at a moment's notice to conduct research or complete a deal, flexibility is another important characteristic.

Financial analysts should be able to work well under pressure, as this line of work often demands long hours and entails strict deadlines. You should have good interpersonal skills and enjoy interacting with others. Social functions and business conferences are good opportunities to make deals and important contacts.

EXPLORING

There are many sources of information dealing with the financial services industry. Read publications such as *Barron's* (http://www.

Questions and Answers about U.S. Coins

Q. Why do some of our coins have grooves along the edges?

A. Originally, the dollar, half-dollar, quarter, and dime coins were made with gold and silver. The grooved edges were used to deter counterfeiting. Although these coins no longer contain precious metals, grooved edges are still used to assist the visually impaired discern coins from one another, such as the penny (no grooves) and the dime (grooves).

Q. Why are coins printed so that if they are flipped, the image appears upside down?

A. The U.S. Treasury produces coins with what is called a "coin turn." The reverse side appears upside down when compared to the front side. Though there is no official reason for this practice, the Treasury still produces coins in this manner for historical reasons.

Q. Why do all the U.S. Presidents pictured on coins face to the left, but Abraham Lincoln, pictured on the penny, faces to the right?

A. The direction that Lincoln is pictured was simply the choice of the designer. The coin was modeled from a plaque of Lincoln, which pictured him facing to the right.

Source: U.S. Mint, http://www.usmint.gov

barrons.com), *The Wall Street Journal* (http://www.wsj.com), *Forbes* (http://www.forbes.com), *BusinessWeek* (http://www.businessweek.com), *Fortune* (http://www.fortune.com), and *Financial Times* (http://www.ft.com). In the print or online versions, you will find a wealth of information on stocks, mutual funds, finance, education, careers, salaries, global business, and more. You can also conduct company research. You might have to become a subscriber to access certain sections online.

AnalystForum (http://www.analystforum.com) is a resource for Chartered Financial Analysts and CFA candidates. Although this site will not be of much use to you until you've launched your career, you can find links to financial, investment, and security analyst society sites. From within these societies, you can perhaps track down a professional who would be willing to do an information interview with you.

While in high school, you might volunteer to handle the bookkeeping for a school club or student government, or help balance the family checking account to become familiar with simple bookkeeping practices. Your school may have an investment club you can join. If not, ask a parent or teacher to help you research and analyze investment opportunities. Choose a specific industry (e.g., telecommunications, technology, or health care), study companies in that industry, and select and track several stocks that appear to have growth potential.

EMPLOYERS

Financial analysts work in the public and private sectors. Employers include banks, brokerage and securities firms, corporations, government agencies, manufacturers, mutual and pension funds, and financial management, insurance, investment, trust, and utility companies. Many financial analysts are self-employed.

According to the *Occupational Outlook Handbook,* about 25 percent of financial analysts work for security and commodity brokers, exchanges, and investment services firms, and 20 percent work for depository and nondepository institutions, including banks, credit institutions, and mortgage bankers and brokers. The rest work mainly for insurance carriers, computer and data processing services, and management and public relations firms.

Since financial analysts often work in Wall Street companies, many employers are found in New York City. They are also concentrated in other large cities but work in smaller cities as well.

Approximately 239,000 financial analysts and personal financial advisers are employed in the United States (financial analysts make up about 60 percent of this total).

STARTING OUT

Representatives from hiring companies (e.g., banks, brokerage firms, or investment companies) may visit college campuses to meet with students interested in pursuing careers as financial analysts. College placement offices will have details on such visits. Company websites may also contain campus recruiting schedules.

Gaining an entry-level position can be difficult. Some companies offer in-house training, but many do not. Working as a research assistant is one way to break into the business. Read member profiles at association sites to see where members have worked as financial analysts. Explore those companies that look appealing.

Make contacts and network with other financial analysts. Your local AIMR society or chapter will probably hold regular meetings, affording ample networking opportunities. You can become an AIMR member whether or not you are a CFA charterholder, but charterholders enjoy full member benefits, such as access to job postings. (Complete details, including listings for local societies and chapters, can be found at the AIMR website: http://www.aimr.org.) Also, internships are an excellent way to make contacts and gain experience in the field.

As an interview tool, the New York Society of Security Analysts suggests that you compile an investment recommendation for potential clients to give them an idea of the kind of research you're capable of and how you present your data.

You can search for job ads online. One resource is the jobsinthemoney.com network (http://www.jobsinthemoney.com). If you know what companies you'd like to work for, visit their websites. Chances are you will find online job listings there.

ADVANCEMENT

Financial analysts who accurately prepare their employer's or client's financial statements and who offer investment advice that results in profits will likely be rewarded for their efforts. Rewards come in the form of promotions and/or bonuses. Successful financial analysts may become senior financial analysts, sometimes in only three or four years. Some become portfolio or financial managers. Rather than simply making recommendations on their company's or client's investment policies, those who advance to a senior position have more decision-making responsibility.

Some financial analysts move on to jobs as investment bankers or advisers. Others become officers in various departments in their company. Positions include chief financial officer and vice president of finance. In time, some cultivate enough contacts to be able to start their own consulting firms.

EARNINGS

The 2001 National Occupational Employment and Wage Estimates, compiled by the U.S. Department of Labor, reports that median annual earnings of financial analysts were $55,130 in 2001. Top earners made more than $107,720, and the lowest salaries were less than $33,520.

As of January 2002, *BusinessWeek Online,* using salary.com's Salary Wizard, reports U.S. salary ranges for several different kinds of analysts. Figures for a financial analyst I (an entry-level position) range from a low of $39,826 to a high of $50,694, whereas the figures for a financial analyst III (a more senior position) range from $61,289 to $76,955. Earnings for a credit analyst I are $29,499–$39,146, and for a credit analyst III, $40,165–$52,317. A treasury analyst I earns $33,283–$40,983, while a treasury analyst III earns $51,641–$70,803.

If the investments of financial analysts' employers or clients perform well, it is not uncommon for those financial analysts to receive a bonus in addition to their salary. With bonuses, skilled financial analysts can make a lot of money in addition to their base salaries.

Benefits include paid vacation, health, disability, life insurance, and retirement or pension plans. Some employers also offer profit-sharing plans. Tuition reimbursement may also be available.

WORK ENVIRONMENT

Most financial analysts work in an office in a corporate setting. Frequently, they work alone (e.g., when conducting research or talking on the phone to clients). Some may work out of their homes. Much time is spent working on a computer, doing research and compiling data. Travel is frequently required—there are meetings and social functions to attend, clients to meet, and companies to research at their place of business. Because financial analysts spend much of their normal business hours talking or meeting with clients, they often conduct research after hours and generally work long days. It is not uncommon for financial analysts to clock well in excess of 50 hours per week.

OUTLOOK

The state of the economy and the stock market has a direct effect on the employment outlook for financial analysts. When the economy is doing well, companies are more likely to make investments, resulting in a need for financial analysts. When the economy is doing poorly, companies are less likely to make investments, and there will be less need for financial analysts. The *Occupational Outlook Handbook* (*OOH*), anticipating an increase in business investments, predicts a faster-than-average employment growth in this field. The *OOH* notes, too, that international securities markets, the complexity of financial products, and business mergers and acquisitions demand financial analysts to sort through all the issues involved. Because of the close scrutiny analysts have been under, it might become more desirable for financial analysts to hold the CFA charter.

Individual investing will also affect the need for financial analysts, in that the more people invest in mutual funds (often through 401-K plans), the greater the need there will be for financial analysts to recommend financial products to the mutual fund companies.

FOR MORE INFORMATION

This organization's website offers an e-library containing a helpful dictionary of financial terminology. Industry news and certification information is also available.

Association for Financial Professionals, Inc.
7315 Wisconsin Avenue, Suite 600 West
Bethesda, MD 20814
Tel: 301-907-2862
http://www.afponline.org

For complete AIMR information, including lists of AIMR societies, publications, news, conference details, and certification information, contact

Association for Investment Management and Research (AIMR)
PO Box 3668
560 Ray C. Hunt Drive
Charlottesville, VA 22903-0668
Tel: 800-247-8132
Email: info@aimr.org
http://www.aimr.org

The NYSSA website includes a list of top employers of financial analysts as well as an article on becoming a security analyst.

New York Society of Security Analysts (NYSSA)
1601 Broadway, 11th Floor
New York, NY 10019-7406
Tel: 212-541-4530
Email: staff@nyssa.org
http://www.nyssa.org

For information on laws and regulations pertaining to investors and the securities markets, contact

U.S. Securities and Exchange Commission
Office of Investor Education and Assistance
450 Fifth Street, NW
Washington, DC 20549
Tel: 202-942-7040
Email: help@sec.gov
http://www.sec.gov

This website has links to financial, investment, and security analyst societies.

AnalystForum
http://www.analystforum.com

For issues of interest to senior finance executives, see

CFO.com
http://www.cfo.com

FINANCIAL INSTITUTION OFFICERS AND MANAGERS

QUICK FACTS

School Subjects
Business
Mathematics

Personal Skills
Communication/ideas
Leadership/management

Work Environment
Primarily indoors
Primarily one location

Minimum Education Level
Bachelor's degree

Salary Range
$37,530 to $55,960 to $136,700 +

Certification or Licensing
Recommended

Outlook
About as fast as the average

DOT
186

GOE
11.06.05

NOC
0122

O*NET-SOC
11-3031.01, 11-3031.02, 13-2071.00, 13-2072.00

OVERVIEW

Financial institution officers and managers oversee the activities of banks and personal credit institutions such as credit unions and finance companies. These establishments serve business, government, and individuals. They lend money, maintain savings, enable people and businesses to write checks for goods and services, rent safe-deposit boxes for storing valuables, manage trust funds, advise clients on investments and business affairs, issue credit cards and traveler's checks, and take payments for gas and electric bills. There are approximately 658,000 financial managers (including those working outside of financial institutions) employed in the United States.

HISTORY

The modern concept of bank notes, or currency, developed in the 17th century. Goldsmiths in London began to issue paper receipts for gold and other valuables that people deposited in their warehouses. The paper money we use today is a modern version of these 17th-century receipts.

The first bank in the United States, Bank of North America, was chartered by the Continental Congress in 1781. By the early 1900s, banks had become so numerous that federal control of banks was needed. The Federal Deposit System, as we know it today, is the result of the efforts to coordinate the activities of the many banks throughout the nation. As banks grew in number and competed to attract new customers, financial professionals developed a variety of new services for banks to offer. Advancements in technology made many of these new services possible and often changed the way people thought about money. For example, in the late 1950s and 1960s banks introduced the first credit cards (Visa, MasterCard, etc.) that were accepted by multiple vendors. The introduction of these credit cards was made possible by the introduction of bank computers that were able to track transactions and signal when spending limits were reached. Today, credit cards have become so commonplace that CardWeb.com estimates that there are approximately 6,000 credit card issuers.

The banking industry continues to use technology developments to expand its services. For example, the American Bankers Association reports that nearly two-thirds of the country's community banks had websites by 2000. As the 21st century began, online banking was quickly becoming an expected option. Within the past 25 years, the number of banks and other financial institutions has grown extensively, and many financial professionals are needed to run the banking industry.

THE JOB

Financial institutions include commercial banks, which provide full banking service for business, government, and individuals; investment banks, which offer their clients financial counseling and brokering; Federal Reserve Banks, whose customers are affiliated banks in their districts; or other organizations such as credit unions and finance companies.

These institutions employ many officers and managers whose duties vary depending on the type and size of the firm as well as on their own area of responsibility. All financial institutions operate under the direction of a president, who is guided by policies set by the board of directors. Vice presidents are department heads who are sometimes also responsible for certain key clients. Controllers handle bank funds, properties, and equipment. Large institutions may also have treasurers, loan officers, and officers in charge of departments such as trust, credit, and investment.

The *financial institution president* directs the overall activities of the bank or consumer credit organization, making sure that its objectives are achieved without violating government regulations or overlooking any legal requirements. The officers are responsible for earning as much of a return as possible on the institution's investments within the restrictions demanded by government and sound business practices. They help set policies pertaining to investments, loans, interest, and reserves. They coordinate the activities of the various divisions and delegate authority to subordinate officers, who administer the operation of their own areas of responsibility. Financial institution presidents study financial reports and other data to keep up with changes in the economy that may affect their firm's policies.

The *vice president* coordinates many of the operations of the institution. This person is responsible for the activities of a regional bank office, branch bank, and often an administrative bank division or department. As designated by the board of directors, the vice president supervises programs such as installment loan, foreign trade, customer service, trust, and investment. The vice president also prepares studies for management and planning, like workload and budget estimates and activity and analysis reports.

The *administrative secretary* usually writes directions for supervisory workers that outline and explain policy. The administrative secretary acts, in effect, as an intermediary between minor supervisory workers and the executive officers.

The *financial institution treasurer* directs the bank's monetary programs, transactions, and security measures in accordance with banking principles and legislation. Treasurers coordinate program activity and evaluate operating practices to ensure efficient operations. They oversee receipt, disbursement, and expenditure of money, and sign documents approving or affecting monetary transactions. They direct the safekeeping and control of assets and securities and maintain specified legal cash reserves. They review financial and operating statements and present reports and recommendations to bank officials or board committees.

Controllers authorize the use of funds kept by the treasurer. They also supervise the maintenance of accounts and records and analyze these records so that the directors or other bank officials will know how much the bank is spending for salaries, operating expenses, and other expenses. Controllers often formulate financial policies.

The *financial institution manager* establishes and maintains relationships with the community. This person's responsibility is to supervise accounting and reporting functions and to establish operating policies and procedures. The manager directs several activities within the bank. The assets, records, collateral, and securities held by the financial institution are in the manager's custody. Managers approve loans of various types, such as credit, commercial, real estate, and consumer loans. They also direct personnel in trust activities.

The *loan officer* and the *credit and collection manager* both deal with customers who are seeking or have obtained loans or credit. The loan officer specializes in examining and evaluating applications for lines of credit, installment credit, or commercial, real estate, and consumer loans and has the authority to approve them within a specified limit or recommend their approval to the loan committee. To determine the feasibility of granting a loan request, the officer analyzes the applicant's financial status, credit, and property evaluation. The job may also include handling foreclosure proceedings. Depending on training and experience, officers may analyze potential loan markets to develop prospects for loans. They negotiate the terms of transaction and draw up the requisite documents to buy and sell contracts, loans, or real estate. Credit and collection managers make up collection notices for customers who already have credit. When the bank has difficulty collecting accounts or receives a worthless check, credit and collection managers take steps to correct the situation. Managers must keep records of all credit and collection transactions.

Loan counselors study the records of the account when payments on a loan are overdue and contact the borrower to discuss payment of the loan. They may analyze the borrower's financial problems and make new arrangements for repayment of the loan. If a bank is unable to collect on a loan, loan counselors prepare a report for the bank or institution's files.

Credit card operations managers are responsible for the credit card policies and operations of a bank, commercial establishment, or credit card company. They establish procedures for verifying the information on application forms, determine applicants' credit worthiness, approve the issuance of credit cards, and set a credit limit on each account. These managers coordinate the work involved with reviewing unpaid balances, collecting delinquent accounts, investigating and preventing fraud, voiding lost or stolen credit cards, keeping records, and exchanging information with the company's branches and other credit card companies.

The *letter of credit negotiator* works with clients who hold letters of credit used in international banking. This person contacts foreign banks, suppliers, and other sources to obtain documents needed to authorize the requested loan. Then the negotiator checks to see if the documents have been completed correctly so that the conditions set forth in the letter of credit meet with policy and code requirements. Before authorizing payment, the negotiator verifies the client's credit rating and may request increasing the collateral or reducing the amount of purchases, amending the contract accordingly. The letter of credit negotiator specifies the method of payment and informs the foreign bank when a loan has gone unpaid for a certain length of time.

The *trust officer* directs operations concerning the administration of private, corporate, and probate trusts. Officers examine or draft trust agreements to ensure compliance with legal requirements and terms creating trusts. They locate, inventory, and evaluate assets of probated accounts. They also direct realization of assets, liquidation of liabilities, payment of bills, preparation of federal and state tax returns on trust income, and collection of earnings. They represent the institution in trust fund negotiations.

Reserve officers maintain the institution's reserve funds according to policy and as required by law. They regulate the flow of money through branches, correspondent banks, and the Federal Reserve Bank. They also consolidate financial statements, calculate the legal reserve, and compile statistical and analytical reports of the reserves.

Foreign-exchange traders maintain the balance that the institution has on deposit in foreign banks to ensure its foreign-exchange position and determine the prices at which that exchange will be purchased and sold. Their conclusions are based on an analysis of demand, supply, and the stability of the currency. They establish local rates of exchange based upon money market quotations or the customer's financial standing. They also buy and sell foreign-exchange drafts and compute the proceeds.

The *securities trader* performs securities investment and counseling service for the bank and its customers. They study financial histories and future trends and advise financial institution officers and customers regarding investments in stocks and bonds. They transmit buy-and-sell orders to a trading desk or broker as directed and recommend purchase, retention, or sale of issues. They compute extensions, commissions, and other charges for billing customers and making payments for securities.

The *operations officer* is in charge of the internal operations in a department or branch office of a financial institution. This person is responsible for the smooth and efficient operation of a particular area. Duties include interviewing, hiring, and directing the training of employees, as well as supervising their activities, evaluating their performance, and making certain that they comply with established procedures. Operations officers audit accounts, records, and certifications and verify the count of incoming cash. They prepare reports on the activities of the department or branch, control the supply of money for its needs, and perform other managerial tasks of a general nature.

The *credit union manager* directs the operations of credit unions, which are chartered by the state or federal government to provide savings and loan services to their members. This manager reviews loan applications, arranges automatic payroll deductions for credit union members wishing to make regular savings deposits or loan payments, and assists in collecting delinquent accounts. Managers prepare financial statements, help the government audit credit union records, and supervise bookkeeping and clerical activities. Acting as management representative of the credit union, credit union managers have the power to sign legal documents and checks on behalf of the board of directors. They also oversee control of the credit union's assets and advise the board on how to invest its funds.

REQUIREMENTS

High School

You will need at least a bachelor's degree if you want to work as a financial institution officer or manager. While you are in high school, therefore, you should take classes that will give you a solid preparation for college. Such classes include mathematics, such as algebra and geometry, science, history, and a foreign language. Take English courses to improve your researching, writing, and communication skills. Also, take computer classes. Computer technology is an integral part of today's financial world, and you will benefit from being familiar with this tool. Finally, if your high school offers classes in economics, accounting, or finance, be sure to take these courses. The course work will not only give you an opportunity to gain knowledge but also allow you to see if you enjoy working with numbers and theories.

Postsecondary Training

Possible majors for you to take in college include accounting, economics, finance, or business administration with an emphasis on accounting or finance. You will need to continue honing your computer skills during this time. Also, you will probably have exposure to business law classes. It is important for you to realize that federal and state laws regarding business and finances change, so you will need to become familiar with current regulations.

Financial institutions increasingly seek candidates with master's degrees in business administration for positions as managers. So keep in mind that you may have to pursue further education even after you have completed your bachelor's degree. No matter what level of degree you obtain, however, you will also need to keep up your education even as you work. Many financial management and banking associations offer continuing education programs in conjunction with colleges or universities. These programs are geared toward advancing and updating your knowledge of subjects such as changing banking regulations, financial analysis, and international banking.

Certification or Licensing

Certification is one way to show your commitment to the field, improve your skills, and increase your possibilities for advancement. Professional certification is available in specialized fields such as investment and credit management. Requirements for earning the designation chartered financial analyst, which is conferred by the Association for Investment Management and Research, include having the educational background to be able to do master's level work, passing three levels of tests, and having three or more years of experience in the field. The National Association of Credit Management offers business credit professionals a three-part certification program that consists of work experience and examinations. Financial managers pass through the level of credit business associate to credit business fellow to certified credit executive. The Association for Financial Professionals confers the certified treasury professional (formerly known as the certified cash manager) designation. Applicants must pass an examination and have working experience in the field.

Other Requirements

In the banking business, the ability to get along well with others is essential. You should be able to show tact and convey a feeling of understanding and confidence. Honesty is perhaps the most important qualification for this job. These officers and managers handle large sums of money and have access to confidential financial information about the individuals and business concerns associated with their institutions. Therefore, if you are interested in this career, you must have a high degree of personal integrity.

EXPLORING

Except for high school courses that are business oriented, you will find few opportunities for experience and exploration during high school. Ask your teacher or guidance counselor to arrange a class tour of a financial institution. This will at least give you a taste of how banking services work. You can gain the most valuable experience by finding a part-time or a summer job in a bank or other institution that sometimes hires qualified high school or college students. Finally, to gain some hands-on experience with managing money, consider joining a school or local club in which you could work as the treasurer.

EMPLOYERS

Financial managers and related workers hold approximately 658,000 jobs. They primarily work for banks and personal credit institutions such as credit unions and finance companies.

STARTING OUT

One way to enter banking as a regular employee is through part-time or summer employment. Anyone can apply for a position by writing to a financial institution officer in charge of personnel or by arranging for an interview appointment. Many institutions advertise in the classified section of local newspapers. The larger banks recruit on college campuses. An officer will visit a campus and conduct interviews at that time. Student placement offices can also arrange interviews.

ADVANCEMENT

There is no one method for advancement among financial institution officers. Advancement depends on the size of the institution, the services it offers, and the qualifications of the employee. Usually, the smaller the employer the slower the advancements.

Financial institutions often offer special training programs that take place at night, during the summer, and in some special instances during scheduled working hours. People who take advantage of these opportunities usually find that advancement comes more quickly. The American Banking Institute (part of the American Bankers Association), for example, offers training in every phase of banking through its own facilities or the facilities of the local universities and banking organizations. The length of this training may vary from six months to two years. Years of service and experience are required for a top-level financial institution officer to become acquainted with policy, operations, customers, and the community. Similarly, the National Association of Credit Management offers training and instruction.

EARNINGS

Those who enter banking in the next few years will find their earnings are dependent on their experience, the size of the institution, and its location. In general, starting salaries in financial institutions are not usually the highest, although among larger financial institutions in big cities, starting salaries often compare favorably with salaries in large corporations. After five to 10 years of experience, financial institution officers' salaries are usually slightly higher than those in large corporations for people of comparable experience.

Financial managers in commercial banks earned a median annual salary of $55,960 in 2000, according to the U.S. Department of Labor. Also according to the Department, the lowest paid 10 percent of financial managers made approximately $37,530 in 2001, while the highest paid 10 percent earned $136,700 or more in 2001.

Group life insurance, paid vacations, profit-sharing plans, and health care and retirement plans are some of the benefits offered to financial officers and managers.

WORK ENVIRONMENT

Working conditions in financial institutions are generally pleasant. They are usually clean, well maintained, and often air-conditioned. They are generally located throughout cities for the convenience of customers and employees, too. Working hours for financial institution officers and managers may be somewhat irregular as many organizations have expanded their hours of business.

OUTLOOK

The number of job openings for financial institution officers and managers is expected to increase about as fast as the average for all other occupations over the next decade, according to predictions by the U.S. Department of Labor. The need for skilled professionals will increase primarily as a result of greater domestic and foreign competition, changing laws affecting taxes and other financial matters, and a growing emphasis on accurate reporting of financial data for both financial institutions and corporations.

However, competition for these jobs will be strong for several reasons. Financial institution officers and managers are often promoted from within the ranks of the organization, and, once established in their jobs, they tend to stay for many years. Also, more qualified applicants are becoming available each year to fill vacancies; workers who have earned master's degrees in business administration will experience the lowest unemployment rates. Chances for employment will be best for workers who are familiar with a range of financial services, such as banking, insurance, real estate, and securities, and for those experienced in computers and data processing systems.

FOR MORE INFORMATION

This organization has information about the banking industry and continuing education available through the American Institute of Banking. It also has information on the Stonier Graduate School of Banking.

American Bankers Association
1120 Connecticut Avenue, NW
Washington, DC 20036
Tel: 800-226-5377
http://www.aba.com

For certification, industry news, and career information, contact

Association for Financial Professionals
7315 Wisconsin Avenue, Suite 600 West
Bethesda, MD 20814
Tel: 301-907-2862
http://www.afponline.org

For information on the chartered financial analyst designation, contact

Association for Investment Management and Research
PO Box 3668
560 Ray C. Hunt Drive
Charlottesville, VA 22903-0668
Tel: 800-247-8132
Email: info@aimr.org
http://www.aimr.org

For information on certification, continuing education, and general information on the banking and credit industry, contact

National Association of Credit Management
8840 Columbia 100 Parkway
Columbia, MD 21045
Tel: 410-740-5560
Email: nacm_info@nacm.org
http://www.nacm.org

FINANCIAL SERVICES BROKERS

QUICK FACTS

School Subjects Business Mathematics	**Certification or Licensing** Required by certain states
Personal Skills Communication/ideas Technical/scientific	**Outlook** Faster than the average
Work Environment Primarily indoors Primarily one location	**DOT** 211
Minimum Education Level Bachelor's degree	**GOE** 07.03.01
Salary Range $25,990 to $59,690 to $145,000+	**NOC** 1113
	O*NET-SOC 41-3031.00, 41-3031.01

OVERVIEW

Financial services brokers, sometimes called *registered representatives, account executives, securities sales representatives,* or *stockbrokers,* work to represent both individuals and organizations who wish to invest in and sell stocks, bonds, or other financial products. Financial services brokers analyze companies offering stocks to see if investing is worth the risk. They also advise clients on proper investment strategies for their own investment goals. Securities, commodities, and financial services brokers hold approximately 367,000 jobs in the United States.

HISTORY

When a government wants to build a new sewer system or a company wants to build a new factory, it rarely has the required money—or capital—readily at hand to do it. It must first raise the capital from investors. Historically, raising capital to finance the needs of government and commerce was—and often still is—an arduous task. European monarchies, particularly during the 18th and 19th centuries, relied heavily upon bankers to meet the costs of the interminable wars that devastated the continent and to assist in early industrial expansion. This system grew obsolete, however, and governments, banks, and industry turned to the burgeoning middle class for funds. They offered middle class investors securities and stocks—a fractional ownership in a company or enterprise—in exchange for their money. Soon, dealers emerged that linked government and industry with the smaller investor. In the United States, the New York Stock Exchange was formed in 1790 and officially established in 1817.

The stock exchange functions as a marketplace where stockbrokers buy and sell securities for individuals or institutions. Stock prices can fluctuate from minute to minute, with the price of a stock at any given time determined by the demand for it. As a direct result of the disastrous stock market crash of 1929, the Federal Securities Act of 1934 set up a federal commission to control the handling of securities and made illegal any manipulation of prices on stock exchanges. Today, the public is protected by regulations that set standards for stock listings, require public disclosure of the financial condition of companies offering stock, and prohibit stock manipulation and trading on inside information.

THE JOB

The most important part of a broker's job is finding customers and building a client base. Beginning brokers spend much of their time searching for customers, relying heavily on telephone solicitation such as "cold calls"—calling people with whom they have never had any contact. Brokers also find customers through business and social contacts or they might be given a list of likely prospects from their brokerage firm.

When financial services brokers open accounts for new customers, they first record all the personal information that is required to allow the customer to trade securities through the brokerage firm. Depending on a customer's knowledge of the market, the broker may explain the meaning of stock market terms and trading practices and offer financial counseling. Then the broker helps the customer to devise an individual financial portfolio, including securities, life insurance, corporate and municipal bonds, mutual funds, certificates of deposit, annuities, and other investments. The broker must determine the customer's investment goals—such as whether the customer wants long-term, steady growth or a quick turnaround of stocks for short-term gains—and then offers advice on investments accordingly. Once an investment strategy has been worked out, brokers execute buy-and-sell orders for their customers by relaying the information to the floor of the stock exchange, where the broker's floor representative pus the order into effect. *Securities traders* also buy and sell securities, but usually as a representative of a private firm.

From the research department of the brokerage firm, brokers obtain information on the activities and projected growth of any company that is currently offering stock or plans to offer stock in the near future. The actual or perceived strength of a company is a major factor in a stock-purchase decision. Brokers must be prepared to answer questions on the technical aspects of stock market operations and also be informed on current economic conditions. They are expected to have the market knowledge to anticipate certain trends and to counsel customers accordingly in terms of their particular stock holdings.

Some financial services brokers specialize in areas such as handling only institutional accounts, bond issues, or mutual funds. Whatever their area of specialization, financial services brokers must keep abreast of all significant political and economic conditions, maintain very accurate records for all transactions, and continually solicit new customers.

REQUIREMENTS

High School

If you are interested in becoming a financial services broker, you should take courses in business, accounting, economics, mathematics, government, and communications.

Postsecondary Training

Because of the specialized knowledge necessary to perform this job properly, a college education is increasingly important, especially in the larger brokerage houses. To make intelligent and insightful judgments, a broker must be able to read and understand financial reports and evaluate statistics. For this reason, although employers seldom require specialized academic training, a bachelor's degree in business administration, economics, or finance is helpful.

Certification or Licensing

Almost all states require brokers to be licensed. Some states administer written examinations and some require brokers to post a personal bond. Brokers must register as representatives of their firms with the National Association of Securities Dealers (NASD). In order to register with NASD, brokers must first pass the General Securities Registered Representative Examination (Series 7 exam) administered by NASD Regulation (a subsidiary of NASD) to demonstrate competence in the areas in which they will work. In addition, they must be employees of a registered firm for at least four months. Many states also require brokers to take and pass a second examination—the Uniform Securities Agents State Law Examination.

Other Requirements

Because they deal with the public, brokers should be well groomed and pleasant and have large reserves of tact and patience. Employers look for ambitious individuals with sales ability. Brokers also need self-confidence and the ability to handle frequent rejections. Above all, they must have a highly developed sense of responsibility, because in many instances they will be handling funds that represent a client's life savings.

EXPLORING

Any sales experience can provide you with a general background for work in financial services. You might be able to find summer employment in a brokerage house. A visit to a local investment office, the New York Stock Exchange, or one of the commodities exchanges located in other major cities will provide a valuable opportunity to observe how transactions are handled and what is required of people in the field.

EMPLOYERS

Financial services brokers and related workers hold 367,000 jobs, and 90,000 of these workers are self-employed. The Department of Labor reports that seven out of 10 brokers work for securities and commodities firms, exchanges, and investment services companies. One in seven are employed by banks, savings institutions, and credit unions.

Financial services brokers work all around the country. Although many employers are very small, the largest employers of financial services brokers are a few large firms that have their main offices in major cities, especially New York.

STARTING OUT

Many firms hire beginning sales workers and train and retain them for a probationary period to determine their talents and ability to succeed in the business. The training period lasts about six months and includes classroom instruction and on-the-job training. Applications for these beginning jobs may be made directly to the personnel offices of the various securities firms.

ADVANCEMENT

Depending upon their skills and ambitions, financial services brokers may advance rapidly in this field. Accomplished brokers may find that the size and number of accounts they service will increase to a point at which they no longer need to solicit new customers. Others become branch managers, research analysts, or partners in their own firms.

EARNINGS

The salaries of trainees and beginners range from $1,200 to $1,500 per month, although larger firms pay a somewhat higher starting wage. Once the financial services broker has acquired a sufficient number of accounts, he or she works solely on a commission basis, with fees resulting from the size and type of security bought or sold. Some firms pay annual bonuses to their brokers when business warrants. Since earnings can fluctuate greatly based on the condition of the market, some brokers may find it necessary to supplement their income through other means during times of slow market activity.

According to the U.S. Department of Labor, the median earnings for brokers were $59,690 a year in 2001; the middle 50 percent earned between $35,790 and $113,460. Ten percent earned less than $25,990 and 10 percent earned more than $145,000.

WORK ENVIRONMENT

Brokers work more flexible hours than workers in other fields. They may work fewer hours during slow trading periods but be required to put in overtime dealing with paperwork during busy periods.

The atmosphere of a brokerage firm is frequently highly charged, and the peaks and drops of market activity can produce a great deal of tension. Watching fortunes being made is exciting, but the reverse occurs frequently, too, and it requires responsibility and maturity to weather the setbacks.

OUTLOOK

The U.S. Department of Labor predicts that job opportunities for financial services brokers are expected to grow faster than the average for all occupations over the next decade because of continued interest in the stock market. Rising personal incomes and greater inherited wealth are increasing the amount of funds people are able to invest. Many people dabble in investing via their personal computers and the Internet. Even those with limited means have the option of investing through a variety of methods such as investment clubs, mutual funds, and monthly payment plans. In addition, the expansion of business activities and new technological breakthroughs will create increased demand for the sale of stock to meet capital requirements for companies around the world.

Demand for financial services brokers fluctuates with the economy. Turnover among beginners is high because they have a hard time soliciting enough clients. Because of potentially high earnings, competition in this business is very intense.

FOR MORE INFORMATION

To learn more about different types of investment professionals and new financial products and to read a glossary of terms and news alerts, visit the individual investor section of the National Association of Securities Dealers (NASD) website. Also visit the website for more information on NASD and its subsidiaries.

NASD/NASD Regulation
One Liberty Plaza, 48th Floor
New York, NY 10006
Tel: 212-858-4020
http://www.nasd.com

To learn more about investing, the securities industry, and industry issues, contact

The Securities Industry Association
120 Broadway, 35th Floor
New York, NY 10271-0080
Tel: 212-608-1500
Email: info@sia.com
http://www.sia.com

FRANCHISE OWNERS

QUICK FACTS

School Subjects Business Mathematics **Personal Skills** Following instructions Leadership/management **Work Environment** Primarily indoors Primarily one location **Minimum Education Level** Some postsecondary training **Salary Range** $0 to $30,000 to $100,000+	**Certification or Licensing** Required by certain franchisers (certification) Required by certain states (licensing) **Outlook** About as fast as the average **DOT** N/A **GOE** N/A **NOC** N/A **O*NET-SOC** N/A

OVERVIEW

A *franchise owner* contracts with a company to sell the company's products or services. After paying an initial fee and agreeing to pay the company a certain percentage of revenue, the franchise owner can use the company's name, logo, and guidance. McDonald's, Subway, and KFC are some of the top franchised companies that have locations all across the country. Franchises, however, are not limited to the fast food industry. Today, franchises are available in a wide variety of business areas including computer service, lawn care, real estate, and even hair salons. According to industry expert FranchiseHelp, franchises account for more than 40 percent of all retail sales in the United States and these sales total approximately $1 trillion a year.

HISTORY

Know anybody with an antique Singer sewing machine? Chances are, it was originally sold by one of the first franchise operations.

During the Civil War, the Singer Sewing Machine Company recognized the cost-efficiency of franchising and allowed dealers across the country to sell its sewing machines. Coca-Cola, as well as the Ford Motor Company and other automobile manufacturers, followed Singer's lead in the early 20th century by granting individuals the rights to sell their products. Franchising, however, didn't quite catch on until after World War II, when the needs for products and services across the country boomed along with the population. Ray Kroc jumped on the bandwagon with his McDonald's restaurants in the 1950s. Since then, the McDonald's franchise has become one of the top money-making franchise opportunities of all time.

Franchises have changed somewhat over the last 20–30 years. Abuses of the franchise system brought new government regulations in the 1970s, and the government has been actively involved in protecting the rights of franchisers and franchisees. Also, single-unit ownership, the "mom and pop" operations, is giving way to multiple-unit ownership. A majority of franchisees own more than one of the franchiser's units.

THE JOB

Today, industry experts report that franchises are responsible for almost 50 percent of all retail sales in the United States, and this figure is expected to grow through the 21st century. Franchisers (those companies that sell franchise businesses) and franchisees (those who buy the businesses) are sharing in the almost $1 trillion a year that franchise businesses take in. While everyone probably has a favorite business or two—maybe the neighborhood Krispy Kreme with its fresh crullers or the 7-Eleven down the street with its Big Gulp sodas—not everyone may realize that these are franchised establishments. For those people interested in starting their own businesses, becoming franchisees may offer just the right mix of risk and security. Any new business venture comes with a certain amount of risk, but franchises offer the security of a name and product that customers are used to and are willing to seek out. Someone with money to invest, the willingness to work hard and sometimes long hours, and the desire to be in the retail world may just be the person able to become the successful franchisee, sharing in the franchiser's success.

There's a franchise for practically every type of product and service imaginable. In addition to the familiar McDonald's and Burger King, other franchise operations are providing opportunities: businesses that offer temporary help, maid services, weight control centers, and custom picture framing, to name a few. The International Franchise Association (IFA), in fact, reports that there are approximately 75 different industries that make use of the franchise system. No matter what business a person is interested in, there are probably franchise opportunities available.

Depending on the size and nature of the franchise, owners' responsibilities differ. Those who are able to make a large initial investment may also be able to hire managers and staff members to assist them. Those running a smaller business will need to handle most, if not all, of the job responsibilities themselves. Though there should be assistance from the franchiser in terms of training, marketing guidance, and established business systems, the business is essentially the franchisee's own. The franchisee has paid an initial franchise fee, makes royalty payments to the franchiser, purchased equipment, and rented business space. Any franchisee must handle administrative details, such as record-keeping, creating budgets, and preparing reports for the franchiser. A franchisee is also responsible for hiring (and firing) employees, scheduling work hours, preparing payroll, and keeping track of inventory. Using the franchiser's marketing methods, the franchisee advertises the business. The practices and systems of franchisers differ, so those interested in this work need to carefully research the franchise before buying into it.

Some owners work directly with the clientele. Of course, someone who owns multiple units of the McDonald's franchise probably won't be taking orders at the counter; but someone who owns a single unit of a smaller operation, like a pool maintenance service, may be actively involved in the work at hand, in dealing with the customers, and in finding new customers.

Donna Weber of Redmond, Washington, owns a Jazzercise franchise. Jazzercise is the world's largest dance fitness franchise corporation, with over 5,000 instructors leading almost half a million participants each year. "I own and teach seven Jazzercise classes a week in two suburbs around the Seattle area," Weber says. After investing with an initial low franchise fee, Weber went through considerable training and testing; the training involves instruction on exercise physiology, dance/exercise technique, and safety issues, as well as instruction on the business aspect of owning a franchise. After training, Weber received certification and started her business. She pays a monthly fee to Jazzercise and in return receives choreography notes to new songs and videos demonstrating the exercises.

In addition to conducting classes, Weber spends some part of every workday preparing paperwork for the corporate headquarters. "I keep track of my students' attendance and write personal postcards to those I haven't seen in a while, those who are having birthdays, those who need some personal recognition for a job well done, etc," says Weber, who must also regularly learn new routines. "I teach three different formats," she says, "regular aerobics, step, and a circuit-training class each week, so there is a lot of prep to do a good, safe class."

The franchisee's experience will be affected by the name recognition of the business. If it's a fairly new business, the franchisee may have to take on much of the responsibility of promoting it. If it is a well-established business, customers and clients already know what to expect from the operation.

REQUIREMENTS

High School

Business, math, economics, and accounting courses will be the most valuable to you in preparing for franchise ownership. Before buying into a franchise, you'll have to do a lot of research into the company, analyzing local demographics to determine whether a business is a sound investment. English classes will help you develop the research skills you'll need. In addition, you will need to hone your communication skills that will be essential in establishing relationships with franchisers and customers. Take computer classes since it is virtually impossible to work in today's business world without knowing how to use a computer or the Web. If you already know of a particular area that interests you—such as food service, fashion, or, like Donna Weber, fitness—take classes that will help you learn more about it. Such classes may include home economics, art, dance, or physical education.

Postsecondary Training

Because there is such a variety of franchise opportunities available, there is no single educational path for everyone to take on the road to owning a franchise. Keep in mind, however, that when franchisers review your application for the right to purchase a unit, they'll take into consideration your previous experience in the area. Obviously, a real estate company is unlikely to take a risk on you if you've never had any experience as a broker. In addition, there are some franchise opportunities that require degrees; for example, to own an environmental consulting agency, a business that helps companies meet government environmental standards, you'll have to be an engineer or geologist. But there are also many companies willing to sell to someone wanting to break into a new business. Franchisers will often include special training as part of the initial franchise fee.

Experts in the field stress the importance of gaining work experience before starting out with your own business. Hone your sales, management, and people skills and take the time to learn about the industry that interests you. Even if you don't plan on getting a college degree, consider taking some college-level courses in subjects such as business and finance. One recent survey of franchisees found that over 80 percent had attended college or had a college degree. This reflects the fact that many franchisees have worked for many years in other professions in order to have the money and security needed for starting new businesses. Some organizations and schools, for example, the Institute for Franchise Management at the University of St. Thomas (http://www.stthomas.edu/franchise), offer courses for prospective franchisees.

Certification or Licensing

Some franchisers have their own certification process and require their franchisees to go through training. You may also want to receive the certified franchise executive certification offered by the Institute of Certified Franchise Executives, an organization affiliated with the IFA's Education Foundation. This certification involves completing a certain number of courses in topics such as economics and franchise law, participating in events such as seminars or conventions, and gaining work experience. Although this certification is voluntary, it will show your level of education and commitment to the field as well as give you the opportunity to network with other franchise professionals.

You may also need to obtain a small business license to own a franchise unit in your state. Regulations vary depending on the state and the type of business, so it is important that you check with your state's licensing board for specifics before you invest in a franchise.

Other Requirements

As with any small business, you need self-motivation and discipline in order to make your franchise unit successful. Though you'll have some help from your franchiser, the responsibilities of ownership are your own. You'll also need a good credit rating to be eligible for a bank loan, or you'll need enough money of your own for the initial investment. You should be a fairly cautious person—many people are taken every year in fraudulent franchise schemes. But at the same time, you should feel comfortable taking some risks.

EXPLORING

One relatively easy way to learn about franchising is to do some research on the Web. The IFA, for example, hosts a very informative website (http://www.franchise.org). The association offers the free online newsletter *Franchise-Enews* as well as the magazine *Franchising World*. Both have information of interest to potential franchisees. Also, check out your public library or bookstores for the many business magazines that report on small business opportunities. Many of these magazines, such as *Entrepreneur* (http://www.entrepreneurmag.com), publish special editions dealing specifically with franchises.

Join your high school's business club, a group that may give you the opportunity to meet business leaders in your community. Find a local franchise owner and ask to meet with him or her for an informational interview. Discuss the pros and cons of franchise ownership, find out about the owner's educational and professional background, and ask them for general advice. Also, most franchise companies will send you brochures about their franchise opportunities. Request some information and read about what's involved in owning a franchise unit.

Think about what industry interests you, such as services, fast food, health and fitness, or computers. Come up with your own ideas for a franchise business and do some research to find out if this business already exists. If it does, there may be a part-time or summer job opportunity there for you. If it doesn't, keep the idea in mind for your future but go ahead and get some work experience now. Many franchises hire high school students, and even if you end up working at a Subway when what you're really interested in is lawn care, you'll still be gaining valuable experience dealing with customers, handling sales, and working with others.

EMPLOYERS

There are a number of franchise directories available that list hundreds of franchise opportunities in diverse areas. While some franchisers sell units all across the country, others only do business in a few states. Some of the most successful franchises can guarantee a franchisee great revenue, but these franchise units can require hundreds of thousands of dollars in initial investment.

Many franchisees own more than one franchise unit with a company; some even tie two different franchises together in a practice called "cross-branding." For example, a franchisee may own a pizza franchise, as well as an ice cream franchise housed in the same restaurant. Another combination owners find popular is having a convenience store that also houses a fast food outlet.

STARTING OUT

Before you invest a cent, or sign any papers, you should do an extensive amount of research into the franchise, particularly if it's a fairly new company. There are many disreputable franchise operations, so you need to be certain of what you're investing in. Lawyers and franchise consultants offer their services to assist people in choosing franchises; some consultants also conduct seminars. The Federal Trade Commission (FTC) publishes *The FTC Consumer Guide to Buying a Franchise* and other relevant publications. IFA also provides free franchise-buying advice.

You'll need money for the initial franchise fee and for the expenses of the first few years of business. You may pursue a loan from a bank, from business associates, or you may use your own savings. In some cases your start-up costs will be very low; in others you'll need money for a computer, rental of work space, equipment, signs, and staff. According to the IFA, total start-up costs can range from $20,000 or less to over $1,000,000, depending on the franchise selected and whether it is necessary to own or lease real estate to operate the business. Moreover, the initial franchise fee for most franchisors is between $20,000 and $28,000.

Some franchises can cost much less. Donna Weber's Jazzercise franchise required an initial $600 franchise fee. Though her business has been successful, she must share her gross income. "Twenty percent of that goes back to Jazzercise each month as a fee, I pay about 23 percent of the gross for monthly rent, and 8.6 percent to the state of Washington for sales tax collected on the price of my tickets. There are lots of women grossing $75,000 a year doing this, and there are some who choose to do this for fun and make nothing in return. It's all in how you make it work for you."

ADVANCEMENT

A new franchise unit usually takes a few years to turn profitable. Once the business has proven a success, franchisees may choose to invest in other franchise units with the same company. Franchise owners may also be able to afford to hire management and other staff to take on some of the many responsibilities of the business.

EARNINGS

The earnings for franchisees vary greatly depending on such factors as the type of franchise they own, the amount of money a franchisee was able to initially invest without taking a loan, the franchise's location, and the number of franchise units the franchisee owns. An IFA survey of 1,000 franchise owners found that the average yearly salary of this group was $91,630. Approximately 24 percent made more than $100,000 annually.

Since franchisees run their own businesses, they generally do not have paid sick days or holidays. In addition, they are typically responsible for providing their own insurance and retirement plans.

WORK ENVIRONMENT

Owning a franchise unit can be demanding, requiring work of 60–70 hours a week, but owners have the satisfaction of knowing that their business's success is a result of their own hard work. Some people look for franchise opportunities that are less demanding and may only require a part-time commitment. "I'm not getting rich," Donna Weber says, "but I love my job, and I love being my own boss. I can schedule my vacations when I want; we usually don't close our classes down, so we hire certified Jazzercise substitutes."

Franchise owners who handle all the business details personally may consider this work to be very stressful. In addition, dealing with the hiring, management, and sometimes firing of staff can also be difficult. In some situations, much of a franchisee's work will be limited to an office setting; in other situations, such as with a home inspection service or a maid service, the franchisee drives to remote sites to work with clients. Some franchises are mobile in nature, and these will involve a lot of traveling within a designated region.

OUTLOOK

While some experts say that the success rate of franchises is very high and a great deal of money can be made with a franchise unit, others say franchising isn't as successful as starting an independent business. According to the Department of Commerce, less than 5 percent of franchised outlets have failed each year since 1971. However, when reporting figures, franchisers don't always consider a unit as failing if it is under different ownership, but still in operation. The employment outlook will depend on factors such as the economy—a downturn in the economy is always most difficult for new businesses—as well as the type of franchise. Overall, though, growth should be steady and about as fast as the average.

FOR MORE INFORMATION

For information about buying a franchise and a list of AAFD-accredited franchisers, contact

American Association of Franchisees and Dealers (AAFD)
PO Box 81887
San Diego, CA 92138-1887
Tel: 800-733-9858
http://www.aafd.org

Contact the FTC for publications regarding franchising. The website also provides the text of some publications as well as current franchise news.

Federal Trade Commission (FTC)
Franchises and Business Opportunities
CRC-240
Washington, DC 20580
Tel: 202-326-2222
http://www.ftc.gov

For more information on franchising as well as a free newsletter, contact

FranchiseHelp
101 Executive Boulevard, 2nd Floor
Elmsford, NY 10523
Tel: 800-401-1446
Email: company@franchisehelp.com
http://www.franchisehelp.com

For general information about franchising, specific franchise opportunities, and the publications Franchise-Enews *and* Franchise NewsBriefs, *contact the IFA.*

International Franchise Association (IFA)
1350 New York Avenue, NW, Suite 900
Washington, DC 20005-4709
Tel: 202-628-8000
Email: ifa@franchise.org
http://www.franchise.org

INFORMATION BROKERS

QUICK FACTS

School Subjects Computer science English Journalism	**Certification or Licensing** None available
Personal Skills Communication/ideas Technical/scientific	**Outlook** Faster than the average
Work Environment Primarily indoors Primarily one location	**DOT** N/A
Minimum Education Level Bachelor's degree	**GOE** N/A
Salary Range $20,000 to $54,500 to $100,000+	**NOC** N/A
	O*NET-SOC N/A

OVERVIEW

Information brokers, sometimes called *online researchers* or *independent information professionals,* compile information from online databases and services. They work for clients in a number of different professions, researching marketing surveys, newspaper articles, business and government statistics, abstracts, and other sources of information. They prepare reports and presentations based on their research. Information brokers have home-based operations, or they work full time for libraries, law offices, government agencies, and corporations.

HISTORY

Strange as it may seem, some of the earliest examples of online researchers are the keepers of a library established by Ptolemy I in

Egypt in the third century B.C. These librarians helped to build the first great library by copying and revising classical Greek texts. The monks of Europe also performed some of the modern-day researcher's tasks by building libraries and printing books. Despite their great efforts, libraries weren't used extensively until the 18th century, when literacy increased among the general population. In 1803, the first public library in the United States opened in Connecticut.

In the late 1800s and early 1900s, many different kinds of library associations evolved, reflecting the number of special libraries already established (such as medical and law libraries). With all the developments of the 20th century, these library associations helped to promote special systems and tools for locating information. These systems eventually developed into the online databases and Internet search engines used today. The Internet, although created in 1969 and subsidized by the government as a communication system for the Department of Defense, didn't become a significant source of information until relaxed government policies allowed for its commercial use in 1991.

THE JOB

An interest in the Internet and computer skills are important to success as an independent information broker, but this specialist needs to understand much more than just search engines. Information brokers need to master Dialog, Lexis/Nexis, and other information databases. They also have to compile information with fax machines, photocopiers, and telephones, as well as personal interviews. If you think this sounds like the work of a private eye, you are not far off; as a matter of fact, some information brokers have worked as private investigators.

A majority of research projects, however, are marketing based. Suppose a company wants to embark on a new, risky venture—maybe a fruit distribution company wants to make figs as popular as apples and oranges. First, the company's leaders might want to know some basic information about fig consumption. How many people have even eaten a fig? What articles about figs have been published in national magazines? What have been recent annual sales of figs, Fig Newtons, and other fig-based treats? What popular recipes include figs? The company hires consultants, marketing experts, and researchers to gather all this information.

Each researcher has his or her own approach to accomplishing tasks, but every researcher must first get to know the subject. A researcher who specializes in retail and distribution might already be familiar with the trade associations, publications, and other sources of industry information. Another researcher might have to learn as much as possible, as quickly as possible, about the lingo and organizations involved with the fruit distribution industry. This includes using the Internet's basic search engines to get a sense of what kind of information is available. The researcher then uses a database service, such as the Dialog system, which makes available billions of pages of text and images, including complete newspaper and magazine articles, wire service stories, and company profiles. Because database services often charge the user for the time spent searching or documents viewed, online researchers must know all the various tips and commands for efficient searching. Once the search is complete, and they've downloaded the information needed, online researchers must prepare the information for the company. They may be expected to make a presentation to the company or write a complete report that includes pie graphs, charts, and other illustrations to accompany the text.

The legal profession hires information brokers to search cases, statutes, and other sources of law; update law library collections; and locate data to support cases, such as finding expert witnesses, or researching the history of the development of a defective product that caused personal injury. The health care industry needs information brokers to gather information on drugs, treatments, devices, illnesses, or clinical trials. An information broker who specializes in public records researches personal records (such as birth, death, marriage, adoption, and criminal records), corporations, and property ownership. Other industries that rely on information brokers include banking and finance, government and public policy, and science and technology.

"This isn't the kind of profession you can do right out of high school or college," says Mary Ellen Bates, an independent information professional based in Washington, D.C. "It requires expertise in searching the professional online services. You can't learn them on your own time; you have to have real-world experience as an online researcher. Many of the most successful information brokers are former librarians." Her success in the business has led her to serve as president of the Association of Independent Information Professionals, to write and publish articles about the business, and to serve as a consultant to libraries and other organizations. Some of her projects have included research on the market for independent living facilities for senior citizens and the impact of large grocery chains on independent grocery stores. She's also been asked to find out what rental car companies do with cars after they're past their prime. "Keep in mind that you need a lot more than Internet research skills," Bates says. "You need the ability to run your business from the top to bottom. That means accounting, marketing, collections, strategic planning, and personnel management."

The expense of the commercial database services has affected the career of another online researcher, Sue Carver of Richland, Washington. Changes in Dialog's usage rates have forced her to seek out other ways to use her library skills. In addition to such services as market research and document delivery, Carver's Web page promotes a book-finding service, helping people to locate collectible and out-of-print books. "I have found this a fun, if not highly lucrative, activity which puts me in contact with a wide variety of people," she says. "This is a case where the Internet opens the door to other possibilities. Much of this business is repackaging information in a form people want to buy. This is limited only by your imagination." But she also emphasizes that the job of online researcher requires highly specialized skills in information retrieval. "Nonlibrarians often do not appreciate the vast array of reference material that existed before the Internet," she says, "nor how much librarians have contributed to the information age." Carver holds a master's degree in library science and has worked as a reference librarian, which involved her with searches on patents, molecular biology, and other technical subjects. She has also worked as an indexer on a nuclear engineering project and helped plan a search and retrieval system on a separate nuclear project.

REQUIREMENTS

High School

Take computer classes that teach word and data processing programs, presentation programs, and how to use Internet search engines. Any class offered by your high school or public library on information retrieval will familiarize you with database searches and such services as Dialog, Lexis/Nexis, and Dow Jones. English and composition courses will teach you to organize information and write clearly. Speech and theater classes will help you develop the skills to give presentations in front of clients. Journalism classes and working on your high school newspaper will involve you directly in information retrieval and writing.

Postsecondary Training

It is recommended that you start with a good liberal arts program in a college or university, then pursue a master's degree in either a subject specialty or in library and information science. Developing expertise in a particular subject will prepare you for a specialty in information brokering.

Many online researchers have master's degrees in library science. The American Library Association accredits library and information science programs and offers a number of scholarships. Courses in library programs deal with techniques of data collection and analysis, use of graphical presentation of sound and text, and networking and telecommunications. Internships are also available in some library science programs.

Continuing education courses are important for online researchers with advanced degrees. Because of the rapidly changing technology, researchers need to attend seminars and take courses through such organizations as the Special Libraries Association and the Information Professionals Institute (IPI). The IPI seminars, conducted in major cities across the country, deal with starting a business, finding clients, online searching, and other topics relevant to both the experienced and the inexperienced information brokers. Many online researchers take additional courses in their subject matter specialization. Mary Ellen Bates attends meetings of the Society of Competitive Intelligence Professionals, since a lot of her work is in the field of competitive intelligence.

Other Requirements

In addition to all the varied computer skills necessary to succeed as an information broker, you must have good communication skills. "You're marketing all the time," Bates says. "If you're not comfortable marketing yourself and speaking publicly, you'll never make it in this business." To keep your business running, you need persistence to pursue new clients and sources of information. You are your own boss, so you have to be self-motivated to meet deadlines. Good record-keeping skills will help you manage the financial details of the business and help you keep track of contacts.

Sue Carver advises that you keep up on current events and pay close attention to detail. You should welcome the challenge of locating hard-to-find facts and articles. "I have a logical mind," Carver says, "and love puzzles and mysteries."

EXPLORING

If you've ever had to write an extensive research paper, then you've probably already had experience with online research. In college, many of your term papers will require that you become familiar with Lexis/Nexis and other library systems. The reference librarians of your school and public libraries should be happy to introduce you to the various library tools available. On the Internet, experiment with the search engines; each service has slightly different features and capabilities. Visit Mary Ellen Bates' website at http://www.batesinfo.com for extensive information about the business and to read articles she's written. She's also the author of *Super Searchers Do Business* (Information Today, Inc., 1999) and a quarterly electronic newsletter called *For Your Information.* Also check out *Researching Online For Dummies,* 2nd edition (Wiley, 2000), by Bates and Reva Basch.

EMPLOYERS

A large number of information professionals are employed by colleges, universities, and corporations, and gain experience in full-time staff positions before starting their own businesses. Those who work for themselves contract with a number of different kinds of businesses and organizations. People seeking marketing information make the most use of the services of information professionals. Attorneys, consulting firms, public relations firms, government agencies, and private investigators also hire researchers. With the Internet, a researcher can work anywhere in the country, serving clients all around the world. However, living in a large city will allow an online researcher better access to more expansive public records when performing manual research.

STARTING OUT

People become researchers through a variety of different routes. They may go into business for themselves after gaining a lot of experience within an industry, such as in aviation or pharmaceuticals. Using their expertise, insider knowledge, and professional connections, they can serve as a consultant on issues affecting the business. Or they may become an independent researcher after working as a special librarian, having developed computer and search skills. The one thing most researchers have in common, however, is extensive experience in finding information and presenting it. Once they have the knowledge necessary to start their own information business, online researchers should take seminars offered by

Who Employs Economics Majors?

Academia/Education

- colleges and universities
- community colleges
- elementary schools
- middle schools
- secondary schools

U.S. Government

- Bureau of Economic Analysis
- Bureau of Labor Statistics
- U.S. Census Bureau
- Congressional Budget Office
- Council of Economic Advisors
- Department of Agriculture, Economic Research Service
- Department of Commerce
- Department of Education
- Department of the Interior
- Department of Justice
- Department of Labor
- Department of State
- Department of the Treasury
- Environmental Protection Agency
- Federal Deposit Insurance Corporation
- Federal Reserve System banks
- Federal Trade Commission
- Food and Drug Administration
- Internal Revenue Service
- National Center for Education Statistics
- Small Business Administration

(continues)

Who Employs Economics Majors?

(continued)

Research Organizations and Think Tanks

- American Enterprise Institute
- Brookings Institution
- CATO Institute
- Economic Policy Institute
- Heritage Foundation
- Hoover Institute
- Institute for International Economics
- Institute for Women's Policy Research

International Organizations

- European Union
- International Monetary Fund
- Organization for Economic Cooperation and Development
- United Nations
- World Bank

Private Sector

- accounting firms
- advertising agencies
- banks and other financial institutions
- insurance companies
- health care companies
- labor unions
- entrepreneurships
- marketing research firms
- nonprofit organizations
- publishing companies

such organizations as the IPI. Amelia Kassel, president and owner of MarketingBase (http://www.marketingbase.com), a successful information brokering company, offers a mentoring program via email. As mentor, she advises on such subjects as online databases, marketing strategies, and pricing.

Before leaving her full-time job, Mary Ellen Bates spent a year preparing for her own business. She says, "I didn't want to spend time doing start-up stuff that I could spend marketing or doing paying work." She saved business cards and established contacts. She saved $10,000 and set up a home-based office with a computer, desk, office supplies, fax, and additional phone lines. To help others starting out, Bates has written *Getting Your First Five Clients,* available through the Association of Independent Information Professionals.

ADVANCEMENT

The first few years of any business are difficult and require long hours of marketing, promotion, and building a clientele. Advancement will depend on the online researcher's ability to make connections and to broaden their client base. Some researchers start out specializing in a particular area, such as in telephone research or public record research, before venturing out into different areas. Once they're capable of handling projects from diverse sources, they can expand their business. They can also take on larger projects as they begin to meet other reliable researchers with whom they can join forces.

EARNINGS

Even if they have a great deal of research experience, self-employed information brokers' first few years in the business may be lean ones, and they should expect to make as little as $20,000. As with any small business, it takes a few years to develop contacts and establish a reputation for quality work. Independent information brokers usually charge between $45 and $100 an hour, depending on the project. Eventually, an online researcher should be able to make a salary equivalent to that of a full-time special librarian—a 2001 salary survey by the Special Library Association puts the national median at $54,500. Some very experienced independent researchers with a number of years of self-employment may make well over $100,000.

Helen Burwell, president of Burwell Enterprises, estimates that the average information broker charges $75 an hour. This hourly rate is affected by factors such as geographic location and the broker's knowledge of the subject matter. Information brokers can make more money in cities like New York and Washington, DC, where their services are in higher demand. Also, someone doing high-level patent research, which requires a great deal of expertise, can charge more than someone retrieving public records.

Information brokers who work full-time for companies earn salaries comparable to other information technology (IT) professionals. According to a 2000 survey by the Society for Technical Communications, IT professionals' salaries can range from $36,000 for entry-level personnel to more than $90,000 for those with more than 10 years' experience. A full-time information broker who works for a large corporation primarily in the area of competitive intelligence can earn $100,000 annually.

WORK ENVIRONMENT

Most independent researchers work out of their own homes. This means they have a lot of control over their environment, but it also means they're always close to their workstations. As a result, online researchers may find themselves working longer hours than if they had an outside office and a set weekly schedule. "This is easily a 50- to 60-hour a week job," Mary Ellen Bates says. Online researchers are their own bosses, but they may work as a member of a team with other researchers and consultants on some projects. They will also need to discuss the project with their clients both before and after they've begun their research.

Information brokers employed by companies work in an office environment. Although most of their work takes place at a computer, they may have to make trips to libraries, government offices, and other places that hold information that's not available online. Whether self-employed or not, information brokers spend some time in boardrooms and conference situations making presentations of their findings.

OUTLOOK

Helen Burwell anticipates that independent information professionals will continue to find a great deal of work, but the growth of the industry won't be as rapid as in the past because of the increasing number of new information science graduates entering the field.

The Internet is making it easier for people and businesses to conduct their own online research; this is expected to help business for online researchers rather than hurt. Alex Kramer, past president of the Association of Independent Information Professionals, predicts that the more people recognize the vast amount of information available to them, the more they'll seek out the assistance of online researchers to efficiently compile that information. There will be continuing demand for information brokers in marketing, competitive intelligence, legal research, and science and technology.

Employment experts predict that with the growing reliance on computer technology, businesses will be willing to pay top dollar for employees and consultants who are flexible, mobile, and able to navigate the technology with ease.

FOR MORE INFORMATION

For information about library science programs and scholarships, contact

American Library Association
50 East Huron
Chicago, IL 60611
Tel: 800-545-2433
http://www.ala.org

To learn more about the benefits of association membership, contact

Association of Independent Information Professionals
7044 South 13th Street
Oak Creek, WI 53154-1429
Tel: 414-766-0421
Email: aiipinfo@aiip.org
http://www.aiip.org

For information about seminars and books on information brokers, contact

Information Professionals Institute
Burwell Enterprises
5619 Plumtree Drive
Dallas, TX 75252
Tel: 972-732-0160
http://www.burwellinc.com

For information on continuing education, contact

Special Libraries Association
1700 18th Street, NW
Washington, DC 20009-2514
Tel: 202-234-4700
Email: sla@sla.org
http://www.sla.org

INSURANCE UNDERWRITERS

QUICK FACTS

School Subjects	Certification or Licensing
Business Mathematics	Recommended

School Subjects
Business
Mathematics

Personal Skills
Following instructions
Leadership/management

Work Environment
Primarily indoors
Primarily one location

Minimum Education Level
Bachelor's degree

Salary Range
$27,720 to $44,060 to $76,750+

Certification or Licensing
Recommended

Outlook
Little or no change

DOT
169

GOE
11.06.03

NOC
1234

O*NET-SOC
13-2053.00

OVERVIEW

Insurance underwriters review individual applications for insurance coverage to evaluate the degree of risk involved. They decide whether the insurance company should accept an applicant, and, if the applicant is accepted, underwriters determine the premium that the policyholder will be charged. There are approximately 107,000 underwriters employed in the United States.

HISTORY

Lloyd's of London is generally considered to have been the first insurance underwriter. Formed in the late 1600s, Lloyd's subscribed marine insurance policies for seagoing vessels. Over the years, the principles of insurance were adopted by various fraternal and trade unions.

Fire and life insurance companies in the United States date from colonial times. Benjamin Franklin helped start the Philadelphia Contributionship for the Insurance of Houses, a fire insurance company, in 1752. The first life insurance company was established in 1759 by the New York and Philadelphia synods of the Presbyterian Church.

Industrial insurance began in the late 19th century, offering life insurance to millions of industrial workers. In 1910, the first workers' compensation policy was issued. Group coverage was introduced in the life insurance field in 1911 and has since been broadened to include disability, hospitalization, and pension benefits. In 1936 the Blue Cross organization pioneered group hospitalization insurance. Private insurance companies began to furnish insurance protection in the early 1900s.

Package insurance, such as automobile and homeowners insurance, which includes a variety of types of insurance, developed on a large scale in the 1950s. Health maintenance organizations were first established during the early 1970s in an attempt to stem the rising cost of health care. Judgments in liability lawsuits had drastically increased by 1980, resulting in rapid growth in purchases of liability insurance. Today, insurance packages and managed care companies provide many options and levels of coverage.

THE JOB

People buy insurance policies to protect themselves against financial loss resulting from injuries, illnesses, or lost or damaged property; policyholders transfer this risk of loss from themselves to their insurance companies. As a result, insurance companies assume billions of dollars in risks each year. Underwriters are responsible for evaluating the degree of risk posed by each policy application to determine whether the insurance company should issue a policy.

Underwriters base their decisions on a number of factors, including the applicant's health, occupation, and income. They review and analyze information in insurance applications, medical reports, reports from loss control specialists, and actuarial studies. If an applicant appears to be at a greater risk level than normal, the underwriter may decide that an extra premium is needed. Underwriters must exercise sound judgment when deciding whether to accept an applicant and in deciding upon the premium; their decisions are crucial to the financial success of the insurance company.

Insurance underwriting is a very competitive business. If the underwriter evaluates risks too conservatively and quotes prices that are too high, the insurance company may lose business to competitors. If the underwriters evaluate risks too liberally and accept applications at inadequate prices, the company will have to pay more claims and will ultimately lose money. It is essential that underwriters evaluate applications very carefully.

Many underwriters specialize in life, property, or health insurance; many further specialize in individual or group policies. *Property or casualty underwriters* may specialize by the type of risk involved, such as fire or automobile. Some underwriters work exclusively with business insurance. These *commercial account underwriters* must often evaluate the firm's entire business operation.

Group contracts are becoming increasingly popular. In a group policy, life or health insurance protection is given to all persons in a certain group at uniform rates. Group contracts may also be given to specified groups as individual policies reflecting individual needs. A labor union, for example, may be given individual casualty policies covering automobiles.

Underwriters must assess the acceptability of risk from a variety of policy applications. They must be able to review and analyze complex technical information.

REQUIREMENTS

High School

Small insurance companies may hire people without a college degree for trainee positions, and high school graduates may be trained for underwriting work after working as underwriting clerks. In general, however, a college education is advantageous, if not required, for employment. In high school you should take mathematics, business, economics, and speech classes to help prepare you for work in this field. A basic knowledge of computers is also necessary.

Postsecondary Training

Most insurance companies prefer to hire college graduates for beginning underwriting jobs. Many different majors are acceptable, but a degree in business administration or finance may be particularly helpful. Accounting classes and business law classes will help to round out your educational background for this field. In addition, keep up your computer skills in college. The computer is a tool you will use throughout your professional career.

Certification or Licensing

Underwriters who become certified, or designated, show commitment to their profession and increase their possibilities for advancement. Several designations are available to underwriters. The Insurance Educational Association offers the associate in underwriting (AU) designation, which was originally developed by the Insurance Institute of America. Requirements for the AU include completion of designated course work (usually lasting two years) and the passage of a comprehensive examination.

The American Institute for Chartered Property Casualty Underwriters offers a more advanced professional certification: chartered property and casualty underwriter (CPCU) designation. Course work for the CPCU usually takes five years, and a candidate must pass a minimum of eight examinations (out of 11 offered) covering such subjects as accounting, finance, business law, and commercial risk management.

For life insurance underwriters, The American College offers the Chartered Life Underwriter (CLU) designation. Like the CPCU, the CLU requires completing a comprehensive series of courses and passing examinations. In addition, the College recently teamed up with The Life Underwriter Training Council (LUTC) to offer the more extensive LUTC fellow designation. To receive this certification, individuals must meet or exceed qualifications and continuing education requirements determined by the College. The American College also offers the registered health underwriter designation to underwriters involved in the sale and service of disability income and health insurance. Candidates must complete three courses, maintain ethical standards, and satisfy experience requirements. Visit the college's website (http://www.amercoll.edu) for more details.

Other Requirements

Underwriting work requires great concentration and mental alertness. Underwriters must be analytical, logical, and detail oriented. They must be able to make difficult decisions based on technical, complicated information. Underwriters must also be able to communicate well both in speech and in writing. Group underwriters often meet with union employees or employer representatives. The ability to communicate well is vital for these underwriters.

Keep in mind that advancement in this career comes through continuing your education. While insurance companies often pay tuition for their employees taking underwriting courses, the underwriters themselves must have the desire to learn continuously.

EXPLORING

There are many different ways to explore the underwriting profession. You may visit insurance companies to talk with underwriters and other insurance employees. Many insurance organizations, such as those listed at the end of this article, will send basic information on underwriting jobs to interested people. You might also consider applying for a part-time or summer job at an insurance company. Even if you handle phones or help file records for the office, you are still gaining basic business experience.

High school graduates may decide to work at insurance companies before going to college to determine their interest in and aptitude for underwriting work. In addition, many insurance companies are willing to hire and train college students during the summer months.

EMPLOYERS

Most of the approximately 107,000 underwriters in the United States work for property and casualty insurance companies. Insurance agents, brokers, and services and life insurance companies are the next two largest employers of underwriters. Opportunities are often best in large cities such as New York, Chicago, San Francisco, Dallas, Philadelphia, and Hartford. Finally, some underwriters work in independent agencies, banks, mortgage companies, or regional offices.

STARTING OUT

The most effective way to enter the underwriting profession is to seek employment after earning a college degree. Most insurance companies prefer to hire college graduates, and college placement offices often assist students in securing employment.

It is possible to enter this field without a college degree. Underwriting clerks who show exceptional promise may be trained for underwriter positions. In addition, some insurance companies will hire people without a college degree for trainee jobs.

ADVANCEMENT

Advancement opportunities for underwriters depend on an individual's educational background, on-the-job performance, and leadership abilities. Continuing education is also very important.

Experienced underwriters who have taken continuing education courses may be promoted to chief underwriter or underwriting manager. Underwriting managers may advance to senior management positions.

EARNINGS

According to the Bureau of Labor Statistics, the median annual salary for underwriters was $44,060 in 2001. At the low end of the scale, 10 percent of underwriters earned less than $27,720 per year. The top 10 percent earned $76,750 or more. Experience, certification, and position within the company are all factors influencing salary levels. In addition, most insurance companies have generous employee benefits, normally including liberal vacation allowances and employer-financed group life and retirement plans.

WORK ENVIRONMENT

Underwriters generally work at a desk in pleasant offices; their jobs entail no unusual physical activity, although at times they may have to work under stressful conditions. The normal work week is 40 hours; overtime may be required from time to time. Occasionally, underwriters may travel away from home to attend meetings or continuing education classes.

OUTLOOK

The U.S. Department of Labor predicts little or no change in employment for underwriters over the next decade. Most job openings will occur as a result of underwriters leaving the field for other professions or retirement. The increasing use of underwriting software programs and the increasing numbers of businesses that self-insure will limit job growth in this field.

There will always be a need for underwriters. New businesses will seek protection for new plants and equipment, insurance for workers' compensation, and product liability. The public's growing security consciousness and the increasing importance of employee benefits will result in more opportunities in this field. The increasing number of Americans over the age of 65 who utilize long-term health care and pension benefits will also create a demand for underwriters.

FOR MORE INFORMATION

For information regarding the LUTC program and the CLU and RHU designations and distance education programs, contact

The American College
270 South Bryn Mawr Avenue
Bryn Mawr, PA 19010-2196
Tel: 888-263-7265
Email: StudentServices@Amercoll.Edu
http://www.amercoll.edu

For information regarding the CPCU certification, contact

American Institute for Chartered Property Casualty Underwriters
720 Providence Road
PO Box 3016
Malvern, PA 19355-0716
Tel: 800-644-2101
Email: cserv@cpcuiia.org
http://www.aicpcu.org

For information about the Insurance Institute of America's AU certification and other programs, contact

Insurance Educational Association
100 California Street, Suite 650
San Francisco, CA 94111
Tel: 800-655-4432
Email: info@ieatraining.com
http://www.ieatraining.com

For general information about health underwriting, contact

National Association of Health Underwriters
2000 North 14th Street, Suite 450
Arlington, VA 22201
Tel: 703-276-0220
Email: info@nahu.org
http://www.nahu.org

For information on life underwriting, contact

National Association of Insurance and Financial Advisors
2901 Telestar Court
PO Box 12012
Falls Church, VA 22042-1205
Tel: 877-TO-NAIFA
http://www.naifa.org

This organization is associated with The American College and has information on industry news and events.

Society of Financial Service Professionals
270 South Bryn Mawr Avenue
Bryn Mawr, PA 19010-2195
Tel: 610-526-2500
http://www.financialpro.org

LAWYERS AND JUDGES

QUICK FACTS

School Subjects English Government Speech	**Outlook** About as fast as the average (lawyers) More slowly than the average (judges)
Personal Skills Communication/ideas Leadership/management	**DOT** 110 (lawyers), 111 (judges)
Work Environment Primarily indoors Primarily multiple locations	**GOE** 11.04.02 (lawyers), 11.04.01 (judges)
Minimum Education Level Master's degree	**NOC** 4112 (lawyers), 4111 (judges)
Salary Range $19,470 to $88,760 to $1,000,000+	**O*NET-SOC** 23-1011.00 (lawyers), 23-1023.00 (judges)
Certification or Licensing Required by all states	

OVERVIEW

Lawyers, or *attorneys,* serve in two ways in our legal system: as advocates and as advisers. As advocates, they represent the rights of their clients in trials and depositions or in front of administrative and government bodies. As advisers, attorneys counsel clients on how the law affects business or personal decisions, such as the purchase of property or the creation of a will. Lawyers represent individuals, businesses, and corporations. Approximately 681,000 lawyers work in the United States today, in various areas of the profession.

Judges are elected or appointed officials who preside over federal, state, county, and municipal courts. They apply the law to citizens and businesses and oversee court proceedings according to the established law. Judges also give new rulings on issues not previously decided. Over 43,000 judges work in all levels of the judiciary arm of the United States.

HISTORY

The tradition of governing people by laws has been established over centuries. Societies have built up systems of law that have been studied and drawn upon by later governments. The earliest known law is the Code of Hammurabi, developed about 1800 B.C. by the ruler of the Sumerians. Another early set of laws was the law of Moses, known as the Ten Commandments. Every set of laws, no matter when they were introduced, has been accompanied by the need for someone to explain those laws and help others live under them.

The great orators of ancient Greece and Rome set up schools for young boys to learn by apprenticeship the many skills involved in pleading a law case. Being an eloquent speaker was the greatest advantage. The legal profession has matured since those earlier times; a great deal of training and an extensive knowledge of legal matters are required of the modern lawyer and judge.

Much modern European law was organized and refined by legal experts assembled by Napoleon; their body of law was known as the Napoleonic Code. English colonists coming to America brought English common law, from which American laws have grown. In areas of the United States that were heavily settled by Spanish colonists, there are traces of Spanish law. As the population in the country grew, along with business, those who knew the law were in high demand. The two main kinds of law are *civil* and *criminal,* but many other specialty areas exist. When our country was young, most lawyers were general law practitioners—they knew and worked with all the laws for their clients' sakes. Today, there are many more lawyers who specialize in areas such as tax law, corporate law, and intellectual property law.

THE JOB

All lawyers may give legal advice and represent clients in court when necessary. No matter what their specialty, their job is to help clients know their rights under the law and then help them achieve these rights before a judge, jury, government agency, or other legal forum, such as an arbitration panel. Lawyers may represent businesses and individuals. For businesses, they manage tax matters, arrange for stock to be issued, handle claims cases, represent the firm in real estate dealings, and advise on all legal matters. For individuals they may be trustees, guardians, or executors; they may draw up wills or contracts or advise on income taxes or on the purchase or sale of a home. Some work solely in the courts; others carry on most of their business outside of court, doing such tasks as drawing up mortgages, deeds, contracts, and other legal documents or by handling the background work necessary for court cases, which might include researching cases in a law library or interviewing witnesses. A number of lawyers work to establish and enforce laws for the federal and state governments by drafting legislation, representing the government in court, or serving as judges.

Lawyers can also take positions as professors in law schools. Administrators, research workers, and writers are also important to the profession. Administrative positions in business or government may be of a nonlegal nature, but the qualities, background, and experience of a lawyer are often helpful in such positions.

Other individuals with legal training may choose not to practice but instead opt for careers in which their background and knowledge of law are important. These careers include tax collectors, credit investigators, FBI agents, insurance adjusters, process servers, and probation officers.

Some of the specialized fields for lawyers include the following:

Civil lawyers work in a field also known as private law. They focus on damage suits and breach-of-contract suits; prepare and draw up deeds, leases, wills, mortgages, and contracts; and act as trustees, guardians, or executors of an estate when necessary.

Criminal lawyers, also known as *defense lawyers,* specialize in cases dealing with offenses committed against society or the state, such as theft, murder, or arson. They interview clients and witnesses to ascertain facts in a case, correlate their findings with known cases, and prepare a case to defend a client against the charges made. They conduct a defense at the trial, examine witnesses, and summarize the case with a closing argument to a jury.

District attorneys, also known as *prosecuting attorneys,* represent the city, county, state, or federal government in court proceedings. They gather and analyze evidence and review legal material relevant to a lawsuit. Then they present their case to the grand jury, which decides whether the evidence is sufficient for an indictment. If it is not, the suit is dismissed and there is no trial. If the grand jury decides to indict the accused, however, the case goes to court, where the district attorney appears before the judge and jury to present evidence against the defendant.

Probate lawyers specialize in planning and settling estates. They draw up wills, deeds of trust, and similar documents for clients who want to plan the distribution of their belongings among their heirs when they die. Upon a client's death, probate lawyers vouch for the validity of the will and represent the executors and administrators of the estate.

Bankruptcy attorneys assist their clients, both individuals and corporations, in obtaining protection from creditors under existing bankruptcy laws and with financial reorganization and debt repayment.

Corporation lawyers advise corporations concerning their legal rights, obligations, or privileges. They study constitutions, statutes, previous decisions, ordinances, and decisions of quasi-judicial bodies that are applicable to corporations. They advise corporations on the pros and cons of prosecuting or defending a lawsuit. They act as agent of the corporation in various transactions and seek to keep clients from expensive litigation.

Maritime lawyers, sometimes referred to as *admiralty lawyers,* specialize in laws regulating commerce and navigation on the high seas and any navigable waters, including inland lakes and rivers. Although there is a general maritime law, it operates in each country according to that country's courts, laws, and customs. Maritime law covers contracts, insurance, property damage, and personal injuries.

Intellectual property lawyers focus on helping their clients with patents, trademarks, and copyright protection. *Patent lawyers* are intellectual property lawyers who specialize in securing patents for inventors from the United States Patent Office and prosecuting or defending suits of patent infringements. They prepare detailed specifications for the patent, may organize a corporation, or advise an existing corporation to commercialize on a patent. Biotechnology patent law is a further specialization of patent law. *Biotechnology patent lawyers* specialize in helping biotechnology researchers, scientists, and research corporations with all legal aspects of their biotechnology patents.

Elder law attorneys are lawyers who specialize in providing legal services for the elderly and, in some cases, the disabled.

Tax attorneys handle cases resulting from problems of inheritance, income tax, estate tax, franchises, and real estate tax, among other things.

Insurance attorneys advise insurance companies about legal matters pertaining to insurance transactions. They approve the wording of insurance policies, review the legality of claims against the company, and draw up legal documents.

An *international lawyer* specializes in the body of rules that are observed by nations in their relations with one another. Some of these laws have been agreed to in treaties, some have evolved from long-standing customs and traditions.

Securities and exchange lawyers monitor the activities of individuals and corporations involved in trading and oversee to make sure they comply with applicable laws. When corporations undergo takeovers and mergers, securities and exchange lawyers are there to represent the corporations' interests and fulfill all legal obligations involved in the transaction.

Real estate lawyers handle the transfer of property and perform such duties as searching public records and deeds to establish titles of property, holding funds for investment in escrow accounts, and acting as trustees of property. They draw up legal documents and act as agents in various real estate transactions.

Title attorneys deal with titles, leases, contracts, and other legal documents pertaining to the ownership of land, and gas, oil, and mineral rights. They prepare documents to cover the purchase or sale of such property and rights, examine documents to determine ownership, advise organizations about legal requirements concerning titles, and participate in the trial or lawsuits in connection with titles.

It is important to note that once you are licensed to practice law, you are legally qualified to practice any one or more of these and many other specialties. Some *general practitioners* handle both criminal and civil matters of all sorts. To become licensed, you must be admitted to the bar of that state. *Bar examiners* test the qualifications of applicants. They prepare and administer written exams covering legal subjects, examine candidates orally, and recommend admission of those who meet the prescribed standards.

Lawyers become judges by either election or appointment, and preside over federal, state, county, or municipal courts. Judges administer court procedures during trials and hearings and establish new rules on questions where standard procedures have not previously been set. They read or listen to claims made by parties involved in civil suits and make decisions based on facts, applicable statutes, and prior court decisions. They examine evidence in criminal cases to see if it supports the charges. Judges listen to the presentation of cases, rule on the admission of evidence and testimony, and settle disputes between attorneys. They instruct juries on their duties and advise them of laws that apply to the case. They sentence defendants found guilty of criminal charges and decide who is responsible in nonjury civil cases. Besides their work in the courtroom, judges also research legal matters, study prior rulings, write opinions, and keep abreast of legislation that may affect their rulings.

Some judges have other titles such as *magistrate* or *justice* and preside over a limited jurisdiction. Magistrates hear civil cases in which damages do not exceed a prescribed maximum, as well as minor misdemeanor cases that do not involve penitentiary sentences or fines that exceed a certain specified amount.

REQUIREMENTS

High School

A high school diploma, a college degree, and three years of law school are minimum requirements for a law degree. A high school diploma is a first step on the ladder of education that a lawyer must climb. If you are considering a career in law, courses such as government, history, social studies, and economics provide a solid background for entering college-level courses. Speech courses are also helpful to build strong communication skills necessary for the profession. Also take advantage of any computer-related classes or experience you can get, because lawyers and judges often use technology to research and interpret the law, from surfing the Internet to searching legal databases.

Postsecondary Training

To enter any law school approved by the American Bar Association, you must satisfactorily complete at least three, and usually four, years of college work. Most law schools do not specify any particular courses for prelaw education. Usually a liberal arts track is most advisable, with courses in English, history, economics, social sciences, logic, and public speaking. A college student planning on specialization in a particular area of law, however, might also take courses significantly related to that area, such as economics, agriculture, or political science. Those interested should write to several law schools to learn more about any requirements and to see if they will accept credits from the college the student is planning to attend.

Currently, over 185 law schools in the United States are approved by the American Bar Association; others, many of them night schools, are approved by state authorities only. Most of the approved law schools, however, do have night sessions to accommodate part-time students. Part-time courses of study usually take four years.

Law school training consists of required courses such as legal writing and research, contracts, criminal law, constitutional law, torts, and property. The second and third years may be devoted to specialized courses of interest to the student, such as evidence, business transactions and corporations, or admiralty. The study of cases and decisions is of basic importance to the law student, who will be required to read and study thousands of these cases. A degree of juris doctor (J.D.) or bachelor of laws (LL.B.) is usually granted upon graduation. Some law students considering specialization, research, or teaching may go on for advanced study.

Most law schools require that applicants take the Law School Admission Test (LSAT), where prospective law students are tested on their critical thinking, writing, and reasoning abilities.

Certification or Licensing

Every state requires that lawyers be admitted to the bar of that state before they can practice. They require that applicants graduate from an approved law school and that they pass a written examination in the state in which they intend to practice. In a few states, graduates of law schools within the state are excused from these written examinations. After lawyers have been admitted to the bar in one state, they can practice in another state without taking a written examination if the states have reciprocity agreements; however, they will be required to meet certain state standards of good character and legal experience and pay any applicable fees.

Other Requirements

Federal courts and agencies have their own rules regulating admission to practice. Other requirements vary among the states. For example, the states of Vermont, New York, Washington, Virginia, California, Maine, and Wyoming allow a person who has spent several years reading law in a law office but has no college training or who has a combination of reading and law school experience to take the state bar examination. Few people now enter law practice in this manner.

A few states accept the study of law by correspondence. Some states require that newly graduated lawyers serve a period of clerkship in an established law firm before they are eligible to take the bar examination.

Almost all judges appointed or elected to any court must be lawyers and members of the bar, usually with many years of experience.

Both lawyers and judges have to be effective communicators, work well with people, and be able to find creative solutions to problems, such as complex court cases.

EXPLORING

There are several ways in which you can learn more about a legal career. First, sit in on a trial or two at your local or state courthouse. Try to focus mainly on the judge and the lawyer and take note of what they do. Write down questions you have and terms or actions you don't understand. Then, talk to your guidance counselor and ask for help in setting up a telephone or in-person interview with a judge or lawyer. Prepare a list of questions before your conversation to help focus your thoughts. Also, talk to your guidance counselor or political science teacher about starting or joining a shadowing program. Shadowing programs allow you to follow a person in a certain career around for a day or two to get an idea of what goes on in a typical day. You may even be invited to help out with a few minor duties.

You can also search the World Wide Web for general information about lawyers and judges and current court cases. Read court transcripts and summary opinions written by judges on issues of importance today. After you've done some research and talked to a lawyer or judge and you still think you are destined for law school, try to get a part-time job in a law office. Ask your guidance counselor for help.

If you are already in law school, you might consider becoming a student member of the American Library Association. Student members receive *Student Lawyer,* a magazine that contains useful information for aspiring lawyers. Sample articles from the magazine can be read at http://www.abanet.org/lsd/stulawyer.

EMPLOYERS

About 75 percent of practicing lawyers in the United States work in private practice, either in law firms or alone. The others are employed in government, often at the local level. Lawyers working for the federal government hold positions in the Departments of Justice, Treasury, and Defense. Lawyers also hold positions as house counsel for public utilities, transportation companies, banks, insurance companies, real estate agencies, manufacturing firms, welfare and religious organizations, and other businesses and nonprofit organizations.

Judges and magistrates work for federal, state, and local levels of government.

STARTING OUT

The first steps in entering the law profession are graduation from an approved law school and passing a state bar examination. Usually beginning lawyers do not go into solo practice right away. It is often difficult to become established, and additional experience is helpful to the beginning lawyer. Also, most lawyers do not specialize in a particular branch of law without first gaining experience. Beginning lawyers usually work as assistants to experienced lawyers. At first they do mainly research and routine work. After a few years of successful experience, they may be ready to go out on their own. Other choices open to the beginning lawyer include joining an established law firm or entering into partnership with another lawyer. Positions are also available with banks, business corporations, insurance companies, private utilities, and with a number of government agencies at different levels.

Many new lawyers are recruited directly from law school. Recruiters from law firms and other organizations come to the school and interview possible hires. Other new graduates can get job leads from local and state bar associations.

ADVANCEMENT

Lawyers with outstanding ability can expect to go a long way in their profession. Novice lawyers generally start as law clerks, but as they prove themselves and develop their abilities, many opportunities for advancement will arise. They may be promoted to junior partner in a law firm or establish their own practice. Lawyers may enter politics and become judges, mayors, congressmen, or other government leaders. Top positions are also available in business for the qualified lawyer. Lawyers working for the federal government advance according to the civil service system. Judges usually advance from lower courts to higher courts either in terms of the matters that are decided or in terms of the level—local, state, or federal.

EARNINGS

Incomes generally increase as the lawyer gains experience and becomes better known in the field. The beginning lawyer in solo practice may barely make ends meet for the first few years. According to the National Association for Law Placement, 2002 median salaries for new lawyers ranged from $53,500 for lawyers employed by firms of two to 25 attorneys to $118,000 for lawyers employed by firms of 501 or more attorneys. Those working for the government made approximately $40,000. Starting salaries for lawyers in business were $60,000. Recent graduates entering private practice made the most, earning approximately $80,000.

Experienced lawyers earn salaries that vary depending on the type, size, and location of their employers. According to the U.S. Department of Labor, the 2001 median salary for practicing lawyers was $88,760, although some senior partners earned well over $1 million a year. Ten percent earned less than $43,000. General attorneys in the federal government received $87,080 in 2000. State and local government attorneys generally made less, earning $64,190 and $66,280, respectively, in 2000.

Judges earned median annual salaries of $87,260 in 2001, according to the U.S. Department of Labor. Salaries ranged from less than $19,470 to more than $139,130.

According to the Administrative Office of the U.S. Courts, federal district court judges earned an average of $145,100 in 2001. The chief justice of the United States earned $198,600, while associate justices of the Supreme Court earned $190,100 in 2002. A survey conducted by the National Center for State Courts reports the 2002 salary average for judges in the states' highest courts was $125,485. At the state level, judges serving in intermediate appellate courts averaged $116,064, and in general jurisdiction trial courts they earned an average of $109,811.

WORK ENVIRONMENT

Offices and courtrooms are usually pleasant, although busy, places to work. Lawyers also spend significant amounts of time in law libraries or record rooms, in the homes and offices of clients, and sometimes in the jail cells of clients or prospective witnesses. Many lawyers never work in a courtroom. Unless they are directly involved in litigation, they may never perform at a trial.

Some courts, such as small claims, family, or surrogate, may have evening hours to provide flexibility to the community. Criminal arraignments may be held at any time of the day or night. Court hours for most lawyers and judges are usually regular business hours, with a one-hour lunch break. Often lawyers have to work long hours, spending evenings and weekends preparing cases and materials and working with clients. In addition to the work, the lawyer must always keep up with the latest developments in the profession. Also, it takes a long time to become a qualified lawyer, and it may be difficult to earn an adequate living until the lawyer gets enough experience to develop an established private practice.

Lawyers who are employed at law firms must often work grueling hours to advance in the firm. Spending long weekend hours doing research and interviewing people should be expected.

OUTLOOK

According to the *Occupational Outlook Handbook*, employment for lawyers is expected to grow about as fast as the average through the next decade, but record numbers of law school graduates have created strong competition for jobs, even though the number of graduates has begun to level off. Continued population growth, typical business activities, and increased numbers of legal cases involving health care, environmental, intellectual property, international law, elder law, and sexual harassment issues, among others, will create a steady demand for lawyers. Law services will be more accessible to the middle-income public with the popularity of prepaid legal services and clinics. However, stiff competition has and will continue to urge lawyers to look elsewhere for jobs, in administrative, managerial, and business positions, where legal training is useful.

The top 10 percent of the graduating seniors of the country's best law schools will have more opportunities with well-known law firms and on legal staffs of corporations, in government agencies, and in law schools in the next few decades. Lawyers in solo practice will find it hard to earn a living until their practice is fully established. The best opportunities exist in small towns or suburbs of large cities, where there is less competition and new lawyers can meet potential clients more easily.

Graduates with lower class standings and from lesser known schools may have difficulty in obtaining the most desirable positions. Banks, insurance companies, real estate firms, government agencies, and other organizations often hire law graduates. Legal positions in the armed forces are also available.

Employment of judges is expected to grow more slowly than the average through the next decade. Judges who retire, however, will need to be replaced. There may be an increase in judges in cities with large population growth, but competition will be high for any openings.

FOR MORE INFORMATION

For information about law student services offered by the ABA, contact

American Bar Association (ABA)
Service Center
541 North Fairbanks Court
Chicago, IL 60611
Tel: 312-988-5522
Email: abasvcctr@abanet.org
http://www.abanet.org

For information on workshops and seminars, contact

Association of American Law Schools
1201 Connecticut Avenue, NW, Suite 800
Washington, DC 20036-2605
Tel: 202-296-8851
Email: aals@aals.org
http://www.aals.org

The FBA provides information for lawyers and judges involved in federal practice.

Federal Bar Association (FBA)
Student Services
2215 M Street, NW
Washington, DC 20037
Tel: 202-785-1614
Email: fba@fedbar.org
http://fedbar.org

For information on choosing a law school, law careers, salaries, and alternative law careers, contact

National Association for Law Placement
1025 Connecticut Avenue, NW, Suite 1110
Washington, DC 20036-5413
Tel: 202-835-1001
Email: info@nalp.org
http://www.nalp.org

LIBERAL ARTS TEACHERS

QUICK FACTS

School Subjects
Art
Economics
English
Foreign language
Government
History
Journalism
Mathematics
Music
Psychology
Religion
Sociology
Speech
Theater/dance

Personal Skills
Communication/ideas
Helping/teaching

Work Environment
Primarily indoors
Primarily one location

Minimum Education Level
Bachelor's degree (elementary and secondary teachers)
Master's degree (college professors)

Salary Range
$27,000 to $40,000 to $108,000+

Certification or Licensing
Required by all states (elementary and secondary teachers)
None available (college professors)

Outlook
About as fast as the average (elementary and secondary teachers)
Faster than the average (college professors)

DOT
090, 091, 092

GOE
11.02.01

NOC
4121, 4131, 4141, 4142, 5133, 5134, 5136, 5244

O*NET-SOC
25-1022.00, 25-1041.00, 25-1042.00, 25-1051.00, 25-1052.00, 25-1054.00, 25-1061.00, 25-1062.00, 25-1063.00, 25-1065.00, 25-1066.00, 25-1067.00, 25-1069.99, 25-1081.00, 25-1121.00, 25-1123.00, 25-1124.00, 25-1125.00, 25-1126.00, 25-1191.00, 25-1199.99, 25-2021.00, 25-2022.00, 25-2031.00, 25-2041.00, 25-3099.99

OVERVIEW

Liberal arts teachers instruct students in the humanities, social sciences, natural sciences, and fine arts. They instruct students from as young as three to adults of all ages. They develop teaching outlines and lesson plans, give lectures, facilitate discussions and activities, keep class attendance records, assign homework, and evaluate student progress. Elementary school teachers instruct younger students in a variety of subjects, while secondary teachers and college professors generally specialize in one subject area, such as English, history, or art. There are close to 4 million teachers employed in the United States.

HISTORY

In the early days of Western elementary education, the teacher only had to have completed elementary school to be considered qualified to teach. There was little incentive for teachers to seek further education. School terms were generally short (about six months) and buildings were often cramped and poorly heated. Elementary and secondary schools often combined all grades into one room, teaching the same course of study for all ages. In these earliest schools, teachers were not well paid and had little status or recognition in the community.

Early secondary education was typically based upon training students to enter the clergy. Benjamin Franklin pioneered the idea of a broader secondary education with the creation of the academy, which offered a flexible curriculum and a wide variety of academic subjects. It was not until the 19th century, however, that children of different social classes commonly attended school into the secondary grades. The first English Classical School, which was to become the model for public high schools throughout the country, was established in 1821 in Boston. By the early 20th century, secondary school attendance was made mandatory in the United States.

Harvard, the first U.S. college, was established in 1636. Its stated purpose was to train men for the ministry; the early colleges were all established for religious training. The University of Virginia established the first liberal arts curriculum in 1825, and these innovations were later adopted by many other colleges and universities.

Although the original colleges in the United States were patterned after Oxford University, they later came under the influence of German universities. During the 19th century, more than nine thousand Americans went to Germany to study. The emphasis in

German universities was on the scientific method. Most of the people who had studied in Germany returned to the United States to teach in universities, bringing this objective, factual approach to education and to other fields of learning.

The junior college movement in the United States has been one of the most rapidly growing educational developments. Junior colleges first came into being just after the turn of the 20th century.

THE JOB

The liberal arts can be generally defined as disciplines that help students to develop critical thinking, analytical skills, creativity, and communication skills. They do not usually provide professional, technical, or vocational training. The liberal arts consist of a broad range of disciplines including the humanities (English, foreign language, philosophy, and religious studies), social sciences (anthropology, economics, history, political science/government, and sociology), natural sciences (biology, chemistry, geology, mathematics, physics, and psychology), and fine arts (performing arts and visual arts). Liberal arts teachers pursue college degrees in these majors and, depending on the educational level they attain, teach students from as young as three to adults of all ages. Liberal arts teachers who have earned a bachelor's degree teach students from age three to the high school level, although some community colleges may hire liberal arts teachers who only have a bachelor's degree. Liberal arts teachers with master's degrees or Ph.D.'s teach students at colleges and universities. The following paragraphs describe the basic duties of elementary, secondary, and college teachers.

Elementary School Teachers

Depending on the school, elementary school teachers teach grades one through six or eight. In smaller schools, grades may be combined. In most cases, teachers instruct approximately 20 to 30 children of the same grade.

In the first and second grades, elementary school teachers cover the basic skills: reading, writing, counting, and telling time. With older students, teachers instruct history, geography, math, English, and handwriting. To capture attention and teach new concepts, they use arts and crafts projects, workbooks, music, and other interactive activities. In the upper grades, teachers assign written and oral reports and involve students in projects and competitions such as spelling bees, science fairs, and math contests. Although they are usually required to follow a curriculum designed by state or local administrators, teachers study new learning methods to incorporate into the classroom, such as using computers to surf the Internet.

Elementary school teachers need to devote a fair amount of time to preparation outside of the classroom. They prepare daily lesson plans and assignments, grade papers and tests, and keep a record of each student's progress. Other responsibilities include communicating with parents through written reports and scheduled meetings, keeping their classroom orderly, and decorating desks and bulletin boards to keep the learning environment visually stimulating.

When working with young children, teachers need to instruct social skills along with general school subjects. They serve as disciplinarians, establishing and enforcing rules of conduct to help students learn right from wrong. To keep the classroom manageable, teachers maintain a system of rewards and punishments to encourage students to behave, stay interested, and participate. In cases of classroom disputes, teachers must also be mediators, teaching their pupils to peacefully work through arguments.

Secondary School Teachers

Secondary school teachers may teach in a traditional area, such as science, English, history, and math, or they may teach more specialized classes, such as theater or music. Though secondary teachers are likely be assigned to one specific grade level, they may be required to teach students in surrounding grades. For example, a secondary school English teacher may teach basic composition to a class of ninth-graders one period and creative writing to high school seniors the next.

Secondary school teachers rely on a variety of teaching methods. They spend a great deal of time lecturing, but they also facilitate student discussion and develop projects and activities to interest the students in the subject. They show films and videos, use computers and the Internet, and bring in guest speakers. They assign essays, presentations, and other projects. Each individual subject calls upon particular approaches and may involve laboratory experiments, role-playing exercises, and field trips.

Outside of the classroom, secondary school teachers prepare lectures, lesson plans, and exams. They evaluate student work and calculate grades. In the process of planning their class, secondary school teachers read textbooks, novels, and workbooks to determine reading assignments; photocopy notes, articles, and other handouts;

and develop grading policies. They also continue to study alternative and traditional teaching methods to hone their skills. They prepare students for special events and conferences and submit student work to competitions. Some secondary school teachers also have the opportunity for extracurricular work as athletic coaches or drama coaches.

College Professors

College and university faculty members teach at junior colleges or at four-year colleges and universities. At four-year institutions, most faculty members are *assistant professors, associate professors,* or *full professors.* These three types of professorships differ in regards to status, job responsibilities, and salary.

College professors' most important responsibility is to teach students. Their role within a college department will determine the level of courses they teach and the number of courses per semester. Most professors work with students at all levels, from college freshmen to graduate students. They may head several classes a semester or only a few a year. Some of their classes will have large enrollment, while graduate seminars may consist of only 12 or fewer students.

Though college professors may spend fewer than 10 hours a week in the actual classroom, they spend many hours preparing lectures and lesson plans, grading papers and exams, and preparing grade reports. They also schedule office hours during the week to be available to students outside of the lecture hall, and they meet with students individually throughout the semester. In the classroom, professors lecture, lead discussions, administer exams, and assign textbook reading and other research. In some courses, they rely heavily on laboratories to transmit course material.

In addition to teaching, most college faculty members conduct research and write publications. Professors publish their research findings in various scholarly journals. They also write books based on their research or on their own knowledge and experience in the field. Publishing a significant amount of work has been the traditional standard by which assistant professors prove themselves worthy of becoming permanent, tenured faculty.

The *junior college instructor* has many of the same kinds of responsibilities, as does the teacher in a four-year college or university. Because junior colleges offer only a two-year program, they teach only undergraduates.

REQUIREMENTS

High School

To prepare for a career in education, follow your school's college preparatory program and take advanced courses in English, mathematics, science, history, and government. Art, music, and extracurricular activities will contribute to a broad base of knowledge necessary to teach a variety of subjects. Composition, journalism, and communications classes are also important for developing your writing and speaking skills.

Postsecondary Training

Your college training will depend on the level at which you plan to teach. All 50 states and the District of Columbia require public elementary education teachers to have a bachelor's degree in either education or in the subject they teach. Prospective teachers must also complete an approved training program called student teaching, which combines subject and educational classes with work experience in the classroom.

If you want to teach at the high school level, you may choose to major in your subject area while taking required education courses, or you may major in secondary education with a concentration in your subject area. Similar to prospective elementary teachers, you will need to student teach in an actual classroom environment.

For prospective professors, you will need at least one advanced degree in your chosen field of study. The master's degree is considered the minimum standard, and graduate work beyond the master's level is usually desirable. If you hope to advance in academic rank above instructor, most institutions require a doctorate. Your graduate school program will be similar to a life of teaching—in addition to attending seminars, you'll research, prepare articles for publication, and teach some undergraduate courses.

Thousands of colleges offer liberal arts majors in the United States. Included in this group are 196 private colleges and 21 public colleges that award at least half of their degrees in the liberal arts discipline. According to *U.S. News & World Report*, the top three private liberal arts colleges in 2002 were Amherst College (http://www.amherst.edu), Swarthmore College (http://www.swarthmore.edu), and Williams College (http://www.williams.edu). The top three public liberal arts colleges (in descending order) were Virginia Military Institute (http://www.vmi.edu), St. Mary's College of

Maryland (http://www.smcm.edu), and Mary Washington College (http://www.mwc.edu).

Certification or Licensing

Elementary and secondary teachers who work in public schools must be licensed under regulations established by the state in which they are teaching. If moving, teachers have to comply with any other regulations in their new state to be able to teach, though many states have reciprocity agreements that make it easier for teachers to change locations.

Licensure examinations test prospective teachers for competency in basic subjects such as mathematics, reading, writing, teaching, and other subject matter proficiency. In addition, many states are moving towards a performance-based evaluation for licensing. In this case, after passing the teaching examination, prospective teachers are given provisional licenses. Only after proving themselves capable in the classroom are they eligible for a full license.

Another growing trend spurred by recent teacher shortages in elementary and high schools is alternative licensure arrangements. For those who have a bachelor's degree but lack formal education courses and training in the classroom, states can issue a provisional license. These workers immediately begin teaching under the supervision of a licensed educator for one to two years and take education classes outside of their working hours. Once they have completed the required coursework and gained experience in the classroom, they are granted a full license.

Other Requirements

Many consider the desire to teach a calling. This calling is based on a love of learning. Teachers of young children and young adults must respect their students as individuals, with personalities, strengths, and weaknesses of their own. They must also be patient and self-disciplined to manage a large group independently. Because they work with students who are at very impressionable ages, they should serve as good role models. Elementary and secondary teachers should also be well organized, as you'll have to keep track of the work and progress of a number of different students.

If you aim to teach at the college level, you should enjoy reading, writing, and researching. Not only will you spend many years studying in school, but your whole career will be based on communicating your thoughts and ideas. People skills are important because you'll be dealing directly with students, administrators, and other faculty members on a daily basis. You should feel comfortable in a role of authority and possess self-confidence.

EXPLORING

To explore a teaching career, look for leadership opportunities that involve working with children. You might find summer work as a counselor in a summer camp, as a leader of a scout troop, or as an assistant in a public park or community center. To get some firsthand teaching experience, volunteer for a peer-tutoring program. If you plan to teach young children, look for opportunities to coach youth athletic teams or help out in day care centers.

If you are interested in becoming a college professor, spend some time on a college campus to get a sense of the environment. Write to colleges for their admissions brochures and course catalogs (or check them out online); read about the faculty members and the courses they teach. Before visiting college campuses, make arrangements to speak to professors who teach courses that interest you. These professors may allow you to sit in on their classes and observe.

EMPLOYERS

There are more than 1.5 million elementary school teachers and 1.1 million secondary teachers employed in the United States. They are needed at public and private institutions, day care centers, juvenile detention centers, vocational schools, and schools of the arts. Although rural areas maintain schools, more teaching positions are available in urban or suburban areas. Teachers are also finding opportunities in charter schools, which are smaller, deregulated schools that receive public funding.

College and university professors hold over 1.3 million jobs. Employment opportunities vary based on area of study and education. Most universities have many different departments that hire faculty. With a doctorate, a number of publications, and a record of good teaching, professors should find opportunities in universities all across the country.

STARTING OUT

Elementary and secondary school teachers can use their college placement offices and state departments of education to find job openings. Many local schools advertise teaching positions in newspapers. Another option is to directly contact the administration in the schools in which you'd like to work. While looking for a full-time position, you can work as a substitute teacher. In more urban areas with many schools, you may be able to find full-time substitute work.

Prospective college professors should start the process of finding a teaching position while in graduate school. You will need to develop a curriculum vitae (a detailed, academic resume), work on your academic writing, assist with research, attend conferences, and gain teaching experience and recommendations. Because of the competition for tenure-track positions, you may have to work for a few years in temporary positions. Some professional associations maintain lists of teaching opportunities in their areas. They may also make lists of applicants available to college administrators looking to fill an available position.

ADVANCEMENT

As elementary and secondary teachers acquire experience or additional education, they can expect higher wages and more responsibilities. Teachers with leadership skills and an interest in administrative work may advance to serve as principals or supervisors, though the number of these positions is limited and competition is fierce. Another move may be into higher education, teaching education classes at a college or university. For most of these positions, additional education is required. Other common career transitions are into related fields. With additional preparation, teachers can become librarians, reading specialists, or counselors.

At the college level, the normal pattern of advancement is from instructor to assistant professor, to associate professor, to full professor. All four academic ranks are concerned primarily with teaching and research. College faculty members who have an interest in and a talent for administration may be advanced to chair of a department or to dean of their college. A few become college or university presidents or other types of administrators.

EARNINGS

According to the Bureau of Labor Statistics, the median annual salary for elementary school teachers was $41,080 in 2001. The lowest 10 percent earned $27,000 or less; the highest 10 percent earned $64,280 or more. The median annual salary for secondary school teachers was $43,280 in 2001. The lowest 10 percent earned $27,980; the highest 10 percent earned $67,940.

The American Federation of Teachers reports that the average salary for beginning teachers with a bachelor's degree was $28,986 in 2001. The estimated average salary of all public elementary and secondary school teachers was $43,250.

College professors' earnings vary depending on their academic department, the size of the school, the type of school (public, private, women's only), and by the level of position the professor holds. The American Association of University Professors (AAUP) reported the average yearly income for all full-time faculty was $60,000 in 2001. The AAUP also reports that professors averaged the following salaries by rank: full professors, $78,912; associate professors, $57,380; assistant professors, $47,358; and instructors, $35,790.

Earnings for college professors also vary by the subject they teach. The U.S. Department of Labor reports the following average salaries for professors by discipline in 2001: anthropology ($58,990); art, drama, music ($47,080); biological science ($57,230); chemistry ($53,750); economics ($62,820); English language/literature ($45,590); foreign language/literature ($45,030); history ($50,400); mathematical science ($49,240); philosophy and religion ($47,740); physics ($54,930); political science ($54,930); psychology ($53,120); and sociology ($51,120).

WORK ENVIRONMENT

Most teachers are contracted to work 10 months out of the year, with a two-month vacation during the summer. During their summer break, many continue their education to renew or upgrade their teaching licenses and earn higher salaries. Teachers in schools that operate year-round work eight-week sessions with one-week breaks in between and a five-week vacation in the winter.

Teachers work in generally pleasant conditions, although some older schools may have poor heating or electrical systems. The work can seem confining, requiring them to remain in the classroom throughout most of the day. Elementary school teachers have to deal with busy children all day, which can be tiring and trying.

Elementary and high school hours are generally 8:00 A.M.–3:00 P.M., but teachers work more than 40 hours a week teaching, preparing for classes, grading papers, and directing extracurricular activities. Similarly, most college teachers work more than 40 hours each week. Although they may teach only two or three classes a semester, they spend many hours preparing for lectures, examining student work, and conducting research.

OUTLOOK

According to the *Occupational Outlook Handbook (OOH)*, employment opportunities for teachers (grades K–12) are expected to grow as fast as the average for all occupations through 2010. The need to replace retiring teachers will provide many opportunities nationwide.

The demand for elementary and secondary school teachers varies widely depending on geographic area. Inner-city schools characterized by poor working conditions and low salaries often suffer a shortage of teachers. In addition, more opportunities exist for those who specialize in a subject in which it is harder to attract qualified teachers, such as mathematics, science, or foreign languages.

The National Education Association (NEA) believes that it will be a challenge to hire enough new elementary and secondary school teachers to meet rising enrollments and replace the large number of retiring teachers, primarily because of low teacher salaries. According to the NEA, approximately 2.4 million teachers will be needed to fill classrooms in the next decade. Higher salaries along with other necessary changes, such as smaller classroom sizes and safer schools, will be necessary to attract new teachers and retain experienced ones. Other challenges for elementary and high schools involve attracting more men into teaching. The percentage of male teachers continues to decline.

The *OOH* predicts faster-than-average employment growth for college and university professors through 2010. College enrollment is projected to grow due to an increased number of 18- to 24-year-olds, an increased number of adults returning to college, and an increased number of foreign-born students. Retirement of current faculty members will also provide job openings. However, competition for full-time, tenure-track positions at four-year schools will be very strong.

FOR MORE INFORMATION

For information about careers, education, and union membership, contact the following organizations:

American Anthropological Association
2200 Wilson Boulevard, Suite 600
Arlington, VA 22201
Tel: 703-528-1902
http://www.aaanet.org

American Council on the Teaching of Foreign Languages
6 Executive Plaza
Yonkers, NY 10701-6801
Tel: 914-963-8830
Email: headquarters@actfl.org
http://www.actfl.org

American Association of University Professors
1012 14th Street, NW, Suite 500
Washington, DC 20005
Tel: 202-737-5900
http://www.aaup.org

American Economic Association
2014 Broadway, Suite 305
Nashville, TN 37203
Tel: 615-322-2595
http://www.vanderbilt.edu/AEA

American Federation of Teachers
555 New Jersey Avenue, NW
Washington, DC 20001
Tel: 202-879-4400
Email: online@aft.org
http://www.aft.org

American Political Science Association
1527 New Hampshire Avenue, NW
Washington, DC 20036-1206
Tel: 202-483-2512
Email: apsa@apsanet.org
https://www.apsanet.org

American Sociological Association
1307 New York Avenue, NW, Suite 700
Washington, DC 20005
Tel: 202-383-9005
http://www.asanet.org

Music Teachers National Association
441 Vine Street, Suite 505
Cincinnati, OH 45202-2811
Email: mtnanet@mtna.org
http://www.mtna.org

The National Association for Music Education
1806 Robert Fulton Drive
Reston, VA 20191
http://www.menc.org

National Council for Accreditation of Teacher Education
2010 Massachusetts Avenue, NW, Suite 500
Washington, DC 20036
Tel: 202-466-7496
Email: ncate@ncate.org
http://www.ncate.org

National Council of Teachers of English
1111 West Kenyon Road
Urbana, IL 61801-1096
Email: public_info@ncte.org
http://www.ncte.org

National Council of Teachers of Mathematics
1906 Association Drive
Reston, VA 20191-1502
Tel: 703-620-9840
http://www.nctm.org

National Education Association
1201 16th Street, NW
Washington, DC 20036
Tel: 202-833-4000
http://www.nea.org

LOBBYISTS

QUICK FACTS

School Subjects	Certification or Licensing
Government Journalism Speech	None available
Personal Skills	**Outlook**
Communication/ideas Leadership/management	About as fast as the average
Work Environment	**DOT**
Primarily indoors One location with some travel	165
Minimum Education Level	**GOE**
Bachelor's degree	11.09.03
Salary Range	**NOC**
$20,000 to $100,000 to $500,000+	N/A
	O*NET-SOC
	N/A

OVERVIEW

A *lobbyist* works to influence legislation on the federal, state, or local level on behalf of clients. Nonprofit organizations, labor unions, trade associations, corporations, and other groups and individuals use lobbyists to voice their concerns and opinions to government representatives. Lobbyists use their knowledge of the legislative process and their government contacts to represent their clients' interests. Though most lobbyists are based in Washington, D.C., many work throughout the country representing client issues in city and state government.

HISTORY

Lobbying has been a practice within government since colonial times. In the late 1700s, the term "lobbyist" was used to describe the special-interest representatives who gathered in the anteroom outside the legislative chamber in the New York state capitol. The term often had a pejorative connotation, with political cartoonists frequently portraying lobbyists as slick, cigar-chomping individuals attempting to buy favors. But in the 20th century, lobbyists came to be looked upon as experts in the fields that they represented, and members of Congress relied upon them to provide information needed to evaluate legislation. During the New Deal in the 1930s, government spending in Washington greatly increased, and the number of lobbyists proliferated proportionately. A major lobbying law was enacted in 1938, but it wasn't until 1946 that comprehensive legislation in the form of the Federal Regulation of Lobbying Act was passed into law. The act requires that anyone who spends or receives money or anything of value in the interests of passing, modifying, or defeating legislation being considered by the U.S. Congress be registered and provide spending reports. However, its effectiveness was reduced by vague language that frequently required legal interpretations. Further regulatory acts have been passed in the years since; most recently, the Lobbying Disclosure Act of 1995 has required registration of all lobbyists working at the federal level.

THE JOB

An example of effective lobbying concerns Medic Alert, an organization that provides bracelets to millions of people in the United States and Canada with health problems. Engraved on the bracelet is a description of the person's medical problem, along with Medic Alert's 24-hour emergency response phone number. The emergency response center is located in a region of California that considered changing the telephone area code. Medic Alert anticipated a lot of confusion—and many possible medical disasters—if the area code was changed from that which is engraved on the millions of bracelets. Medic Alert called upon doctors, nurses, and the media to get word out about the danger to lives. Through this lobbying, the public and the state's policy makers became aware of an important aspect of the area code change they may not have otherwise known.

The Medic Alert organization, like the thousands of associations, unions, and corporations in the United States, benefited from using lobbyists with an understanding of state politics and influence. The American Society of Association Executives estimates that the number of national trade and charitable associations is over 23,000. With 2,500 of these associations based in Washington, D.C., associations are the third-largest industry in the city, behind government and tourism. Lobbyists may work for one of these associations as a director of government relations, or they may work for an industry, company, or other organization to act on its behalf in government concerns. Lobbyists also work for lobbying firms that work with many different clients on a contractual basis.

Lobbyists have years of experience working with the government, learning about federal and state politics, and meeting career politicians and their staffs. Their job is to make members of Congress aware of the issues of concern to their clients and the effect that legislation and regulations will have on them. They provide the members of Congress with research and analysis to help them make the most informed decisions possible. Lobbyists also keep their clients informed with updates and reports.

Tom McNamara is the president of a government relations firm based in Washington, D.C. He first became involved in politics by working on campaigns before he was even old enough to vote. Throughout his years in government work, he has served as the Chief of Staff for two different members of Congress and was active in both the Reagan and Bush presidential campaigns. "Clients hire me for my advice," McNamara says. "They ask me to do strategic planning, relying on my knowledge of how Congress operates." After learning about a client's problem, McNamara researches the issue, then develops a plan and a proposal to solve the problem. Some of the questions he must ask when seeking a solution are: What are our assets? Who can we talk to who has the necessary influence? Do we need the media? Do we need to talk to Congressional staff members? "With 22 years in the House of Representatives," McNamara says, "I have a tremendous base of people I know. Part of my work is maintaining these relationships, as well as developing relationships with new members and their staff."

Lobbying techniques are generally broken down into two broad categories: direct lobbying and indirect, or "grassroots," lobbying. Direct lobbying techniques include making personal contacts with members of Congress and appointed officials. It is important for lobbyists to know who the key people are in drafting legislation that is significant to their clientele. They hire technical experts to develop reports, charts, graphs, or schematic drawings that may help in the legislative decision-making process that determines the passage, amendment, or defeat of a measure. Sometimes a lobbyist with expertise on a particular issue works directly with a member of

Congress in the drafting of a bill. Lobbyists also keep members of Congress tuned in to the voices of their constituents.

Indirect, or grassroots, lobbying involves persuading voters to support a client's view. If the Congress member knows that a majority of voters favor a particular point of view, he or she will support or fight legislation according to the voters' wishes. Probably the most widely used method of indirect lobbying is the letter-writing campaign. Lobbyists use direct mail, newsletters, media advertising, and other methods of communication to reach the constituents and convince them to write to their member of Congress with their supporting views. Lobbyists also use phone campaigns, encouraging the constituents to call their Congress member's office. Aides usually tally the calls that come in and communicate the volume to the legislator.

Indirect lobbying is also done through the media. Lobbyists try to persuade newspaper and magazine editors and radio and television news managers to write or air editorials that reflect the point of view of their clientele. They write op-ed pieces that are submitted to the media for publication. They arrange for experts to speak in favor of a particular position on talk shows or to make statements that are picked up by the media. As a persuasive measure, lobbyists may send a legislator a collection of news clippings indicating public opinion on a forthcoming measure or provide tapes of aired editorials and news features covering a relevant subject.

REQUIREMENTS

High School

Becoming a lobbyist requires years of experience in other government and related positions. To prepare for a government job, take courses in history, social studies, and civics to learn about the structure of local, state, and federal government. English and composition classes will help you develop your communication skills. Work on the student council or become an officer for a school club. Taking journalism courses and working on the school newspaper will prepare you for the public relations aspect of lobbying. As a reporter, you'll research current issues, meet with policy makers, and write articles.

Postsecondary Training

As a rule, men and women take up lobbying after having left an earlier career. As mentioned earlier, Tom McNamara worked for over 20 years as a congressional staff member before moving on to this other aspect of government work. Schools do not generally offer a specific curriculum that leads to a career as a lobbyist; your experience with legislation and policy making is what will prove valuable to employers and clients. Almost all lobbyists have college degrees, and many have graduate degrees. Degrees in law and political science are among the most beneficial for prospective lobbyists, just as they are for other careers in politics and government. Journalism, public relations, history, and economics are other areas of study that would be helpful in the pursuit of a lobbying career.

Certification or Licensing

Lobbyists do not need a license or certification, but are required to register. The Lobbying Disclosure Act of 1995 requires all lobbyists working on the federal level to register with the Secretary of the Senate and the Clerk of the House. You may also be required to register with the states in which you lobby and possibly pay a small fee.

There is no union available to lobbyists. Some lobbyists join the American League of Lobbyists, which provides a variety of support services for its members. Membership in a number of other associations, including the American Society of Association Executives and the American Association of Political Consultants, can also be useful to lobbyists.

Other Requirements

"I've had practical, everyday involvement in government and politics," McNamara says about the skills and knowledge most valuable to him as a lobbyist. "I know what motivates Congress members and staff to act."

In addition to this understanding, McNamara emphasizes that lobbyists must be honest in all their professional dealings with others. "The only way to be successful is to be completely honest and straightforward." Your career will be based on your reputation as a reliable person, so you must be very scrupulous in building that reputation.

You also need people skills to develop good relationships with legislators in order to serve your clients' interests. Your knowledge of the workings of government, along with good communication skills, will help you to explain government legislation to your clients in ways that they can clearly understand.

EXPLORING

To explore this career, become an intern or volunteer in the office of a lobbyist, legislator, government official, special interest group, or nonprofit institution (especially one that relies on government grants). Working in these fields will introduce you to the lobbyist's world and provide early exposure to the workings of government.

Another good way to learn more about this line of work is by becoming involved in your school government; writing for your school newspaper; doing public relations, publicity, and advertising work for school and community organizations; and taking part in fund-raising drives. When major legislative issues are being debated, you can write to your congressional representatives to express your views or even organize a letter writing or telephone campaign; these actions are in themselves forms of lobbying.

EMPLOYERS

Organizations either hire government liaisons to handle lobbying or they contract with law and lobby firms. Liaisons who work for one organization work on only those issues that affect that organization. Independent lobbyists work on a variety of different issues, taking on clients on a contractual basis. They may contract with large corporations, such as a pharmaceutical or communications company, as well as volunteer services to nonprofit organizations. Lobbying firms are located all across the country. Those executives in charge of government relations for trade associations and other organizations are generally based in Washington, D.C.

STARTING OUT

Lobbyist positions are not listed in the classifieds. It takes years of experience and an impressive list of connections to find a government relations job in an organization. Tom McNamara retired at age 50 from his work with the House of Representatives. "Lobbying was a natural progression into the private sector," he says. His love for public policy, campaigns, and politics led him to start his own lobbying firm. "I had an institutional understanding that made me valuable," he says.

Professional lobbyists usually have backgrounds as lawyers, public relations executives, congressional aides, legislators, government officials, or professionals in business and industry. Once established in a government or law career, lobbyists begin to hear about corporations and associations that need knowledgeable people for their government relations departments. The American Society of Association Executives (ASAE) hosts a website, http://www.asaenet.org, which lists available positions for executives with trade associations.

ADVANCEMENT

Lobbyists focus on developing long-standing relationships with legislators and clients and become experts on policy making and legislation. Association or company executives may advance from a position as director of government relations into a position as president or vice president. Lobbyists who contract their services to various clients advance by taking on more clients and working for larger corporations.

EARNINGS

Because of the wide range of salaries for lobbyists, it is difficult to compile an accurate survey. The ASAE, however, regularly conducts surveys of association executives. According to ASAE's 2001 Association Executive Compensation Study, directors of government relations within trade associations earned an average of $93,666 annually. The report notes, however, that compensation varies greatly depending on location. Highest earnings of directors were reported in New York City ($185,300), Washington, D.C. ($174,000), and Chicago ($168,000). The size of an association's staff and budget also affects compensation levels.

Like lawyers, lobbyists are considered very well paid; also like lawyers, a lobbyist's income depends on the size of the organization he or she represents. Experienced contract lobbyists with a solid client base can earn well over $100,000 a year and some make more than $500,000 a year. Beginning lobbyists may make less than $20,000 a year as they build a client base. In many cases, a lobbyist may take on large corporations as clients for the bulk of the annual income, then volunteer services to nonprofit organizations.

WORK ENVIRONMENT

Lobbyists spend much of their time communicating with the people who affect legislation—principally the legislators and officials of federal and state governments. This communication takes place in person, by telephone, and by memoranda. Most of a lobbyist's time is spent gathering information, writing reports, creating publicity, and staying in touch with clients. They respond to the public and the news media when required. Sometimes their expertise is required at hearings or they may testify before a legislature.

Tom McNamara has enjoyed the change from congressional Chief of Staff to lobbyist. "I'm an integral part of the system of government," he says, "albeit in a different role." He feels that every day is distinctly different, and he has the opportunity to meet new and interesting people. "It's intellectually challenging," he says. "You have to stay on top of the issues, and keep track of the personalities as well as the campaigns."

OUTLOOK

The number of special interest groups in the United States continues to grow, and as long as they continue to plead their causes before state and federal governments, lobbyists will be needed. However, lobbying cutbacks often occur in corporations. Because lobbying doesn't directly earn a profit for a business, the government relations department is often the first in a company to receive budget cuts. The American League of Lobbyists anticipates that the career will remain stable, though it's difficult to predict. In recent years, there has been a significant increase in registrations, but that is most likely a result of the Lobbying Disclosure Act of 1995 requiring registration.

The methods of grassroots advocacy will continue to be affected by the Internet and other new communication technology. Lobbyists and organizations use Web pages to inform the public of policy issues. These Web pages often include ways to immediately send email messages to state and federal legislators. Constituents may have the choice of composing their own messages or sending messages already composed. With this method, a member of Congress can easily determine the feelings of the constituents based on the amount of email received.

FOR MORE INFORMATION

For information about a lobbyist career, visit the following website or contact

American League of Lobbyists
PO Box 30005
Alexandria, VA 22310
Tel: 703-960-3011
Email: alldc.org@erols.com
http://www.alldc.org

For information about government relations and public policy concerns within trade associations, contact

American Society of Association Executives
1575 I Street, NW
Washington, DC 20005-1103
Tel: 202-626-2723
http://www.asaenet.org

MANAGEMENT ANALYSTS AND CONSULTANTS

QUICK FACTS

School Subjects	Certification or Licensing
Business Computer science Speech	Voluntary

School Subjects
Business
Computer science
Speech

Personal Skills
Communication/ideas
Leadership/management

Work Environment
Primarily indoors
Primarily multiple locations

Minimum Education Level
Bachelor's degree

Salary Range
$35,020 to $57,970 to $250,000+

Certification or Licensing
Voluntary

Outlook
Faster than the average

DOT
161

GOE
05.01.06

NOC
1122

O*NET-SOC
13-1111.00

OVERVIEW

Management analysts and consultants analyze business or operating procedures to devise the most efficient methods of accomplishing work. They gather and organize information about operating problems and procedures and prepare recommendations for implementing new systems or changes. They may update manuals outlining established methods of performing work and train personnel in new applications. There are approximately 501,000 management analysts and consultants employed in the United States.

HISTORY

A number of people in business began experimenting with accepted management practices after the Industrial Revolution. For example, in the 1700s Josiah Wedgwood applied new labor- and work-saving methods to his pottery business and was the first to formulate the concept of mass-producing articles of uniform quality. He believed the manufacturing process could be organized into a system that would use, and not abuse, the people harnessed to it. He organized the interrelationships between people, material, and events in his factory and took the time to reflect upon them. In short, he did in the 18th century what management analysts and consultants do today.

Frederick W. Taylor was the creator of the "efficiency cult" in American business. Taylor invented the world-famous "differential piecework" plan, in which a productive worker could significantly increase take-home pay by stepping up the pace of work. Taylor's well-publicized study of the Midvale Steel plant in Pennsylvania was the first time-and-motion study. This study broke down elements of each part of each job and timed it; the study was therefore able to quantify maximum efficiency. Taylor earned many assignments and inspired James O. McKinsey, in 1910, to found a firm dealing with management and accounting problems.

Today, management analysts and consultants are thriving. As technological advances lead to the possibility of dramatic loss or gain in the business world, many executives feel more secure relying on all the specialized expertise they can find.

THE JOB

Management analysts and consultants are called in to solve any of a vast array of organizational problems. They are often needed when a rapidly growing small company needs a better system of control over inventories and expenses.

The role of the consultant is to come into a situation in which a client is unsure or inexpert and to recommend actions or provide assessments. There are many different types of management analysts and consultants, all of whom require knowledge of general management, operations, marketing, logistics, materials management and physical distribution, finance and accounting, human resources, electronic data processing and systems, and management science.

Management analysts and consultants may be called in when a major manufacturer must reorganize its corporate structure when acquiring a new division. For example, they assist when a company relocates to another state by coordinating the move, planning the new facility, and training new workers.

The work of management analysts and consultants is quite flexible and varies from job to job. In general, management analysts and consultants collect, review, and analyze data, make recommendations, and assist in the implementation of their proposals. Some projects require that several consultants work together, each specializing in a different area. Other jobs require the analysts to work independently.

Public and private organizations use management analysts for a variety of reasons. Some organizations lack the resources necessary to handle a project. Other organizations, before they pursue a particular course of action, will consult an analyst to determine what resources will be required or what problems will be encountered. Some companies seek outside advice on how to resolve organizational problems that have already been identified or to avoid troublesome problems that could arise.

Firms providing consulting practitioners range in size from solo practitioners to large international companies employing hundreds of people. The services are generally provided on a contract basis. A company will choose a consulting firm that specializes in the area that needs assistance, and then the two firms negotiate the conditions of the contract. Contract variables include the proposed cost of the project, staffing requirements, and the deadline.

After getting a contract, the analyst's first job is to define the nature and extent of the project. He or she analyzes statistics, such as annual revenues, employment, or expenditures. He or she may also interview employees and observe the operations of the organization on a day-to-day basis.

The next step for the analyst is to use his or her knowledge of management systems to develop solutions. While preparing recommendations, he or she must take into account the general nature of the business, the relationship of the firm to others in its industry, the firm's internal organization, and the information gained through data collection and analysis.

Once they have decided on a course of action, management analysts and consultants usually write reports of their findings and recommendations and present them to the client. They often make formal oral presentations about their findings as well. Some projects require only reports; others require assistance in implementing the suggestions.

REQUIREMENTS

High School

High school courses that will give you a general preparation for this field include business, mathematics, and computer science.

Management analysts and consultants must pass on their findings through written or oral presentations, so be sure to take English and speech classes, too.

Postsecondary Training

Employers generally prefer to hire management analysts and consultants with a master's degree in business or public administration, or at least a bachelor's degree and several years of appropriate work experience. Many fields of study provide a suitable formal educational background for this occupation because of the diversity of problem areas addressed by management analysts and consultants. These include many areas in the computer and information sciences, engineering, business and management, education, communications, marketing and distribution, and architecture and environmental design.

When hired directly from school, management analysts and consultants often participate in formal company training programs. These programs may include instruction on policies and procedures, computer systems and software, and management practices and principles. Regardless of their background, most management analysts and consultants routinely attend conferences to keep abreast of current developments in the field.

Certification and Licensing

The Institute of Management Consultants offers the certified management consultant designation to those who pass an examination and meet minimum educational and experience criteria. Certification is voluntary but may provide an additional advantage to job seekers.

Other Requirements

Management analysts and consultants are often responsible for recommending layoffs of staff, so it is important that they learn to deal with people diplomatically. Their job requires a great deal of tact, enlisting cooperation while exerting leadership, debating their points, and pointing out errors. Consultants must be quick thinkers, able to refute objections with finality. They also must be able to make excellent presentations.

A management analyst must also be unbiased and analytical, with a disposition toward the intellectual side of business and a natural curiosity about the way things work best.

EXPLORING

The reference departments of most libraries include business areas that will have valuable research tools such as encyclopedias of business consultants and "who's who" of business consultants. These books should list management analysis and consulting firms across the country, describing their annual sales and area of specialization, like industrial, high tech, small business, and retail. After doing some research, you can call or write to these firms and ask for more information.

For more general business exploration, see if your school has a business or young leaders club. If there is nothing of the sort, you may want to explore Junior Achievement, a nationwide association that connects young business-minded students with professionals in the field for mentoring and career advice. Visit http://www.ja.org for more information.

EMPLOYERS

About a third of all management analysts and consultants are self-employed. Federal, state, and local governments employ many of the others. The Department of Defense employs the majority of those working for the federal government. The remainder work in the private sector for companies providing consulting services. Although management analysts and consultants are found throughout the country, the majority are concentrated in major metropolitan areas.

STARTING OUT

Most government agencies offer entry-level analyst and consultant positions to people with bachelor's degrees and no work experience. Many entrants are also career changers who were formerly mid- and upper-level managers. With one-third of the practicing management consultants self-employed, career changing is a common route into the field.

Anyone with some degree of business expertise or an expert field can begin to work as an independent consultant. The number of one- and two-person consulting firms in this country is well over 100,000. Establishing a wide range of appropriate personal contacts is by far the most effective way to get started in this field. Consultants have to sell themselves and their expertise, a task far tougher than selling a tangible product the customer can see and handle. Many consultants get their first clients by advertising in newspapers, magazines, and trade or professional periodicals. After some time in the field, word-of-mouth advertising is often the primary force.

ADVANCEMENT

A new consultant in a large firm may be referred to as an *associate* for the first couple of years. The next progression is to *senior associate,* a title that indicates three to five years' experience and the ability to supervise others and do more complex and independent work. After about five years, the analyst who is progressing well may become an *engagement manager* with the responsibility to lead a consulting team on a particular client project. The best managers become *senior engagement managers,* leading several study teams or a very large project team. After about seven years, those who excel will be considered for appointment as *junior partners* or *principals.* Partnership involves responsibility for marketing the firm and leading client projects. Some may be promoted to senior partnership or *director,* but few people successfully run this full course. Management analysts and consultants with entrepreneurial ambition may open their own firms.

EARNINGS

In 2001, management analysts and consultants had median annual earnings of $57,970, according to the Bureau of Labor Statistics. The lowest 10 percent earned less than $35,020, and the highest 10 percent earned more than $109,620.

Salaries and hourly rates for management analysts and consultants vary widely, according to experience, specialization, education, and employer. The *Occupational Outlook Handbook* reports that analysts and consultants working in the management and public relations industries earned median annual earnings of $61,290 in 2000, while those employed in the computer and data processing services industry earned $56,070. Management analysts and consultants employed by state government earned a median of $43,470.

Many consultants can demand between $400 and $1,000 per day. Their fees are often well over $40 per hour. Self-employed management consultants receive no fringe benefits and generally have to maintain their own office, but their pay is usually much higher than salaried consultants. They can make more than $2,000 per day or $250,000 in one year from consulting just two days per week.

Typical benefits for salaried analysts and consultants include health and life insurance, retirement plans, vacation and sick leave, profit sharing, and bonuses for outstanding work. All travel expenses are generally reimbursed by the employer.

WORK ENVIRONMENT

Management analysts and consultants generally divide their time between their own offices and the client's office or production facility. They can spend a great deal of time on the road.

Most management analysts and consultants work at least 40 hours per week plus overtime depending on the project. The nature of consulting projects—working on location with a single client toward a specific goal—allows these professionals to immerse themselves totally in their work. They sometimes work 14–16-hour days, and six- or seven-day workweeks can be fairly common.

While self-employed, consultants may enjoy the luxury of setting their own hours and doing a great deal of their work at home; the tradeoff is sacrificing the benefits provided by the large firms. Their livelihood depends on the additional responsibility of maintaining and expanding their clientele on their own.

Although those in this career usually avoid much of the potential tedium of working for one company all day, every day, they face many pressures resulting from deadlines and client expectations. Because the clients are generally paying generous fees, they want to see dramatic results, and the management analyst can feel the weight of this.

OUTLOOK

Employment of management analysts is expected to grow faster than the average for all occupations through the next decade, according to the U.S. Department of Labor. Industry and government agencies are expected to rely more and more on the expertise of these professionals to improve and streamline the performance of their organizations. Many job openings will result from the need to replace personnel who transfer to other fields or leave the labor force.

Competition for management consulting jobs will be strong. Employers can choose from a large pool of applicants who have a wide variety of educational backgrounds and experience. The challenging nature of this job, coupled with high salary potential, attracts many. A graduate degree, experience and expertise in the industry, as well as a knack for public relations, are needed to stay competitive.

Trends that have increased the growth of employment in this field include advancements in information technology and e-commerce, the growth of international business, and fluctuations in the economy that have forced businesses to streamline and downsize.

FOR MORE INFORMATION

For industry information, contact the following organizations:

American Institute of Certified Public Accountants
1211 Avenue of the Americas
New York, NY 10036
Tel: 212-596-6200
http://www.aicpa.org

American Management Association
1601 Broadway
New York, NY 10019
Tel: 800-262-9699
http://www.amanet.org

Association of Management Consulting Firms
380 Lexington Avenue, Suite 1700
New York, NY 10168
Tel: 212-551-7887
Email: info@amcf.org
http://www.amcf.org

For information on certification, contact

Association of Internal Management Consultants, Inc.
19 Harrison Street
Framingham, MA 01702
Tel: 508-820-3434
Email: info@aimc.org
http://aimc.org

For information on certification, contact

Institute of Management Consultants
2025 M Street, NW, Suite 800
Washington, DC 20036-3309
Tel: 800-221-2557
http://www.imcusa.org

MARKETING RESEARCH ANALYSTS

QUICK FACTS

School Subjects Business Mathematics	**Certification or Licensing** None available
Personal Skills Following instructions Technical/scientific	**Outlook** Faster than the average
Work Environment Primarily indoors Primarily one location	**DOT** 050
Minimum Education Level Bachelor's degree	**GOE** 11.06.03
Salary Range $28,500 to $53,450 to $96,980+	**NOC** N/A
	O*NET-SOC 19-3021.00

OVERVIEW

Marketing research analysts collect, analyze, and interpret data to determine potential demand for a product or service. By examining the buying habits, wants, needs, and preferences of consumers, research analysts are able to recommend ways to improve products, increase sales, and expand customer bases.

HISTORY

Knowing what customers want and what prices they are willing to pay have always been concerns of manufacturers and producers of goods and services. As industries have grown and competition for consumers of manufactured goods has increased, businesses have turned to marketing research as a way to measure public opinion and assess customer preferences.

Marketing research formally emerged in Germany in the 1920s and in Sweden and France in the 1930s. In the United States, emphasis on marketing research began after World War II. With a desire to study potential markets and gain new customers, U.S. firms hired marketing research specialists, professionals who were able to use statistics and refine research techniques to help companies reach their marketing goals. By the 1980s, research analysts could be found even in a variety of Communist countries, where the quantity of consumer goods being produced was rapidly increasing.

Today, the marketing research analyst is a vital part of the marketing team. By conducting studies and analyzing data, research professionals help companies address specific marketing issues and concerns.

THE JOB

Marketing researchers collect and analyze all kinds of information to help companies improve their products, establish or modify sales and distribution policies, and make decisions regarding future plans and directions. In addition, research analysts are responsible for monitoring both in-house studies and off-site research, interpreting results, providing explanations of compiled data, and developing research tools.

One area of marketing research focuses on company products and services. In order to determine consumer likes and dislikes, research analysts collect data on brand names, trademarks, product design, and packaging for existing products, items being test-marketed, and those in experimental stages. Analysts also study competing products and services that are already on the market to help managers and strategic planners develop new products and create appropriate advertising campaigns.

In the sales methods and policy area of marketing research, analysts examine firms' sales records and conduct a variety of sales-related studies. For example, information on sales in various geographical areas is analyzed and compared to previous sales figures, changes in population, and total and seasonal sales volume. By analyzing this data, marketing researchers can identify peak sales periods and recommend ways to target new customers. Such information helps marketers plan future sales campaigns and establish sales quotas and commissions.

Advertising research is closely related to sales research. Studies on the effectiveness of advertising in different parts of the country are conducted and compared to sales records. This research is helpful in planning future advertising campaigns and in selecting the appropriate media to use.

Marketing research that focuses on consumer demand and preferences solicits opinions of the people who use the products or services being considered. In addition to actually conducting opinion studies, marketing researchers often design the ways to obtain the information. They write scripts for telephone interviews, develop direct-mail questionnaires and field surveys, and design focus group programs.

Through one or a combination of these studies, market researchers are able to gather information on consumer reaction to the need for and style, design, price, and use of a product. The studies attempt to reveal who uses various products or services, identify potential customers, or get suggestions for product or service improvement. This information is helpful for forecasting sales, planning design modifications, and determining changes in features.

Once information has been gathered, marketing researchers analyze the findings. They then detail their findings and recommendations in a written report and often orally present them to management.

A number of professionals compose the marketing research team. The *project supervisor* is responsible for overseeing a study from beginning to end. The *statistician* determines the sample size—the number of people to be surveyed—and compares the number of responses. The project supervisor or statistician, in conjunction with other specialists (such as *demographers* and *psychologists*), often determines the number of interviews to be conducted as well as their locations. *Field interviewers* survey people in various public places, such as shopping malls, office complexes, and popular attractions. *Telemarketers* gather information by placing calls to current or potential customers, to people listed in telephone books, or to those who appear on specialized lists obtained from list houses. Once questionnaires come in from the field, *tabulators* and *coders* examine the data, count the answers, code non-categorical answers, and tally the primary counts. The marketing research analyst then analyzes the returns, writes up the final report, and makes recommendations to the client or to management.

Marketing research analysts must be thoroughly familiar with research techniques and procedures. Sometimes the research problem is clearly defined, and information can be gathered readily. Other times, company executives may know only that a problem exists as evidenced by a decline in sales. In these cases, the market research analyst is expected to collect the facts that will aid in revealing and resolving the problem.

Top Economics Graduate Programs by Specialty

U.S. News & World Report prepares annual ranking lists for graduate school programs. The following lists show the top ranked schools for various economics specialties.

Microeconomics

1. Massachusetts Institute of Technology
   http://econ-www.mit.edu
2. Harvard University (Mass.)
   http://www.economics.harvard.edu
3. Stanford University (Calif.)
   http://www-econ.stanford.edu
4. Princeton University (N.J.)
   http://www.econ.princeton.edu
5. University of Chicago
   http://economics.uchicago.edu
6. Yale University (Conn.)
   http://www.econ.yale.edu
7. Northwestern University (Ill.)
   http://www.econ.northwestern.edu
8. University of California-Berkeley
   http://emlab.berkeley.edu/econ
9. University of Pennsylvania
   http://www.econ.upenn.edu
10. California Institute of Technology
    http://www.hss.caltech.edu/ss/phd/overview

Macroeconomics

1. University of Chicago
   http://economics.uchicago.edu
2. Harvard University (Mass.)
   http://www.economics.harvard.edu
3. Massachusetts Institute of Technology
   http://econ-www.mit.edu
4. Stanford University (Calif.)
   http://www-econ.stanford.edu

(continues)

Top Economics Graduate Programs by Specialty

(continued)

5. Princeton University (N.J.)
   http://www.econ.princeton.edu
6. University of Minnesota-Twin Cities
   http://www.econ.umn.edu
7. University of California-Berkeley
   http://emlab.berkeley.edu/econ
8. University of Rochester
   http://www.econ.rochester.edu
9. Northwestern University (Ill.)
   http://www.econ.northwestern.edu
10. Yale University (Conn.)
    http://www.econ.yale.edu

International Economics

1. Princeton University (N.J.)
   http://www.econ.princeton.edu
2. Harvard University (Mass.)
   http://www.economics.harvard.edu
3. Massachusetts Institute of Technology
   http://econ-www.mit.edu
4. Columbia University (N.Y.)
   http://www.columbia.edu/cu/economics
5. University of California-Berkeley
   http://emlab.berkeley.edu/econ
6. Stanford University (Calif.)
   http://www-econ.stanford.edu
7. University of California-Los Angeles
   http://econweb.sscnet.ucla.edu
8. University of Michigan-Ann Arbor
   http://www.econ.lsa.umich.edu
9. Yale University (Conn.)
   http://www.econ.yale.edu
10. University of Pennsylvania
    http://www.econ.upenn.edu

(continues)

Top Economics Graduate Programs by Specialty

(continued)

Public Finance

1. Harvard University (MA)
   http://www.economics.harvard.edu
2. Massachusetts Institute of Technology
   http://econ-www.mit.edu
3. Stanford University (CA)
   http://www-econ.stanford.edu
4. Princeton University (NJ)
   http://www.econ.princeton.edu
5. University of Chicago
   http://economics.uchicago.edu
6. University of California-Berkeley
   http://emlab.berkeley.edu/econ
7. University of Michigan-Ann Arbor
   http://www.econ.lsa.umich.edu
8. University of Wisconsin-Madison
   http://www.ssc.wisc.edu/econ
9. University of Pennsylvania
   http://www.econ.upenn.edu
10. Northwestern University (IL)
    http://www.econ.northwestern.edu

Industrial Organization

1. Massachusetts Institute of Technology
   http://econ-www.mit.edu
2. Northwestern University (Ill.)
   http://www.econ.northwestern.edu
3. Stanford University (Calif.)
   http://www-econ.stanford.edu
4. Harvard University (Mass.)
   http://www.economics.harvard.edu
5. University of California-Berkeley
   http://emlab.berkeley.edu/econ

(continues)

Top Economics Graduate Programs by Specialty

(continued)

6. University of Chicago
http://economics.uchicago.edu
7. Princeton University (N.J.)
http://www.econ.princeton.edu
8. Yale University (Conn.)
http://www.econ.yale.edu
9. University of Wisconsin-Madison
http://www.ssc.wisc.edu/econ
10. University of Pennsylvania
http://www.econ.upenn.edu

Source: *U.S. News & World Report* (ranked in 2001)

REQUIREMENTS

High School

Most employers require their marketing research analysts to hold at least a bachelor's degree, so a college preparatory program is advised. Classes in English, marketing, mathematics, psychology, and sociology are particularly important. Courses in computing are especially useful, since a great deal of tabulation and statistical analysis is required in the marketing research field.

Postsecondary Training

A bachelor's degree is essential for careers in marketing research. Majors in marketing, business administration, statistics, computer science, or economics provide a good background for most types of research positions. In addition, course work in sociology and psychology is helpful for those who are leaning toward consumer demand and opinion research. Since quantitative skills are important in various types of industrial or analytic research, students interested in these areas should take statistics, econometrics, survey design, sampling theory, and other mathematics courses.

Many employers prefer that a marketing research analyst hold a master's degree as well as a bachelor's degree. A master's of business administration, for example, is frequently required on projects calling for complex statistical and business analysis. Graduate work at the doctorate level is not necessary for most positions, but it is highly desirable for those who plan to become involved in advanced research studies.

Other Requirements

To work in this career, you should be intelligent, detail oriented, and accurate; have the ability to work easily with words and numbers; and be particularly interested in solving problems through data collection and analysis. In addition, you must be patient and persistent, since long hours are often required when working on complex studies.

As part of the market research team, you must be able to work well with others and have an interest in people. The ability to communicate, both orally and in writing, is also important, since you will be responsible for writing up detailed reports on the findings in various studies and presenting recommendations to management.

EXPLORING

You can find many opportunities in high school to learn more about the necessary skills for the field of marketing research. For example, experiments in science, problems in student government, committee work, and other school activities provide exposure to situations similar to those encountered by marketing research analysts.

You can also seek part-time employment as a survey interviewer at local marketing research firms. Gathering field data for consumer surveys offers valuable experience through actual contact with both the public and marketing research supervisors. In addition, many companies seek a variety of other employees to code, tabulate, and edit surveys; monitor telephone interviews; and validate the information entered on written questionnaires. You can search for job listings in local newspapers and on the Web or apply directly to research organizations.

EMPLOYERS

Marketing research analysts are employed by large corporations, industrial firms, advertising agencies, data collection businesses, and private research organizations that handle local surveys for companies on a contract basis. While many marketing research organizations offer a broad range of services, some firms subcontract parts of an overall project out to specialized companies. For example, one research firm may concentrate on product interviews, while another might focus on measuring the effectiveness of product advertising. Similarly, some marketing analysts specialize in one industry or area. For example, agricultural marketing specialists prepare sales forecasts for food businesses, which use the information in their advertising and sales programs.

Although many smaller firms located all across the country outsource studies to marketing research firms, these research firms, along with most large corporations that employ marketing research analysts, are located in such big cities as New York or Chicago. Private industry employs about 90 percent of salaried marketing research analysts, but opportunities also exist in government and academia, as well as at hospitals, public libraries, and a variety of other types of organizations.

STARTING OUT

Students with a graduate degree in marketing research and experience in quantitative techniques have the best chances of landing jobs as marketing research analysts. Since a bachelor's degree in marketing or business is usually not sufficient to obtain such a position, many employees without postgraduate degrees start out as research assistants, trainees, interviewers, or questionnaire editors. In such positions, those aspiring to the job of research analyst can gain valuable experience conducting interviews, analyzing data, and writing reports.

Use your college placement office, the Web, and help wanted sections of local newspapers to look for job leads. Another way to get into the marketing research field is through personal and professional contacts. Names and telephone numbers of potential employers may come from professors, friends, or relatives. Finally, students who have participated in internships or have held marketing research-related jobs on a part-time basis while in school or during the summer may be able to obtain employment at these firms or at similar organizations.

ADVANCEMENT

Most marketing research professionals begin as junior analysts or research assistants. In these positions, they help in preparing questionnaires and related materials, training survey interviewers, and tabulating and coding survey results. After gaining sufficient experience in these and other aspects of research project development, employees are often assigned their own research projects, which usually involve supervisory and planning responsibilities. A typical promotion path for those climbing the company ladder might be from assistant researcher to marketing research analyst to assistant manager and then to manager of a branch office for a large private research firm. From there, some professionals become market research executives or research directors for industrial or business firms.

Since marketing research analysts learn about all aspects of marketing on the job, some advance by moving to positions in other departments, such as advertising or sales. Depending on the interests and experience of marketing professionals, other areas of employment to which they can advance include data processing, teaching at the university level, statistics, economics, and industrial research and development.

In general, few employees go from starting positions to executive jobs at one company. Advancement often requires changing employers. Therefore, marketing research analysts who want to move up the ranks frequently go from one company to another, sometimes many times during their careers.

EARNINGS

Beginning salaries in marketing research depend on the qualifications of the employee, the nature of the position, and the size of the firm. Interviewers, coders, tabulators, editors, and a variety of other employees usually get paid by the hour and may start at $6 or more per hour. The Bureau of Labor Statistics reported that in 2001, median annual earnings of market research analysts were $53,450. The middle 50 percent earned between $38,280 and $74,460. Salaries ranged from less than $28,500 to more than $96,980. Experienced analysts working in supervisory positions at large firms can have even higher earnings. Market research directors earn up to $200,000.

Because most marketing research workers are employed by business or industrial firms, they receive fringe benefit packages that include health and life insurance, pension plans, and paid vacation and sick leave.

WORK ENVIRONMENT

Marketing research analysts usually work a 40-hour week. Occasionally, overtime is necessary in order to meet project deadlines. Although they frequently interact with a variety of marketing research team members, analysts also do a lot of independent work, analyzing data, writing reports, and preparing statistical charts.

While most marketing research analysts work in offices located at the firm's main headquarters, those who supervise interviewers may go into the field to oversee work. Regular travel is required of many market research analysts.

OUTLOOK

The U.S. Department of Labor predicts that employment for marketing research analysts will grow faster than the average through the next decade. Increasing competition among producers of consumer goods and services and industrial products, combined with a growing awareness of the value of marketing research data, will contribute to opportunities in the field. Opportunities will be best for those with graduate degrees who seek employment in marketing research firms, financial services organizations, health care institutions, advertising firms, manufacturing firms producing consumer goods, and insurance companies.

While many new graduates are attracted to the field, creating a competitive situation, the best jobs and the highest pay will go to those individuals who hold a master's degree or doctorate in marketing research, statistics, economics, or computer science.

FOR MORE INFORMATION

For information on college chapters, internship opportunities, and financial aid opportunities, contact

American Advertising Federation
1101 Vermont Avenue, NW, Suite 500
Washington, DC 20005-6306
Tel: 202-898-0089
Email: aaf@aaf.org
http://www.aaf.org

For career resources and job listings, contact or check out the following website:

American Marketing Association
311 South Wacker Drive, Suite 5800
Chicago, IL 60606
Tel: 800-262-1150
Email: info@ama.org
http://www.marketingpower.com

POLITICAL SCIENTISTS

QUICK FACTS

School Subjects Government Sociology	**Certification or Licensing** None available
Personal Skills Communication/ideas Helping/teaching	**Outlook** About as fast as the average
Work Environment Primarily indoors Primarily one location	**DOT** 051
Minimum Education Level Doctorate degree	**GOE** 11.03.02
Salary Range $21,900 to $81,040 to $100,000+	**NOC** 4169
	O*NET-SOC 19-3094.00, 25-1065.00

OVERVIEW

Political scientists study the structure and theory of government, usually as part of an academic faculty. They constantly seek both theoretical and practical solutions to political problems. They divide their responsibilities between teaching and researching. After compiling facts, statistics, and other research, they present their analyses in reports, lectures, and journal articles.

HISTORY

Political science is the oldest of the social sciences and is currently one of the most popular subjects of undergraduate study. The ideas of many early political scientists still influence current political theories. Machiavelli, the 16th-century Italian statesman and philosopher, believed that politics and morality are two entirely different spheres of human activity and that they should be governed by different standards and different laws. In the 17th century, Thomas Hobbes thought of government as a police force that prevented people from plundering their neighbors. John Locke was a 17th-century Englishman from whom we get the philosophy of "the greatest good for the greatest number." Some people call him the originator of "beneficent paternalism," which means that the state or ruler acts as a kindly leader to citizens, deciding what is best for them, then seeing that the "best" is put into effect, whether the citizens like it or not.

Common among theorists today is the assumption that politics is a process, the constant interaction of individuals and groups in activities that are directly or indirectly related to government. By 1945, political science in the United States was much more than the concern for institutions, law, formal structures of public government, procedures, and rules. It had expanded to include the dynamics of public governance. Instead of studying the rules of administrative procedure in a political group, for example, political scientists had begun to study the actual bureaucratic processes at work within the group. This signified the start of what would become systems theory in political science.

THE JOB

While many government careers involve taking action that directly impacts political policy, political scientists study and discuss the results of these actions. "You can look into just about anything that interests you," says Chris Mooney, an associate professor and director of graduate studies for the political science department of West Virginia University, "but you have to be able to argue that it's relevant to some basic theory in political science."

Political scientists may choose to research political lyrics in rock music, or study how teenagers form their political ideas. They may research the history of women in politics, the role of religion in politics, and the political histories of other countries. In addition to his teaching responsibilities, Mooney is currently researching the reasons why some states have the death penalty. Many political scientists specialize in one area of study, such as public administration, history of political ideas, political parties, public law, American government, or international relations.

About 80 percent of all political scientists are employed as college and university professors. Depending on the institution for which they work, political scientists divide their time between teaching and researching. Mooney estimates that 45 percent of his time is devoted to teaching, 45 percent to research, and the remaining time is for service to the university, such as committee work. Though he works for a research-oriented university, "teaching drives everything," he says.

In addition to teaching and researching, political scientists write books and articles based on their studies. A number of political science associations publish journals, and there are small presses devoted to publishing political theory. Mooney has published two books, and many scholarly articles in such journals as *Policy Studies Journal, Health Economics*, and the *American Journal of Political Science*. His area of study is behavioral political science. For his current study of the death penalty, he is compiling economic, social, and demographic facts. This data is then fed into the computer, and Mooney attempts to draw conclusions. Sometimes graduate students are involved with the research; they assist with the collection of data, computer work, and copy editing.

In researching policy issues, political scientists use a variety of different methods. They work with historians, economists, policy analysts, demographers, and statisticians. The Internet has become a very important resource tool for political scientists. The federal government has been dedicated to expanding the World Wide Web, including making available full text of legislation, recent Supreme Court decisions, and access to the Library of Congress. Political scientists also use the data found in yearbooks and almanacs, material from encyclopedias, clippings from periodicals or bound volumes of magazines or journals. They refer to law books, to statutes, to records of court cases, to the *Congressional Record*, and to other legislative records. They consult census records, historical documents, personal documents such as diaries and letters, and statistics from public opinion polls. They use libraries and archives to locate rare and old documents and records. For other information, political scientists use the "participant observer" method of research. In this method, they become part of a group and participate in its proceedings, while carefully observing interaction. They may also submit questionnaires. Questions will be carefully worded to elicit the facts needed, and the questionnaire will be administered to a selected sample of people.

When conducting research, political scientists must avoid letting their own biases distort the way in which they interpret the gathered facts. Then, they must compare their findings and analyses with those of others who have conducted similar investigations. Finally, they must present the data in an objective fashion, even though the findings may not reveal the kinds of facts they anticipated.

Those political scientists who are not employed as teachers work for labor unions, political organizations, or political interest groups. Political scientists working for government may study organizations ranging in scope from the United Nations to local city councils. They may study the politics of a large city like New York or a small town in the Midwest. Their research findings may be used by a city's mayor and city council to set public policy concerning waste management or by an organization, such as the National Organization for Women, to decide where to focus efforts on increasing the participation of women in local politics. Political scientists who work for the U.S. Department of State in either this country or in the foreign service use their analyses of political structures to make recommendations to the U.S. government concerning foreign policy.

Political scientists may also be employed by individual members of Congress. In this capacity, they might study government programs concerned with low-income housing and make recommendations to help the member of Congress write new legislation. Businesses and industries also hire political scientists to conduct polls on political issues that affect their operations. A tobacco company might want to know, for example, how the legislation restricting advertising by tobacco companies affects the buying habits of consumers of tobacco products.

REQUIREMENTS

High School

Take courses in government, American history, and civics to gain insight into politics. Math is also important because, as a political scientist, you'll be evaluating statistics, demographics, and other numerical data. English and composition classes will help you develop the writing and communication skills you'll need for teaching, publishing, and presenting papers. Take a journalism course and work for your high school newspaper to develop research, writing, and editing skills. Join a speech and debate team to gain experience researching current events, analyzing data, and presenting the information to others.

Postsecondary Training

Though you'll be able to find some government jobs with a bachelor's degree in political science, you won't be able to pursue work in major academic institutions without a doctorate.

The American Political Science Association (APSA) publishes directories of undergraduate and graduate political science programs. An undergraduate program requires general courses in English, economics, statistics, and history, as well as courses in American politics, international politics, and political theory. Look for a school with a good internship program that can involve you with the U.S. Congress or state legislature. *U.S. News & World Report* publishes rankings of graduate schools. In 2001, Harvard was deemed the top-ranked political science department. Stanford, University of California (Berkeley), and University of Michigan (Ann Arbor) all tied for second place, and Yale came in fifth place.

Your graduate study will include courses in political parties, public opinion, comparative political behavior, and foreign policy design. You'll also assist professors with research, attend conferences, write articles, and teach undergraduate courses.

Other Requirements

Because you'll be compiling information from a number of different sources, you must be well-organized. You should also enjoy reading and possess a curiosity about world politics. "You have to really enjoy school," Chris Mooney says, "but it should all be fairly fascinating. You'll be studying and telling people about what you're studying." People skills are important, as you'll be working closely with students and other political scientists.

EXPLORING

Write to college political science departments for information about their programs. You can learn a lot about the work of a political scientist by looking at college course lists and faculty bios. Political science departments also have Web pages with information, and links to the curricula vitae (C.V.) of faculty. A C.V. is an extensive resume including lists of publications, conferences attended, and other professional experience. A C.V. can give you an idea of a political scientist's career and education path.

Contact the office of your state's senator or representative in the U.S. Congress about applying to work as a page. Available to students at least 16 years old, and highly competitive, page positions allow students to serve members of Congress, running messages across Capitol Hill in Washington, D.C. This experience would be very valuable to you in learning about the workings of government.

EMPLOYERS

Political science is a popular major among undergraduates, so practically every college and university has a political science department. Political scientists find work at public and private universities, and at community colleges. They teach in undergraduate, master's, and doctorate programs. Teaching jobs at doctoral institutions are usually better paying and more prestigious. The most sought-after positions are those that offer tenure.

STARTING OUT

"Go to the best school you can," Chris Mooney advises, "and focus on getting into a good graduate school." Most graduate schools accept a very limited number of applicants every semester, so there's a lot of competition for admittance into some of the top programs. Applicants are admitted on the basis of grade point averages, test scores, internships performed, awards received, and other achievements.

Once you're in graduate school, you'll begin to perform the work you'll be doing in your career. You'll teach undergraduate classes, attend conferences, present papers, and submit articles to political science journals. Your success as a graduate student will help you in your job search. After completing a graduate program, you'll teach as an adjunct professor or visiting professor at various schools until you can find a permanent tenure-track position.

Membership in APSA and other political science associations entitles you to job placement assistance. APSA can also direct you to a number of fellowship and grant opportunities. Michigan State University posts job openings on its H-Net (Job Guide for the Humanities and Social Sciences) Web page at http://www.matrix.msu.edu/jobs. Due to the heavy competition for these jobs, you'll need an impressive C.V., including a list of publications in respected political science journals, a list of conferences attended, and good references attesting to your teaching skills.

ADVANCEMENT

In a tenure-track position, political scientists work their way up through the ranks from assistant professor, to associate professor, to full professor. They will probably have to work a few years in temporary, or visiting, faculty positions before they can join the permanent faculty of a political science department. They can then expect to spend approximately seven years working toward tenure. Tenure provides political scientists job security and prominence within their department, and is awarded on the basis of publications, research performed, student evaluations, and teaching experience.

EARNINGS

The *Occupational Outlook Handbook* reports that median annual earnings for social scientists in 2000 were $81,040. Starting federal government salaries for political scientists with a bachelor's degree and no experience were $21,900 or $27,200, depending on academic record, in 2001. Those with a master's degree earned an average starting salary of $33,300, while those with a Ph.D. averaged $40,200.

The American Association of University Professors (AAUP) conducts an annual survey of the salaries of college professors. With the 2001–02 survey, the AAUP found that full professors (with varying educational backgrounds) received an average of $83,282 a year, and associate professors received an average of $59,496 annually.

WORK ENVIRONMENT

Political scientists who work as tenured faculty members enjoy pleasant surroundings. Depending on the size of the department, they will have their own office and be provided with a computer, Internet access, and research assistants. With good teaching skills, they will earn the respect of their students and colleagues. Political science professors are also well-respected in their communities.

Political science teachers work a fairly flexible schedule, teaching two or three courses a semester. The rest of their 40- to-50-hour workweek will be spent meeting individually with students, conducting research, writing, and serving on committees. Some travel may be required, as teachers attend a few conferences a year on behalf of their department, or as they take short-term assignments at other institutions. Teachers may teach some summer courses, or have the summer off. They will also have several days off between semesters.

OUTLOOK

Overall employment of social scientists is expected to grow about as fast as the average over the next several years, according to the *Occupational Outlook Handbook.*

The survival of political science departments depends on continued community and government support of education. The funding of humanities and social science programs is often threatened, resulting in budget cuts and hiring freezes. This makes for heavy competition for the few graduate assistantships and new faculty positions available. Also, there's not a great deal of mobility within the field; professors who achieve tenure generally stay in their positions until retirement.

The pay inequity between male and female professors is of some concern. In the workplace in general, women are paid less than men, but this inequity is even greater in the field of academics. The AAUP is fighting to correct this, and female professors are becoming more cautious when choosing tenure-track positions.

More and more professors are using computers and the Internet, not just in research, but in conducting their classes. According to an annual survey conducted by the Campus Computing Project, computers and CD-ROMs are used increasingly in the lecture hall, and many professors use Web pages to post class materials and other resources.

FOR MORE INFORMATION

For more information on a political science career, contact

American Political Science Association
1527 New Hampshire Avenue, NW
Washington, DC 20036-1206
Tel: 202-483-2512
Email: apsa@apsanet.org
http://www.apsanet.org

For employment opportunities, mail resume and cover letters to

U.S. House of Representatives
Office of Human Resources
175 Ford House Office Building
Washington, DC 20515-6610
Tel: 202-225-2450
http://www.house.gov

U.S. Senate Placement Office
Room SH-142B
Washington, DC 20510
Tel: 202-224-9167
http://www.senate.gov

PRESS SECRETARIES AND POLITICAL CONSULTANTS

QUICK FACTS

School Subjects	Certification or Licensing
English Government Journalism	None available
Personal Skills Communication/ideas Leadership/management	**Outlook** About as fast as the average
Work Environment Primarily indoors One location with some travel	**DOT** N/A **GOE** N/A
Minimum Education Level Bachelor's degree	**NOC** N/A **O*NET-SOC** N/A
Salary Range $23,930 to $41,010 to $200,000+	

OVERVIEW

Press secretaries, political consultants, and other media relations professionals help politicians promote themselves and their issues among voters. They advise politicians on how to address the media. Sometimes called "spin doctors," these professionals use the media to either change or strengthen public opinion. Press secretaries work for candidates and elected officials, while political consultants work with firms, contracting their services to politicians. The majority of press secretaries and political consultants work in Washington, D.C.; others work all across the country, involved with local and state government officials and candidates.

HISTORY

The practice of using the media for political purposes is nearly as old as the U.S. government itself. The news media developed alongside the political parties, and early newspapers served as a battleground for the Federalists and the Republicans. The first media moguls of the late 1800s often saw their newspapers as podiums from which to promote themselves. George Hearst bought the *San Francisco Examiner* in 1885 for the sole purpose of helping him campaign for Congress.

The latter half of the 20th century saw the introduction of whole other forms of media, which were quickly exploited by politicians seeking offices. Many historians mark the Kennedy-Nixon debate of 1960 as the moment when television coverage first became a key factor in the election process. Those who read of the debate in the next day's newspapers were under the impression that Nixon had easily won, but it was Kennedy's composure and appeal on camera that made the most powerful impression. Negative campaigning first showed its powerful influence in 1964, when Democratic presidential candidate Lyndon Johnson ran ads featuring a girl picking a flower while a nuclear bomb exploded in the background, which was a commentary on Republican candidate Barry Goldwater's advocacy of strong military action in Vietnam.

Bill Clinton was probably the first president to benefit from the art of "spin," as his press secretaries and political managers were actively involved in dealing with his scandals and keeping his approval ratings high among the public. James Carville and George Stephanopoulos, working for Clinton's 1992 campaign, had the task of playing up Clinton's strengths as an intelligent, gifted politician, while downplaying his questionable moral background. Their efforts were portrayed in the documentary *The War Room*, and their success earned them national renown as "spin doctors."

THE JOB

If you were to manage a political campaign, how would you go about publicizing the candidate to the largest number of voters? You'd use TV, of course. The absolute need for TV and radio spots during a campaign is what makes running for political office so expensive. This is also the reason many politicians hire professionals with an understanding of media relations to help them get elected. Once elected, a politician continues to rely on media relations experts, such as press secretaries, political consultants, and political managers, to use the media to portray the politician in the best light. In recent years, such words as "spin," "leak," and "sound bite" have entered the daily vocabulary of news and politics to describe elements of political coverage in the media.

Political consultants usually work independently, or as members of consulting firms, and contract with individuals. Political consultants are involved in producing radio and TV ads, writing campaign plans, and developing themes for these campaigns. A theme may focus on a specific issue or on the differences between the client and the opponent. Their client may be new to the political arena or someone established looking to maintain an office. They conduct polls and surveys to gauge public opinion and to identify their client's biggest competition. Political consultants advise their clients in the best ways to use the media. In addition to TV and radio, the Internet has proven to be invaluable to politicians. Consultants launch campaign websites and also chase down rumors that spread across the Internet. A consultant may be hired for an entire campaign, to produce one ad, or to come up with a sound bite (or catchy quote) for the media.

Though voters across the country complain about negative campaigning, or "mudslinging," such campaigns have proven effective. In his 1988 presidential campaign, George H. Bush ran TV ads featuring the now notorious Willie Horton, a convict who was released from prison only to commit another crime. The ad was intended to draw attention to what Bush considered his opponent's soft approach to crime. It proved very effective in undermining the campaign of Michael Dukakis and putting him on the defensive. Many consultants believe they must focus on a few specific issues in a campaign, emphasizing their client's strengths as well as the opponent's weaknesses.

Press secretaries serve on the congressional staffs of senators and representatives and on the staffs of governors and mayors. The president also has a press secretary. Press secretaries and their assistants write press releases and opinion pieces to publicize the efforts of the government officials for whom they work. They also help prepare speeches and prepare their employers for press conferences and interviews. They maintain websites, posting press releases and the results of press conferences.

Media relations experts are often called *spin doctors* because of their ability to manipulate the media or put a good spin on a news story to best suit the purposes of their clients. Corporations also rely on spin for positive media coverage. Media relations experts are often called upon during a political scandal, or after corporate blunders, for damage control. Using the newspapers and radio and TV broadcasts, spin doctors attempt to downplay public relations disasters, helping politicians and corporations save face. In highly sensitive situations, they must answer questions selectively and carefully, and they may even be involved in secretly releasing, or leaking, information to the press. Because of these manipulations, media relations professionals are often disrespected. They're sometimes viewed as people who conceal facts and present lies, prey on the emotions of voters, or even represent companies responsible for illegal practices. However, many political consultants and media representatives are responsible for bringing public attention to important issues and good political candidates. They also help organizations and nonprofit groups advocate for legislative issues and help develop support for school funding, environmental concerns, and other community needs.

REQUIREMENTS

High School

English composition, drama, and speech classes will help you develop good communication skills, while government, history, and civics classes will teach you about the structure of local, state, and federal government. Take math, economics, and accounting courses to prepare for poll taking and for analyzing statistics and demographics.

While in high school, work with your school newspaper, radio station, or TV station. This will help you recognize how important reporters, editors, and producers are in putting together newspapers and shaping news segments. You should also consider joining your school's speech and debate team to gain experience in research and in persuasive argument.

Postsecondary Training

Most people in media relations have bachelor's degrees, and some also hold master's degrees, doctorates, and law degrees. As an undergraduate, you should enroll in a four-year college and pursue a well-rounded education. Press secretaries and political consultants need a good understanding of the history and culture of the United States and foreign countries. Some of the majors you should consider as an undergraduate are journalism, political science, English, marketing, and economics. You should take courses in government, psychology, statistics, history of western civilization, and a foreign language.

You might then choose to pursue a graduate degree in journalism, political science, public administration, or international relations.

Seek a college with a good internship program. You might also pursue internships with local and state officials and your congressional members in the Senate and House of Representatives. Journalism internships will involve you with local and national publications, or the news departments of radio and TV stations.

Other Requirements

In this career, you need to be very organized and capable of juggling many different tasks, from quickly writing ads and press releases to developing budgets and expense accounts. You need good problem-solving skills and some imagination when putting a positive spin on negative issues. Good people skills are important so that you can develop contacts within government and the media. You should feel comfortable with public speaking, leading press conferences, and speaking on behalf of your employers and clients. You should also enjoy competition. You can't be intimidated by people in power or by journalists questioning the issues addressed in your campaigns.

EXPLORING

Get involved with your school government as well as with committees and clubs that have officers and elections. You can also become involved in local, state, and federal elections by volunteering for campaigns; though you may just be making phone calls and putting up signs, you may also have the opportunity to write press releases and schedule press conferences and interviews, and you will see firsthand how a campaign operates.

Working for your school newspaper will help you learn about conducting research, interviews, and opinion polls, which all play a part in managing media relations. You may be able to get a part-time job or an internship with your city's newspaper or broadcast news station, where you will gain experience with election coverage and political advertising. Visit the websites of U.S. Congress members. Many sites feature lists of recent press releases, which will give you a sense of how a press office publicizes the efforts and actions of Congress members. Read some of the many books examining recent political campaigns and scandals, and read magazines like *Harper's* (http://www.harpers.org), *The Atlantic* (http://www.theatlantic.com), and the online magazine *salon.com* (http://www.salonmag.com) for political commentary.

EMPLOYERS

Though a majority of press secretaries and political consultants work in Washington, D.C., others work in state capitals and major cities all across the country. Press secretaries work for local, state, and federal government officials. They also find work with public relations agencies, and the press offices of large corporations. Celebrities, and others in the public eye also hire press agents to help them control rumors and publicity.

Political consultants are generally self-employed, or work for consulting firms that specialize in media relations. They contract with politicians, corporations, nonprofit groups, and trade and professional associations. They participate in the campaigns of mayors, governors, and Congress members as well as in the political campaigns of other countries.

STARTING OUT

Media relations jobs are not advertised, and there is no predetermined path to success. It is recommended that you make connections with people in both politics and the media. Volunteer for political campaigns, and also advocate for public policy issues of interest to you. You can make good connections, and gain valuable experience, working or interning in the offices of your state capital. You might also try for an internship with one of your state's members of Congress; contact their offices in Washington, D.C., for internship applications. If you're more interested in the writing and producing aspects of the career, work for local newspapers or the broadcast news media, or work as a producer for a television production crew or for an ad agency that specializes in political campaigns. A political consulting firm may hire assistants for writing and for commercial production. Whereas some people pursue the career directly by working in the press offices of political candidates, others find their way into political consulting after having worked as lawyers, lobbyists, or journalists.

ADVANCEMENT

A press secretary who has worked closely with a successful government official may advance into a higher staff position, like chief of staff or legislative director. Political consultants, after winning many elections and establishing credentials, will begin to take on more prominent clients and major campaigns. Network TV, cable, and radio news departments also hire successful media relations experts to serve as political analysts on the air. Some consultants also write columns for newspapers and syndicates and publish books about their insights into politics.

EARNINGS

According to the U.S. Bureau of Labor Statistics, public relations specialists (which includes press secretaries and political consultants) had median annual earnings of $41,010 in 2001, with salaries ranging from less than $23,930 to more than $72,910. In 2000, median earnings for those who worked in local government were $40,760, and for those in state government, $39,560.

According to the Congressional Management Foundation (CMF), a consulting firm in Washington, D.C., press secretaries working in the U.S. House of Representatives earned less than their counterparts in the Senate. The CMF found that the average pay of a House press secretary was $45,301, while those employed by the Senate earned an average of $116,573. This pay differential is probably even greater, because the CMF info for the Senate is from 1999, while the House data is from 2000.

The incomes of political consultants vary greatly. Someone contracting with local candidates, or with state organizations and associations, may make around $40,000 a year; someone consulting with high-profile candidates may earn hundreds of thousands of dollars a year. A study by the Pew Research Center showed that more than half of its respondents had family incomes of more than $150,000 a year; one-third reported annual incomes of more than $200,000.

WORK ENVIRONMENT

Representing politicians can be thankless work. Press secretaries may have to speak to the press about sensitive, volatile issues and deal directly with the frustrations of journalists unable to get the answers they want. When working for prominent politicians, they may become the subject of personal attacks.

Despite these potential conflicts, the work can be exciting and fast-paced. Press secretaries and political consultants see the results of their efforts in the newspapers and on television, and they have the satisfaction of influencing voters and public opinion. If working on a campaign as a consultant, their hours will be long and stressful. In some cases, they'll have to scrap unproductive media ads and start from scratch with only hours to write, produce, and place new commercials. They'll also have to be available to their clients around the clock.

OUTLOOK

Employment for press secretaries and political consultants is expected to grow about as fast as the average. Consultants and media representatives will become increasingly important to candidates and elected officials. Television ads and Internet campaigns have become almost necessary to reach the public. The work of press secretaries will expand as more news networks and news magazines more closely follow the decisions and actions of government officials.

The Pew Research Center, which surveys public opinion on political issues, has found that most Americans are concerned about negative campaigning, while most political consultants see nothing wrong with using negative tactics in advertising. Despite how the general public may feel about negative campaigning, it remains a very effective tool for consultants. In some local elections, candidates may mutually agree to avoid the mudslinging, but the use of negative ads in general is likely to increase.

This negative campaigning may be affected somewhat by developing technology. Voters are now able to access more information about candidates and issues via the Internet. Also, the increase in the number of channels available to cable TV watchers makes it more difficult for candidates to advertise to a general audience. However, the greater number of outlets for media products will employ more writers, TV producers, and Web designers in the process of creating a political campaign.

FOR MORE INFORMATION

This organization provides professional guidance, assistance, and education to members and maintains a code of ethics.

American Association of Political Consultants
600 Pennsylvania Avenue, SE, Suite 330
Washington, DC 20003
Tel: 202-544-9815
Email: info@theaapc.org
http://www.theaapc.org

For general information about careers in broadcast media, contact

National Association of Broadcasters
1771 N Street, NW
Washington, DC 20036
Tel: 202-429-5300
Email: nab@nab.org
http://www.nab.org

Visit the websites of the House and the Senate for press releases and links to sites for individual members of Congress. To write to your state representatives, contact

Office of Senator (Name)
United States Senate
Washington, DC 20510
http://www.senate.gov

Office of Congressperson (Name)
U.S. House of Representatives
Washington, DC 20510
http://www.house.gov

The Pew Research Center is an opinion research group that studies attitudes toward press, politics, and public policy issues. To read some of their survey results, visit their website.

The Pew Research Center for the People and the Press
1150 18th Street, NW, Suite 975
Washington, DC 20036
Tel: 202-293-3126
Email: mailprc@people-press.org
http://www.people-press.org

REGIONAL AND LOCAL OFFICIALS

QUICK FACTS

School Subjects Economics Government History	**Certification or Licensing** None available
Personal Skills Communication/ideas Leadership/management	**Outlook** Little or no change
Work Environment Primarily indoors One location with some travel	**DOT** 188
Minimum Education Level Bachelor's degree	**GOE** 11.05.03
Salary Range $0 to $40,000 to $100,000+	**NOC** 0011
	O*NET-SOC 11-1031.00

OVERVIEW

Regional and local officials hold positions in the legislative, executive, and judicial branches of government at the local level. They include mayors, commissioners, and city and county council members. These officials direct regional legal services, public health departments, and police protection. They serve on housing, budget, and employment committees and develop special programs to improve communities.

HISTORY

The first U.S. colonies adopted the English "shire" form of government. This form was 1,000 years old and served as the administrative arm of both the national and local governments; a county in medieval England was overseen by a sheriff (originally a "shire reeve") appointed by the crown and was represented by two members in Parliament.

The framers of the U.S. Constitution didn't make any specific provisions for the governing of cities and counties. This allowed state governments to compose their own definitions; when drawing up their own constitutions, the states essentially considered county governments to be extensions of the state government.

City governments, necessary for dealing with increased industry and trade, evolved during the 19th century. Population growth and suburban development helped to strengthen local governments after World War I. The county governments grew even stronger after World War II, due to rising revenues and increased independence from the states.

THE JOB

There are a variety of different forms of local government across the country, but they all share similar concerns. County and city governments make sure that the local streets are free of crime as well as free of potholes. They create and improve regional parks and organize music festivals and outdoor theater events to be staged in these parks. They identify community problems and help to solve them in original ways. For example, in an effort to solve the problem of unemployment among those recently released from jail, King County, Washington, developed a baking training program for county inmates. The inmates' new talents with danishes and bread loaves opened up well-paying job opportunities in grocery store bakeries all across the county. King County also has many youth programs, including the Paul Robeson Scholar-Athlete Award to recognize students who excel in both academics and athletics.

The Innovative Farmer Program in Huron County, Michigan, was developed to introduce new methods of farming to maintain the role of agriculture as part of the county's economy. The program is studying new cover-crops, tillage systems, and herbicides. In Onondaga County, New York, the public library started a program of basic reading instruction for deaf adults. In Broward County, Florida, a program provides a homelike setting for supervised visitation and parenting training for parents who are separated from their children due to abuse or domestic violence.

The needs for consumer protection, water quality, and affordable housing increase every year. Regional or local officials are elected to deal with issues such as public health, legal services, housing, and budget and fiscal management. They attend meetings and serve on committees. They know about the industry and agriculture of the area as well as the specific problems facing constituents, and they offer educated solutions, vote on laws, and generally represent the people in their districts.

There are two forms of county government: the *commissioner/administrator form,* in which the county board of commissioners appoints an administrator who serves the board, and the *council/executive form,* in which a county executive is the chief administrative officer of the district and has the power to veto ordinances enacted by the county board. A county government may include a *chief executive,* who directs regional services; *council members,* who are the county legislators; a *county clerk,* who keeps records of property titles, licenses, etc.; and a *county treasurer,* who is in charge of the receipt and disbursement of money.

A county government doesn't tax its citizens, so its money comes from state aid, fees, and grants. A city government funds its projects and programs with money from sales and other local taxes, block grants, and state aid. Elected executives direct these funds and services. *Mayors* serve as the heads of city governments and are elected by the general populace. Their specific functions vary depending on the structure of their government. In mayor-council governments, both the mayor and the city council are popularly elected. The council is responsible for formulating city ordinances, but the mayor exercises control over the actions of the council. In such governments, the mayor usually plays a dual role, serving not only as chief executive officer but also as an agent of the city government responsible for such functions as maintaining public order, security, and health. In a commission government, the people elect a number of *commissioners,* each of whom serves as head of a city department. The presiding commissioner is usually the mayor. The final type of municipal government is the council/manager form. Here, the council members are elected by the people, and one of their functions is to hire a *city manager* to administer the city departments. A mayor is elected by the council to chair the council and officiate at important municipal functions.

REQUIREMENTS

High School

Courses in government, civics, and history will give you an understanding of the structure of government. English courses are important because you will need good writing skills to communicate with constituents and other government officials. Math, accounting, and economics will help you develop analytical skills for examining statistics and demographics. Journalism classes will develop research and interview skills for identifying problems and developing programs.

Postsecondary Training

To serve on a local government, your experience and understanding of the city or county are generally more important than your educational background. Some mayors and council members are elected to their positions because they've lived in the region for a long time and have had experience with local industry and other concerns. For example, someone with years of farming experience may be the best candidate to serve a small agricultural community. Voters in local elections may be more impressed by a candidate's previous occupations and roles in the community than they are by a candidate's postsecondary degrees.

That said, most regional and local officials still hold an undergraduate degree, and many hold a graduate degree. Popular areas of study include public administration, law, economics, political science, history, and English. Regardless of your major as an undergraduate, you are likely to be required to take classes in English literature, statistics, foreign language, western civilization, and economics.

Other Requirements

To be successful in this field, you must understand deeply the city and region you serve. You need to be knowledgeable about the local industry, private businesses, and social problems. You should also have lived for some time in the region in which you hope to hold office.

You also need good people skills to be capable of listening to the concerns of constituents and other officials and exchanging ideas with them. Other useful qualities are problem-solving skills and creativity to develop innovative programs.

EXPLORING

Depending on the size of your city or county, you can probably become involved with your local government at a young age. Your council members and other government officials should be more accessible to you than state and federal officials, so take advantage of that. Visit the county court house and volunteer in whatever capacity you can with county-organized programs, such as tutoring in a literacy program or leading children's reading groups at the public library. Become involved with local elections.

Many candidates for local and state offices welcome young people to assist with campaigns. As a volunteer, you may make calls, post signs, and get to see a candidate at work. You will also have the opportunity to meet others who have an interest in government, and the experience will help you to gain a more prominent role in later campaigns.

Another way to learn about government is to become involved in an issue that interests you. Maybe there's an old building in your neighborhood you'd like to save from destruction, or maybe you have some ideas for youth programs or programs for senior citizens. Research what's being done about your concerns and come up with solutions to offer to local officials.

EMPLOYERS

Every city in the United States requires the services of local officials. In some cases, the services of a small town or suburb may be overseen by the government of a larger city or by the county government. According to the National Association of Counties, 48 states have operational county governments—a total of over 3,000 counties. (Connecticut and Rhode Island are the only two states without counties.) The counties with the largest populations are Los Angeles County, California; Cook County, Illinois; and Harris County, Texas. There are also 31 governments that are consolidations of city and county governments; New York, Denver, and San Francisco are among them.

STARTING OUT

There is no direct career path for gaining public office. The way you pursue a local office will be greatly affected by the size and population of the region in which you live. When running for mayor or council of a small town, you may have no competition at all. On the other hand, to become mayor of a large city, you need extensive experience in the city's politics. If you're interested in pursuing a local position, research the backgrounds of your city mayor, county commissioner, and council members to get an idea of how they approached their political careers.

Some officials stumble into government offices after some success with political activism on the grassroots level. Others have had success in other areas, such as agriculture, business, and law enforcement, and use their particular understanding of an area to help improve the community. Many local politicians started their careers by assisting in someone else's campaign or advocating for an issue.

ADVANCEMENT

Some successful local and regional officials maintain their positions for many years. Others hold local office for only one or two terms, then return full time to their businesses and other careers. You might also choose to use a local position as a stepping stone to a position of greater power within the region or to a state office. Many mayors of the largest cities run for governor or state legislature and may eventually move into federal office.

EARNINGS

In general, salaries for government officials tend to be lower than what the official could make working in the private sector. In many local offices, officials volunteer their time or work only part time. According to a salary survey published in 2001 by the International City/County Management Association, the chief elected official of a city makes an average salary of $20,719 a year. The average salary for city managers was $85,587. A county's chief elected official averages $35,118 a year. County clerks average about $44,680, and treasurers earn $43,985.

A job with a local or regional government may or may not provide benefits. Some positions may include accounts for official travel and other expenses.

WORK ENVIRONMENT

Most government officials work in a typical office setting. Some may work a regular 40-hour week, while others work long hours and weekends. Though some positions may only be considered part time, they may take up nearly as many hours as full-time work. Officials have the opportunity to meet with the people of the region, but they also devote a lot of time to clerical duties. If serving a large community, they may have assistants to help with phones, filing, and preparing documents.

Because officials must be appointed or elected in order to keep their jobs, determining long-range career plans can be difficult. There may be extended periods of unemployment, where living off of savings or other jobs may be necessary. Because of the low pay of some positions, officials may have to work another job even while they serve in office. This can result in little personal time and the need to juggle many different responsibilities at once.

OUTLOOK

Though the form and structure of state and federal government are not likely to change, the form of your local and county government can be altered by popular vote. Every election, voters somewhere in the country are deciding whether to keep their current forms of government or to introduce new forms. But these changes don't greatly affect the number of officials needed to run your local government. The chances for holding office are greater in small communities. The races for part-time and nonpaying offices are also less competitive.

The issues facing a community will have the most effect on the jobs of local officials. In a city with older neighborhoods, officials deal with historic preservation, improvements in utilities, and water quality. In a growing city of many suburbs, officials have to make decisions regarding development, roads, and expanded routes for public transportation.

The federal government has made efforts to shift costs to the states. If this continues, states may offer less aid to counties. A county government's funds are also affected by changes in property taxes.

FOR MORE INFORMATION

For information about the forms of city and county governments around the country and to learn about programs sponsored by local and regional governments, contact the following organizations:

International City/County Management Association
777 North Capitol Street, NE, Suite 500
Washington, DC 20002
Tel: 202-289-4262
http://www.icma.org

National Association of Counties
440 First Street, NW, Suite 800
Washington, DC 20001
Tel: 202-393-6226
http://www.naco.org

REPORTERS

QUICK FACTS

School Subjects English Journalism	**Certification or Licensing** None available
Personal Skills Communication/ideas Helping/teaching	**Outlook** More slowly than the average
Work Environment Indoors and outdoors Primarily multiple locations	**DOT** 131
Minimum Education Level Bachelor's degree	**GOE** 11.08.02
Salary Range $17,320 to $30,060 to $68,020+	**NOC** 5123 **O*NET-SOC** 27-3022.00

OVERVIEW

Reporters are the foot soldiers for newspapers, magazines, and television and radio broadcast companies. They gather and analyze information about current events and write stories for publication or for broadcasting. News analysts, reporters, and correspondents hold about 78,000 jobs in the United States.

HISTORY

Newspapers are the primary disseminators of news in the United States. People read newspapers to learn about the current events that are shaping their society and societies around the world. Newspapers give public expression to opinion and criticism of government and societal issues, and, of course, provide the public with entertaining, informative reading.

Newspapers are able to fulfill these functions because of the freedom given to the press. However, this was not always the case. The first American newspaper, published in 1690, was suppressed four days after it was published. And it was not until 1704 that the first continuous newspaper appeared.

One early newspaperman who later became a famous writer was Benjamin Franklin. Franklin worked for his brother at a Boston newspaper before publishing his own paper in 1723 in Philadelphia.

A number of developments in the printing industry made it possible for newspapers to be printed more cheaply. In the late 19th century, new types of presses were developed to increase production, and the Linotype machine was invented. The Linotype mechanically set letters so that handset type was no longer necessary. This dramatically decreased the amount of prepress time needed to get a page into print. Newspapers could respond to breaking stories more quickly, and late editions with breaking stories became part of the news world.

These technological advances, along with an increasing population, factored into the rapid growth of the newspaper industry in the United States. In 1776, there were only 37 newspapers in the United States. Today there are more than 1,500 daily and nearly 7,500 weekly newspapers in the country.

As newspapers grew in size and widened the scope of their coverage, it became necessary to increase the number of employees and to assign them specialized jobs. Reporters have always been the heart of newspaper staffs. However, in today's complex world, with the public hungry for news as it occurs, reporters and correspondents are involved in all media—not only newspapers, but magazines, radio, and television as well. Today, with the advent of the Internet, many newspapers are going online, causing many reporters to participate actively in the online world.

THE JOB

Reporters collect information on newsworthy events and prepare stories for newspaper or magazine publication or for radio or television broadcast. The stories may simply provide information about local, state, or national events, or they may present opposing points of view on issues of current interest. In this latter capacity, the press plays an important role in monitoring the actions of public officials and others in positions of power.

Stories may originate as an assignment from an editor or as the result of a lead or news tip. Good reporters are always on the lookout for good story ideas. To cover a story, they gather and verify facts by interviewing people involved in or related to the event, examining documents and public records, observing events as they happen, and researching relevant background information. Reporters generally take notes or use a tape recorder as they collect information and write their stories once they return to their offices. To meet deadlines, reporters may have to telephone the stories to *rewriters,* who write or transcribe the stories for them. After the facts have been gathered and verified, the reporters transcribe their notes, organize their material, and determine what emphasis, or angle, to give the news. The story is then written to meet prescribed standards of editorial style and format.

The basic functions of reporters are to observe events objectively and impartially, record them accurately, and explain what the news means in a larger, societal context. Within this framework, there are several types of reporters.

The most basic is the *news reporter.* This job sometimes involves covering a beat, which means that the reporter may be assigned to consistently cover news from an area such as the local courthouse, police station, or school system. It may involve receiving general assignments, such as a story about an unusual occurrence or an obituary of a community leader. Large daily papers may assign teams of reporters to investigate social, economic, or political events and conditions.

Many newspaper, wire service, and magazine reporters specialize in one type of story, either because they have a particular interest in the subject or because they have acquired the expertise to analyze and interpret news in that particular area. *Topical reporters* cover stories for a specific department, such as medicine, politics, foreign affairs, sports, consumer affairs, finance, science, business, education, labor, or religion. They sometimes write features explaining the history that has led up to certain events in the field they cover. *Feature writers* generally write longer, broader stories than news reporters, usually on more upbeat subjects, such as fashion, art, theater, travel, and social events. They may write about trends, for example, or profile local celebrities. *Editorial writers* and *syndicated news columnists* present viewpoints that, although based on a thorough knowledge, are opinions on topics of popular interest. *Columnists* write under a byline and usually specialize in a particular subject, such as politics or government activities. *Critics* review restaurants, books, works of art, movies, plays, musical performances, and other cultural events.

Specializing allows reporters to focus their efforts, talent, and knowledge on one area of expertise. It also gives them more opportunities to develop deeper relationships with contacts and sources, which is necessary to gain access to the news.

Correspondents report events in locations distant from their home offices. They may report news by mail, telephone, fax, or computer from rural areas, large cities throughout the United States, or countries. Many large newspapers, magazines, and broadcast companies have one correspondent who is responsible for covering all the news for the foreign city or country where they are based. These reporters are known as *foreign correspondents.*

Reporters on small or weekly newspapers not only cover all aspects of the news in their communities, but also may take photographs, write editorials and headlines, lay out pages, edit wire-service copy, and help with general office work. *Television reporters* may have to be photogenic as well as talented and resourceful. They may at times present live reports, filmed by a mobile camera unit at the scene where the news originates, or they may tape interviews and narration for later broadcast.

REQUIREMENTS

High School

High school courses that will provide you with a firm foundation for a reporting career include English, journalism, history, social studies, communications, typing, and computer science. Speech courses will help you hone your interviewing skills, which are necessary for

Project Nothing

Economists are concerned with levels of consumption—including how to limit purchasing when resources are scarce. A class of nine-year-olds in Canada took up this cause to encourage people to buy less to help our environment. In fact, they started an online project to encourage people to buy nothing for one day of the year. Because the average North American creates 3.5 pounds of garbage every day, these young students established the International Buy Nothing Day to make people aware of their spending habits and its possible effect on the environment and society. Buy Nothing Day has been celebrated on the last Friday of November since 1991. Learn more at http://www3.sympatico.ca/dalia/buy0/buytoc.htm.

success as a reporter. In addition, it will be helpful to take college prep courses, such as foreign language, math, and science.

Postsecondary Training

You will need at least a bachelor's degree to become a reporter, and a graduate degree will give you a great advantage over those entering the field with lesser degrees. Most editors prefer applicants with degrees in journalism because their studies include liberal arts courses as well as professional training in journalism. Some editors consider it sufficient for a reporter to have a good general education from a liberal arts college. Others prefer applicants with an undergraduate degree in liberal arts and a master's degree in journalism. The great majority of journalism graduates hired today by newspapers, wire services, and magazines have majored specifically in news-editorial journalism.

More than 400 colleges offer programs in journalism leading to a bachelor's degree. In these schools, around three-fourths of a student's time is devoted to a liberal arts education and one-fourth to the professional study of journalism, with required courses such as introductory mass media, basic reporting and copyediting, history of journalism, and press law and ethics. Students are encouraged to select other journalism courses according to their specific interests.

Many community and junior colleges also offer journalism courses and programs. Graduates of these programs are prepared to work as general assignment reporters, but they may encounter difficulty when competing with graduates of four-year programs. Credit earned in community and junior colleges may be transferable to four-year programs in journalism at other colleges and universities. Journalism training may also be obtained in the armed forces. Names and addresses of newspapers and a list of journalism schools and departments are published in the annual *Editor & Publisher International Year Book: The Encyclopedia of the Newspaper Industry* (New York: Editor & Publisher, 2003) which is available for reference in most public libraries and newspaper offices.

Approximately 120 schools offer master's degree programs in journalism, and about 35 schools offer journalism doctorates. Graduate degrees may prepare students specifically for careers in news or as journalism teachers, researchers, and theorists, or for jobs in advertising or public relations.

A reporter's liberal arts training should include courses in English (with an emphasis on writing), sociology, political science, economics, history, psychology, business, speech, and computer science.

Knowledge of foreign languages is also useful. To be a reporter in a specialized field, such as science or finance, requires concentrated course work in that area.

Other Requirements

You need to be a good typist to be a successful reporter, as you will type your stories using word processing programs. Although it is not essential, a knowledge of shorthand or speedwriting makes note taking easier, and an acquaintance with news photography is an asset.

You must also be inquisitive, aggressive, persistent, and detail-oriented. You should enjoy interaction with people of various races, cultures, religions, economic levels, and social statuses.

EXPLORING

You can explore a career as a reporter in a number of ways. You can talk to reporters and editors at local newspapers and radio and TV stations. You can interview the admissions counselor at the school of journalism closest to your home.

In addition to taking courses in English, journalism, social studies, speech, computer science, and typing, high school students can acquire practical experience by working on school newspapers or on a church, synagogue, or mosque newsletter. Part-time and summer jobs on newspapers provide invaluable experience to the aspiring reporter.

College students can develop their reporting skills in the laboratory courses or workshops that are part of the journalism curriculum. College students might also accept jobs as campus correspondents for selected newspapers. People who work as part-time reporters covering news in a particular area of a community are known as *stringers* and are paid only for those stories that are printed.

Universities, newspapers, foundations, and professional organizations offer more than 3,000 journalism scholarships, fellowships, and assistantships to college students. Many newspapers and magazines offer summer internships to journalism students to provide them with practical experience in a variety of basic reporting and editing duties. Students who successfully complete internships are usually placed in jobs more quickly upon graduation than those without such experience.

EMPLOYERS

Of the approximately 78,000 reporters and correspondents employed in the United States, nearly 50 percent work for newspapers of all sizes. About 28 percent work in radio and television broadcasting. The rest are employed by wire services and magazines.

STARTING OUT

Jobs in this field may be obtained through college placement offices or by applying directly to the personnel departments of individual employers. If you have some practical experience, you will have an advantage; you should be prepared to present a portfolio of material you wrote as a volunteer or part-time reporter, or other writing samples.

Most journalism school graduates start out as general assignment reporters or copy editors for small publications. A few outstanding journalism graduates may be hired by large city newspapers or national magazines. They are trained on the job, but they are the exception, as large employers usually require several years' experience. As a rule, novice reporters cover routine assignments, such as reporting on civic and club meetings, writing obituaries, or summarizing speeches. As you become more skilled in reporting, you will be assigned to more important events or to a regular beat, or you may specialize in a particular field.

ADVANCEMENT

Reporters may advance by moving to larger newspapers or press services, but competition for such positions is unusually keen. Many highly qualified reporters apply for these jobs every year.

A select number of reporters eventually become columnists, correspondents, editorial writers, editors, or top executives. These important and influential positions represent the top of the field, and competition is strong for them.

Many reporters transfer the contacts and knowledge developed in newspaper reporting to related fields, such as public relations, advertising, or preparing copy for radio and television news programs.

EARNINGS

There are great variations in the earnings of reporters. Salaries are related to experience, the type of employer for which the reporter works, geographic location, and whether the reporter is covered by a contract negotiated by the Newspaper Guild.

According to the *National Occupational Employment and Wage Estimates,* a salary survey by the U.S. Department of Labor, the median salary for news analysts, reporters, and correspondents was $30,060 in 2001. The lowest paid 10 percent of these workers earned $17,320 or less per year, while the highest paid 10 percent made $68,020 or more annually.

According to the Newspaper Guild, the average top minimum salary for reporters with about five years' experience was $43,820 in 2002. Salaries range from $20,000 to $65,000 or more.

The U.S. Department of Labor reported that reporters and correspondents who worked in radio and television broadcasting had median annual earnings of $33,550 in 2000.

WORK ENVIRONMENT

Reporters work under a great deal of pressure in settings that differ from the typical business office. Their jobs generally require a five-day, 35–40-hour week, but overtime and irregular schedules are very common. Reporters employed by morning papers start work in the late afternoon and finish around midnight, while those on afternoon or evening papers start early in the morning and work until early or mid-afternoon. Foreign correspondents often work late at night to send the news to their papers in time to meet printing deadlines.

The day of the smoky, ink-stained newsroom has passed, but newspaper offices are still hectic places. Reporters have to work amid the clatter of computer keyboards and other machines, loud voices engaged in telephone conversations, and the bustle created by people hurrying about. An atmosphere of excitement prevails, especially as press deadlines approach.

Travel is often required in this occupation, and some assignments may be dangerous, such as covering wars, political uprisings, fires, floods, and other events of a volatile nature.

OUTLOOK

Employment for reporters and correspondents through 2010 is expected to grow more slowly than the average for all occupations, according to the *Occupational Outlook Handbook.* The U.S. Bureau of Labor Statistics projects that the number of employed reporters and correspondents will grow by 2.8 percent between 2000 and 2010. While the number of self-employed reporters and correspondents is expected to grow, newspaper jobs are expected to decrease because of mergers, consolidations, and closures in the newspaper industry.

Because of an increase in the number of small community and suburban daily and weekly newspapers, opportunities will be best for journalism graduates who are willing to relocate and accept relatively low starting salaries. With experience, reporters on these small papers can move up to editing positions or may choose to transfer to reporting jobs on larger newspapers or magazines.

Openings will be limited on big city dailies. While individual papers may enlarge their reporting staffs, little or no change is expected in the total number of these newspapers. Applicants will face strong competition for jobs on large metropolitan newspapers. Experience is a definite requirement, which rules out most new graduates unless they possess credentials in an area for which the publication has a pressing need. Occasionally, a beginner can use contacts and experience gained through internship programs and summer jobs to obtain a reporting job immediately after graduation.

A significant number of jobs will be provided by magazines and in radio and television broadcasting, but the major news magazines and larger broadcasting stations generally prefer experienced reporters. For beginning correspondents, small stations with local news broadcasts will continue to replace staff who move on to larger stations or leave the business. Network hiring has been cut drastically in the past few years and will probably continue to decline.

Stronger employment growth is expected for reporters in online newspapers and magazines.

Overall, the prospects are best for graduates who have majored in news-editorial journalism and completed an internship while in school. The top graduates in an accredited program will have a great advantage, as will talented technical and scientific writers. Small newspapers prefer to hire beginning reporters who are acquainted with the community and are willing to help with photography and other aspects of production. Without at least a bachelor's degree in journalism, applicants will find it increasingly difficult to obtain even an entry-level position.

Those with doctorates and practical reporting experience may find teaching positions at four-year colleges and universities, while highly qualified reporters with master's degrees may obtain employment in journalism departments of community and junior colleges.

Poor economic conditions do not drastically affect the employment of reporters and correspondents. Their numbers are not severely cut back even during a downturn; instead, employers forced to reduce expenditures will suspend new hiring.

FOR MORE INFORMATION

This organization provides general educational information on all areas of journalism, including newspapers, magazines, television, and radio.

Association for Education in Journalism and Mass Communication
234 Outlet Pointe Boulevard
Columbia, SC 29210-5667
Tel: 803-798-0271
Email: aejmchq@aejmc.org
http://www.aejmc.org

To receive a copy of The Journalist's Road to Success, *which lists schools offering degrees in news-editorial and financial aid to those interested in print journalism, contact*

Dow Jones Newspaper Fund
PO Box 300
Princeton, NJ 08543-0300
Tel: 609-452-2820
Email: newsfund@wsj.dowjones.com
http://djnewspaperfund.dowjones.com

For information on careers in newspapers and industry facts and figures, contact

Newspaper Association of America
1921 Gallows Road, Suite 600
Vienna, VA 22182-3900
Tel: 703-902-1600
Email: IRC@naa.org
http://www.naa.org

For information on union membership, contact

Newspaper Guild-Communication Workers of America
501 Third Street, NW, Suite 250
Washington, DC 20001
Tel: 202-434-7177
Email: guild@cwa-union.org
http://www.newsguild.org

RESEARCH ASSISTANTS

QUICK FACTS

School Subjects English History Journalism	**Certification or Licensing** None available
Personal Skills Communication/ideas Following instructions	**Outlook** About as fast as the average
Work Environment Primarily indoors Primarily multiple locations	**DOT** 109
Minimum Educational Level Bachelor's degree	**GOE** 11.03.03
Salary Range $12,000 to $26,000 to $74,000	**NOC** 4122 **O*NET-SOC** N/A

OVERVIEW

Research assistants work to help writers, scientists, radio, film, and television producers, marketing and advertising executives, attorneys, professors, publishers, politicians, museum curators, and a wide variety of other professionals with their jobs. They are information specialists who find the facts, data, and statistics that their employers need, leaving the employers free to pursue the larger task at hand.

HISTORY

The position of assistant is one of the oldest in the world. After all, assistants have been around for as long as people have worked: The job of research assistant was created the first time a worker sent an assistant out to gather information, whether it was to scout hunting grounds or survey land for possible dwelling places.

Although the job of the research assistant has changed little since the early days, the tools used to gather information have changed dramatically. An assistant to a doctor a hundred years ago would have had to travel to libraries and other information centers to gather data on a disease from books and then laboriously take down notes on paper. Today that same research assistant could do an Internet search and print the findings in only a few minutes. As technology becomes more advanced, research assistants will have the convenience of using new methods to complete their research, but they will also bear the burden of having to master the techniques to get the information they need.

THE JOB

Although the fields in which they work may differ greatly, all research assistants work to help their employers complete a job more easily and more thoroughly. A research assistant may work for one person, such as a university professor, or for a team of people, such as the writers of brochures, newsletters, and press releases at a large nonprofit organization. If the research assistant works for more than one person, he or she needs to follow a system to determine whose work will be done when. Sometimes the team assigning the work determines the order in which jobs should be done; other times, research assistants keep sign-up sheets and perform the research requests in the order they are listed. An urgent job often necessitates that the research assistant disregard the sheet and jump quickly to the new task. Sometimes research assistants help with clerical duties, such as transcription, word processing, and reception, or, in the case of scientific research assistants, with cleaning and maintaining laboratories and equipment.

After receiving a research assignment from the person or people they assist, research assistants must first determine how to locate the desired information. Sometimes this will be as simple as making a single phone call and requesting a brochure. Other times it may involve anywhere from hours to weeks of research in libraries, archives, museums, laboratories, and on the Internet until all of the necessary information is compiled and consolidated. Research assistants must then prepare the material for presentation to the person who requested it. If specific brochures or catalogs are requested, the research assistant need only hand them over when they arrive. More often than not, however, the research assistant has to write up notes or even a report outlining the research efforts and presenting the information they were asked to locate. These reports may include graphs, charts, statistics, and drawings or photographs. They include a listing of sources and the exact specifications of any interviews conducted, surveys taken, or experiments performed. Sometimes research assistants are asked to present this information verbally as well.

Research assistants work in almost every field imaginable. The following are some of the most common areas or situations in which research assistants work.

Research assistants work for writers in a wide variety of circumstances. They may work for commercial magazines and newspapers, where they might locate possible interview candidates, conduct surveys, scan other periodicals for relevant articles and features, or help a writer gather information for an article. For example, a writer doing an article on the history of rap music might send a research assistant to compile statistics on rap music sales from over the years or create a comprehensive list of artists signed by a specific record label. Some research assistants working for periodicals and other publications do nothing but confirm facts, such as dates, ages, and statistics. These researchers are called *fact checkers*. Research assistants who work in radio, film, or television often help locate and organize historical facts, find experts to be interviewed, or help follow up on ideas for future programs.

Many large companies, agencies, and organizations hire research assistants to help their in-house writing staff produce brochures, newsletters, and press releases. Research assistants may gather facts and statistics, retrieve applicable quotes, and conduct preliminary phone interviews.

Advertising and marketing agencies hire research assistants to help them discover consumer desires and the best ways to advertise and market products. Imagine that a small toy company is considering marketing a new toy. Research assistants for the company might be assigned to help find out how much it would cost to make the toy, whether or not there is already a similar toy on the market, who might buy the toy, and who might sell the toy. This would help the marketing department decide in what ways the toy should be marketed. In advertising, research assistants may be asked to provide executives with statistics and quotes so that the executives may determine whether a product is appealing to a certain portion of the population.

University professors hire research assistants to help them in their research in all fields. For example, a history professor working on a paper about the Italian military might send a research assistant to the library to uncover everything possible about the Italian military presence in Greece during World War II. A research assistant in microbiology will help a biologist prepare and perform experiments and record data. Often, professors hire graduate students as research assistants, either during the summer or in addition to the student's regular course load. Sometimes a research assistantship is part of a financial aid package; this ensures that the professor has help with research and gives the students an opportunity to earn money while learning more about their chosen field.

Politicians hire research assistants to help find out how a campaign is succeeding or failing, to find statistics on outcomes of past elections, and to determine the issues that are especially important to the constituents, among other things. Research assistants who work for politicians may also follow the opponent's campaign, trying to find ways to win over new supporters.

Some research assistants work for museums where they try to determine ways to add to a collection, develop signs and explanations for public education, and keep an inventory of all collection pieces. Research assistants may also do research to help curators learn more about the pieces in the museum's collection.

REQUIREMENTS

High School

Requirements for becoming a research assistant vary depending upon the field in which you hope to work. In high school, take a wide variety of college preparatory courses, including English, history, mathematics, and the sciences. Knowledge of at least one foreign language can be extremely helpful in gaining employment as a research assistant, especially in the fields of marketing, publishing, and the arts. Since writing and presenting research are important aspects of the research assistant's work, you should take classes that strengthen these skills, such as public speaking, journalism, and statistics. Knowledge of computers and excellent library skills are absolutely vital to this profession. If you will be working in the hard sciences or engineering, laboratory skills are essential.

Postsecondary Training

In college you should begin thinking about a specific field you are interested in and take courses in that field. If you are interested in advertising research but your college does not offer an advertising degree, you should plan to major in English or psychology but take a large concentration of communications, business, and economics courses. Often, English and journalism are good majors for the research assistant career, as the work requires so much reading, researching, and writing. Some employers prefer research assistants to have a degree in library science.

Some fields require degrees beyond a bachelor's degree for research assistants. This is often true in the hard sciences, engineering, medicine, and law. Depending on the field, some employers require a master's degree, or some advanced study in the area. For instance, an insurance company that hires a research assistant may require the employee to take insurance courses in order to become more knowledgeable about the industry. Research assistants in the social sciences or arts will find more high-paying employment opportunities with a master's in library science.

Other Requirements

To succeed as a research assistant, you must be naturally curious and enjoy doing research, finding and organizing facts, working with other people, and handling a variety of tasks. You should also be self-motivated, take instruction well, and be resourceful. For example, a research assistant assigned by an attorney to research marriage records at the county clerk's office should not be calling the law firm every few minutes to ask for further direction. A good research assistant must be able to take an assignment, immediately ask any questions necessary to clarify the task, and then begin retrieving the requested information.

EXPLORING

You can begin exploring this career while working on your own school assignments. Use different types of resources, such as newspapers, magazines, library catalogs, computers, the Internet, and official records and documents. If you are interested in becoming a research assistant in the sciences or medicine, pay close attention to procedures and methods in your laboratory classes.

Consider joining groups in your school devoted to research or fieldwork. Work as a reporter for your school newspaper, or volunteer to write feature articles for your yearbook. Both of these positions will provide you with experience in research and fact-finding. You can also create your own research opportunities. If you are a member of the marching band, for instance, you could research the history of the clarinet and write an article for the band newsletter.

Occasionally, small newspapers, nonprofit groups, political campaigns, and other organizations will accept student interns, volunteers, or even summer employees to help out with special projects. If you obtain such a position, you may have the opportunity to help with research, or at least, to see professionals in action, learn valuable work skills, and help support a good cause.

There are many books available describing the techniques of basic research skills. Ask a librarian or bookstore worker to help you locate them, or better yet, begin developing your research skills by tracking down materials yourself. The Internet is also full of helpful information on all subjects. To get tips on designing research surveys and analyzing data, visit http://www.hostedsurvey.com.

EMPLOYERS

All types of companies, organizations, and private individuals employ research assistants. Most college and university professors have a research assistant on staff to help them with articles and books they are writing. Newspapers and magazines use research assistants to find information for articles and verify facts. Museums employ research assistants to find information to add to museum collections, as well as to search museum archives for information requested by outside historians, scientists, writers, and other scholars. Companies in all fields need people to help find information on products, ingredients, production techniques, and competitors.

The government is a major employer of research assistants. Local, state, and federal government offices often hire research assistants to conduct interviews, gather statistics, compile information, and synthesize data. Research assistants for the government work for the U.S. Census Bureau, the U.S. Bureau of Labor Statistics, and the Library of Congress, among other divisions.

STARTING OUT

How you begin a career as a research assistant depends largely upon the field in which you are interested in working. In college, you may wish to pursue an assistantship with a professor. He or she can act as a mentor while you are earning your degree and offer valuable advice and feedback on your research techniques.

After receiving a bachelor's degree, you might begin by contacting agencies, firms, or companies where you'd like to work. For example, if you are interested in doing research to support writers, you might apply to newspapers, magazines, and large companies that produce their own publications. Also, some college and university career offices have listings of job openings in the research fields; occasionally these jobs are advertised in newspapers and magazines.

There may also be freelance opportunities for the beginning research assistant. Try marketing your services in the school newspaper or bulletin boards of your alma mater. You can also set up a Web page that lists your qualifications and the services you offer. Ask for referrals from professors with whom you have studied or worked. If you do a thorough, competent job on research assignments, you can use positive word-of-mouth to get more work.

ADVANCEMENT

A research assistant who gains a high skill level and demonstrates dedication to the employer and the field may earn the opportunity to lead other assistants on a special project. Some research assistants who work for writers and prove to have excellent writing skills themselves may get hired to write newsletter articles or brochures for publications. Depending on departmental needs, research assistants who work for a university while earning a degree may be offered a full-time position upon completion of their studies. Research assistants who work for clients on a freelance basis may find that they get more assignments and can command higher fees as they gain experience and a good reputation.

Advancement in this field is usually up to the individual. You will need to seek out opportunities. If you are interested in getting better assignments, you will probably need to ask for them. If you would like to supervise a newsletter or brochure project within your company, try making a proposal to your manager. With a proven track record and a solid idea of how a project can be accomplished, you will likely receive increased responsibility.

EARNINGS

Earnings vary widely, depending on field, level of education, and employer. Generally, large companies pay their research assistants more than smaller businesses and nonprofit organizations do. Research assistants with advanced degrees make more than those with bachelor's degrees only. Research assistants who work for large pharmaceutical companies or engineering laboratories and have advanced science degrees make some of the highest wages in the field.

Each college and university has its own salary budget for graduate student research assistants. There are often set minimum salaries for academic year employment and for full 12-month employment. Most student research assistants work part time and receive a percentage of these minimums based on the number of hours they work (usually 50 percent, 25 percent, or 33 percent). Some schools have an hourly rate that averages about $10–$15. Annual salaries for university research assistants can range from $12,000 to $42,000.

According to *The Scientist* and Abbott, Langer & Associates, Inc., senior researchers in the life sciences who work in academia earn from $30,000 to $74,000 annually, and postdoctorate researchers earn from $26,000 to $39,000. In industry, senior researchers earn from $30,000 to $72,000, and junior/postdoctorate researchers earn from $26,000 to $44,000.

Self-employed research assistants are paid by the hour or by assignment. Depending on the experience of the research assistant, the complexity of the assignment, and the location of the job, pay rates may be anywhere from $7 to $25 per hour, although $10–$12 is the norm.

Benefits such as health insurance, vacation, and sick leave vary by field and employer. Universities generally provide health care coverage, paid vacations, sick time, and a pension plan for full-time employees. Research assistants employed full-time by a private company are also eligible for similar benefits; some companies may provide benefits to part-time or contract workers. Freelancers must provide their own benefits.

Research assistants who work in some fields may receive additional bonuses. A person working on a research project about movies, for instance, may receive free passes to a local theater. A woman's magazine may send research assistants cosmetics samples so they can test different lipsticks for staying power. Research assistants charged with finding information about another country's economy may even be sent abroad. All of these perks, of course, vary depending on the needs of the employer and the experience of the researcher.

WORK ENVIRONMENT

Most research assistants work indoors in clean, climate-controlled, pleasant facilities. Many spend most of their time at the business that employs them, checking facts over the phone, finding data on a computer, searching the company's records, writing up reports, or conducting laboratory research. Others spend a great deal of time in libraries, government offices, courthouses, museums, archives, and even in such unlikely places as shopping malls and supermarkets. Research assistants go wherever they must to obtain the information requested.

Most assignments require that research assistants do their work on their own, with little direct supervision. Research assistants need to be very self-motivated in order to get the work done since they often do not have someone readily available to support them. It is important for research assistants who leave their offices for work to remember that they are representatives of their company or employer and to act and dress according to the employer's standards.

Full-time research assistants work 35–40 hours a week. They may have to work overtime or on weekends right before deadlines or when involved in special projects. Some research assistants, especially those who work for smaller organizations or for professors or private employers, work only part time. They may work as little as 10 hours a week. These research assistants are usually graduate students or freelancers who have a second job in a related field.

OUTLOOK

The outlook for the research assistant career generally depends upon the outlook for the field in which the researcher works. That is, a field that is growing quickly will usually need many new researchers, whereas a field with little growth will not. A researcher with a good background in many fields will be in higher demand, as will a researcher with specialized knowledge and research techniques specific to a field.

Although definite statistical data as to the present and future of all researchers is sketchy at best, as technology becomes more advanced and the amount of information available through newer media like the Internet increases, knowledgeable research assistants will be essential to find, sort, compile, present, and analyze this information. As a result of technological advancements, a new career niche has developed for *information brokers,* who compile information from online databases and services.

Since many people take research assistant positions as steppingstones to positions with more responsibility or stability, positions are often available to beginning researchers. Research assistants with good experience, excellent work ethics, and the drive to succeed will rarely find themselves out of work. Jobs will be available, but it may take some creative fact finding for research assistants to locate positions that best meet their needs and interests.

FOR MORE INFORMATION

To find out about health care research projects and opportunities with the U.S. Department of Health and Human Services, contact

Agency for Healthcare Research and Quality
2101 East Jefferson Street, Suite 501
Rockville, MD 20852
Tel: 301-594-1364
Email: info@ahrq.gov
http://www.ahcpr.gov

For a list of research opportunities and student internships with National Institutes of Health, contact

National Institutes of Health
Office of Human Resources Management
6100 Executive Boulevard, Room 3E01 MSC 7509
Bethesda, MD 20892-7509
http://ohrm.cc.nih.gov

For information on research assistant positions with the U.S. Census Bureau, contact

U.S. Census Bureau
Washington, DC 20233
Tel: 301-457-4608
Email: recruiter@ccmail.census.gov
http://www.census.gov

For a national list of research opportunities in physics, contact

The University of Pennsylvania School for Arts and Sciences
http://dept.physics.upenn.edu/undergraduate/lablist.html

RISK MANAGERS

QUICK FACTS

School Subjects Economics Mathematics	**Certification or Licensing** Recommended
Personal Skills Communication/ideas Leadership/management	**Outlook** About as fast as the average
Work Environment Primarily indoors One location with some travel	**DOT** 186
Minimum Education Level Bachelor's degree	**GOE** 11.06.03
Salary Range $37,530 to $77,753 to $175,000	**NOC** 0111
	O*NET-SOC 11-3031.00

OVERVIEW

Risk managers help businesses control risks and losses while maintaining the highest production levels possible. They work in industrial, service, nonprofit, and public-sector organizations. By protecting a company against loss, the risk manager helps it to improve operating efficiency and meet strategic goals.

HISTORY

Entrepreneurs have always taken steps to prevent losses or damage to their businesses. During the industrial revolution, business owners recognized that as production levels increased, risks increased at the same rate. The risks were often managed at the expense of worker health and safety.

Only since the mid-1950s, however, has risk management developed into a specialized field. With the rapid growth of technology came greater and more varied risks. Risk management changed from simply buying insurance against risks to planning a wide variety of programs to prevent, minimize, and finance losses.

THE JOB

Risk management protects people, property, and inventory. For example, factories that use hazardous chemicals require employees to wear protective clothing; department stores use closed-circuit surveillance to minimize shoplifting and vandalism; and manufacturers have a plan of action to follow should their products injure consumers. The five general categories of risks are damage to property, loss of income from property damage, injury to others, fraud or criminal acts, and death or injury of employees.

Risk managers first identify and analyze potential losses. They examine the various risk-management techniques and select the best ones, including how to pay for losses that may occur. After the chosen techniques are implemented, they closely monitor the results.

Risk management has two basic elements: risk control and risk finance. Risk control involves loss-prevention techniques to reduce the frequency and lower the severity of losses. Risk managers make sure operations are safe. They see that employees are properly trained and that workers have and use safety equipment. This often involves conducting safety and loss-prevention programs for employees. They make recommendations on the safe design of the workplace, and make plans in case of machinery breakdowns. They examine company contracts with suppliers to ensure a steady supply of raw materials.

Risk finance programs set aside funds to pay for losses not anticipated by risk control. Some losses can be covered by the company itself; others are covered by outside sources, such as insurance firms. Risk finance programs try to reduce costs of damage or loss, and include insurance programs to pay for losses.

Large organizations often have a risk-management department with several employees who each specialize in one area, such as employee-related injuries, losses to plant property, automobile losses, and insurance coverage. Small organizations have risk managers who may serve as safety and training officers in addition to handling workers' compensation and employee benefits.

REQUIREMENTS

High School

If you are interested in becoming a risk manager, you should plan on getting a bachelor's degree and may at some point consider getting an advanced degree, such as master's of business administration (M.B.A.) or a master's in risk management. In high school, therefore, you should take classes that will prepare you for college as well as help you explore this type of work. Take plenty of mathematics classes. Also, take accounting, business, and economics if your school offers these classes. To round out your education, take a variety of science, history, government, and computer classes. And of course, take English classes, which will help you hone your research and writing skills and make you ready for college-level work.

Postsecondary Training

Risk managers generally need a college degree with a broad business background. Depending on the college or university you attend, you may be able to major in risk management or insurance. There are about 100 schools that offer courses or degrees in insurance and risk management. If your school does not offer these degrees, consider a major in other management or finance areas, such as accounting, economics, engineering, finance, law, management, or political science. No matter what your particular major, your class schedule will most likely include economics, accounting, and mathematics, such as calculus. Computer classes that deal with using a variety of software programs will also be essential. Insurance and even banking classes will give you an understanding of these industries and the financial tools they use.

Certification or Licensing

Many organizations require their risk managers to earn the designation associate in risk management (ARM) or certified risk manager (CRM). The ARM program is run jointly by the American Institute for Chartered Property Casualty Underwriters and the Insurance Institute of America. You must take courses and pass exams in the following areas: risk management, risk control, and financing. The Institute also offers the associate in risk management for public entities for risk managers who are interested in working in the public sector.

The Certified Risk Managers International, a member of the National Alliance for Insurance Education and Research, offers the CRM program. To earn this designation, you must pass exams in five courses covering all major areas of risk management.

The Risk and Insurance Management Society (RIMS) offers an advanced designation in risk management, the RIMS fellow. The program consists of workshops covering advanced issues in business, insurance, and risk management.

Other Requirements

Communications skills are important for risk managers. They must regularly interact with other departments, such as accounting, engineering, finance, human resources, environmental, legal, research and development, safety, and security. They must also be able to communicate with outside sources, such as attorneys, brokers, union officials, consultants, and insurance agents.

Risk managers must have analytical and problem-solving skills in order to foresee potential problem situations and recommend appropriate solutions. They must be able to examine and prepare reports on risk costs, loss statistics, cost-versus-benefit data, insurance costs, and depreciation of assets.

A knowledge of insurance fundamentals and risk financing is necessary for this career. Risk managers must know loss-control issues such as employee health, worker and product safety, property safeguards, fire prevention, and environmental protection.

Management skills help risk managers set goals, plan strategies, delegate tasks, and measure and forecast results. Computer skills and familiarity with business law are also very helpful.

EXPLORING

You may wish to ask your family's insurance agent to help you contact a colleague who has commercial accounts and might introduce you to a risk manager for one of their larger clients.

The Risk and Insurance Management Society, Inc., is the largest organization for risk managers. It offers books, monographs, a bimonthly newsletter, education programs, and an annual conference. Students may be able to attend local chapter meetings. The Spencer Educational Foundation, affiliated with RIMS, provides annual scholarships to academically outstanding full-time students of risk management and insurance. (See the end of this article for contact information.)

EMPLOYERS

Airlines, banks, insurance companies, manufacturers, government agencies, municipalities, hospitals, retailers, school districts, and universities employ risk managers.

STARTING OUT

College placement offices can put students in touch with recruiting officers from industries that employ risk managers. Recent graduates can also send resumes to employers of risk managers, such as corporations, service providers, government agencies, and other public and private organizations. Some risk managers join insurance companies, insurance brokerage firms, or consulting firms that provide risk-management services to clients.

Some individuals gain experience and education while working in accounting or personnel departments and later move into risk-management positions.

ADVANCEMENT

There is good potential for advancement in the risk-management field. Many risk managers work in a related field, such as in a human resources department handling employee benefits.

Risk managers may eventually head a personnel or finance department, become a human resources director, or join the insurance industry. Some become independent consultants. Membership in professional associations that offer networking opportunities can lead to better positions in the field.

Risk managers usually hold mid-level management positions and often report to a financial officer. Some, however, become vice presidents or presidents of their organizations.

EARNINGS

Risk managers' salaries vary depending on level of responsibility and authority, type of industry, organization size, and geographic region. The U.S. Department of Labor, which classifies risk managers with financial managers, reported a median yearly income for financial managers of $70,210 in 2001. The lowest 10 percent had earnings of less than $37,530, while the top 10 percent earned more than $136,700. According to a survey by the Global Association of Risk Professionals (GARP), risk professionals in the United States earned an average salary of $77,753. Compensation ranged from $175,000 for a senior market risk manager to $130,000 for a senior executive within the credit risk department and just over $100,000 for an operational risk professional.

Risk managers usually receive benefits, bonuses, paid vacation, health and life insurance, pensions, and stock options.

WORK ENVIRONMENT

Risk managers work in a variety of settings from schools, stores, and government agencies to manufacturers and airlines. Most work in offices, not on the production line, but they may be required to spend some time in production departments. They may have to travel to study risks in other companies or to attend seminars.

Risk managers usually work a 40-hour week, Monday through Friday. They may have to spend much of their time at a computer, analyzing statistics and preparing reports.

OUTLOOK

Since advanced technology continues to increase productivity as well as the potential for disaster, the need for risk management will continue to grow. Organizations now recognize risk management as an integral and effective tool for cost-containment. The profession will continue to gain recognition in the next decade, so salaries and career opportunities are expected to continue to escalate. The U.S. Department of Labor predicts the growth rate for financial managers (including risk managers) to be about as fast as the average over the next several years.

FOR MORE INFORMATION

For information about the associate in risk management designation, contact

American Institute for Chartered Property Casualty Underwriters Insurance Institute of America
720 Providence Road
PO Box 3016
Malvern, PA 19355-0716
Tel: 800-644-2101
http://www.aicpcu.org

For information on education, research, student memberships, and publications, contact

American Risk and Insurance Association
716 Providence Road
PO Box 3028
Malvern, PA 19355-3402
Tel: 610-640-1997
Email: aria@cpcuiia.org
http://www.aria.org

For information about the certified risk manager designation, contact

National Alliance for Insurance Education and Research
PO Box 27027
Austin, TX 78755-2027
Tel: 800-633-2165
Email: alliance@scic.com
http://www.scic.com

For industry news and training programs aimed at risk managers employed in municipal and state governments, contact

Public Risk Management Association
1815 North Fort Myer Drive, Suite 1020
Arlington, VA 22209-1805
Tel: 703-528-7701
http://www.primacentral.org

For information on continuing education and the Spencer Educational Foundation, contact

Risk and Insurance Management Society, Inc.
655 Third Avenue, Second Floor
New York, NY 10017
Tel: 212-286-9292
http://www.rims.org

SALES REPRESENTATIVES

QUICK FACTS

School Subjects Business Mathematics Speech	DOT 250, 251, 252, 253, 254, 259, 260, 261, 262, 269, 270, 271, 272, 273, 274, 275, 276, 277, 279, 291
Personal Skills Communication/ideas Helping/teaching	GOE 08.01.01, 08.01.02, 08.02.01, 08.02.02, 08.02.03, 08.02.05, 08.02.06, 08.02.08
Work Environment Indoors and outdoors Primarily multiple locations	NOC 6221, 6411, 6421, 6433
Minimum Education Level High school diploma	O*NET-SOC 41-4011.00, 41-4011.01, 41-4011.02, 41-4011.03, 41-4011.04, 41-4011.05, 41-4011.06, 41-4012.00, 41-9031.00, 41-9091.00
Salary Range $13,220 to $41,510 to $106,560+	
Certification or Licensing None available	
Outlook More slowly than the average	

OVERVIEW

Sales representatives, also called *sales reps,* sell the products and services of manufacturers and wholesalers. They look for potential customers or clients such as retail stores, other manufacturers or wholesalers, government agencies, hospitals, and other institutions; explain or demonstrate their products to these clients; and attempt to make a sale. The job may include follow-up calls and visits to ensure the customer is satisfied.

Sales representatives work under a variety of titles. Those employed by manufacturers are typically called *manufacturers' sales workers* or *manufacturers' representatives*. Those who work for wholesalers are sometimes called *wholesale trade sales workers* or *wholesale sales representatives*. A *manufacturers' agent* is a self-employed salesperson who agrees to represent the products of various companies. A *door-to-door sales worker* usually represents just one company and sells products directly to consumers, typically in their homes. Approximately 1.8 million people work as manufacturers' and wholesale sales representatives in the United States.

HISTORY

Sales representatives for manufacturers and wholesalers have long played an important role in the U.S. economy. By representing products and seeking out potential customers, they have helped in the efficient distribution of large amounts of merchandise.

The earliest wholesalers were probably the ship "chandlers," or suppliers, of colonial New England. Chandlers assembled in large quantities the food and equipment required by merchant ships and military vessels. Ship owners found that a centralized supply source enabled them to equip their vessels quickly.

Various developments in the 19th century made wholesalers more prominent. Factories were becoming larger, thus allowing for huge amounts of merchandise to be manufactured or assembled in a single location. New forms of transportation, especially the railroad, made it more practical for manufacturers to sell their products over great distances. Although some manufacturers would sell their goods directly to retail outlets and elsewhere, many found it easier and more profitable to let wholesalers do this job. Retail stores, moreover, liked working with wholesalers, who were able to sell them a wide range of merchandise from different manufacturers and from different areas of the country and the world.

The sales representatives hired by manufacturers and wholesalers were typically given a specific territory in which to sell their goods. Armed with illustrated product catalogs, special promotional deals, and financial support for advertising, they traveled to prospective customers and tried to explain the important qualities of their products. Competition between sales representatives sometimes was fierce, leading some to be less than scrupulous. Product claims were exaggerated, and retail stores were sometimes supplied with shoddy merchandise. Eventually more fact-based sales pitches were emphasized by manufacturers and wholesalers, who in the long run benefited from having responsible, honest, well-informed representatives. Products also began to be backed by written guarantees of quality.

Meanwhile, some manufacturers employed door-to-door sales workers to sell products directly to consumers. Direct selling in the United States goes back to the famous "Yankee Peddler" who, during colonial times, traveled by wagon, on horseback, and sometimes on foot, bringing to isolated settlers many products that were not easily available otherwise. A forerunner of the modern door-to-door sales worker, peddlers also tried to anticipate the settlers' needs and wants. They frequently represented new or unknown products with the hope of creating a demand for them.

Changes in the 20th century, once again including improvements in transportation, brought still more possibilities for sales representatives. Automobiles allowed representatives to travel to many more communities and to carry more product samples and descriptive catalogs. Trucks provided a new means of transporting merchandise. The growth of commercial aviation further expanded the opportunities for salespeople. Sales representatives would eventually be able to travel to customers in New York, Atlanta, Los Angeles, and Minneapolis, for example, all during a single week.

By the late 20th century, the food products industry was one of the largest employers of sales representatives. Other important fields included printing, publishing, fabricated metal products, chemicals and dyes, electrical and other machinery, and transportation equipment. Among the many establishments helped by sales representatives were retail outlets, who needed a constant supply of clothing, housewares, and other consumer goods, and hospitals, who purchased specialized surgical instruments, drugs, rubber gloves, and thousands of other products from representatives.

THE JOB

Manufacturers' representatives and wholesale sales representatives sell goods to retail stores, other manufacturers and wholesalers, government agencies, and various institutions. They usually do so within a specific geographical area. Some representatives concentrate on just a few products. An electrical appliance salesperson, for example, may sell 10–30 items ranging from food freezers and air-conditioners to waffle irons and portable heaters. Representatives of drug wholesalers, however, may sell as many as 50,000 items.

The duties of sales representatives usually include locating and contacting potential new clients, keeping a regular correspondence with existing customers, determining their clients' needs, and informing them of pertinent products and prices. They also travel to meet with clients, show them samples or catalogs, take orders, arrange for delivery, and possibly provide installation. A sales representative also must handle customer complaints, keep up to date on new products, and prepare reports. Many salespeople attend trade conferences, where they learn about products and make sales contacts.

Finding new customers is one of the most important tasks. Sales representatives often follow leads suggested by other clients, from advertisements in trade journals, and from participants in trade shows and conferences. They may make "cold calls" to potential clients. Sales representatives frequently meet with and entertain prospective clients during evenings and weekends.

Representatives who sell highly technical machinery or complex office equipment often are referred to as *sales engineers* or *industrial sales workers.* Because their products tend to be more specialized and their clients' needs more complex, the sales process for these workers tends to be longer and more involved. Before recommending a product, they may, for example, carefully analyze a customer's production processes, distribution methods, or office procedures. They usually prepare extensive sales presentations that include information on how their products will improve the quality and efficiency of the customer's operations.

Some sales engineers, often with the help of their company's research and development department, adapt products to a customer's specialized needs. They may provide the customer with instructions on how to use the new equipment or work with installation experts who provide this service. Some companies maintain a sales assistance staff to train customers and provide specific information. This permits sales representatives to devote a greater percentage of their time to direct sales contact.

Other sales workers, called *detail people,* do not engage in direct selling activities but strive instead to create a better general market for their companies' products. A detail person for a drug company, for example, may call on physicians and hospitals to inform them of new products and distribute samples.

The particular products sold by the sales representative directly affect the nature of the work. Salespeople who represent sporting goods manufacturers may spend most of their time driving from town to town calling on retail stores that carry sporting equipment. They may visit with coaches and athletic directors of high schools and colleges. A representative in this line may be a former athlete or coach who knows intimately the concerns of his or her customers.

Food manufacturers and wholesalers employ large numbers of sales representatives. Because these salespeople usually know the grocery stores and major chains that carry their products, their main focus is to ensure the maximum sales volume. Representatives negotiate with retail merchants to obtain the most advantageous store and shelf position for displaying their products. They encourage the store or chain to advertise their products, sometimes by offering to pay part of the advertising costs or by reducing the selling price to the merchant so that a special sale price can be offered to customers. Representatives check to make sure that shelf items are neatly arranged and that the store has sufficient stock of their products.

Sales transactions can involve huge amounts of merchandise, sometimes worth millions of dollars. For example, in a single transaction, a washing-machine manufacturer, construction company, or automobile manufacturer may purchase all the steel products it needs for an extended period of time. Salespeople in this field may do much of their business by telephone because the product they sell is standardized and, to the usual customer, requires no particular description or demonstration.

Direct, or door-to-door, selling has been an effective way of marketing various products, such as appliances and housewares, cookware, china, tableware and linens, foods, drugs, cosmetics and toiletries, costume jewelry, clothing, and greeting cards. Like other sales representatives, door-to-door sales workers find prospective buyers, explain and demonstrate their products, and take orders. In recent years, Internet sales have taken over much of the door-to-door market.

Several different arrangements are common between companies and their door-to-door sales workers. Under the *direct company plan,* for example, a sales representative is authorized to take orders for a product, and the company pays the representative a commission for each completed order. Such workers may be employees of the company and may receive a salary in addition to a commission, or they may be independent contractors. They usually are very well trained. Sales workers who sell magazine subscriptions may be hired, trained, and supervised by a *subscription crew leader,* who assigns representatives to specific areas, reviews the orders they take, and compiles sales records.

Under the *exhibit plan* a salesperson sets up an exhibit booth at a place where large numbers of people are expected to pass, such as a state fair, trade show, or product exposition. Customers approach the booth and schedule appointments with the salespersons for later demonstrations at home.

The *dealer plan* allows a salesperson to function as the proprietor of a small business. The salesperson, or *dealer,* purchases the product wholesale from the company and then resells it to consumers at the retail price, mainly through door-to-door sales.

Under various *group plans,* a customer is contacted by a salesperson and given the opportunity to sponsor a sales event. In the *party plan,* for example, the sales representative arranges to demonstrate products at the home of a customer, who then invites a group of friends for the party. The customer who hosts the party receives free or discounted merchandise in return for the use of the home and for assembling other potential customers for the salesperson.

Finally, the *COD plan* allows representatives to sell products on a cash-on-delivery (COD) basis. In this method, the salesperson makes a sale, perhaps collecting an advance deposit, and sends the order to the company. The company, in turn, ships the merchandise directly to the customer, who in this case makes payment to the delivery person, or to the salesperson, who then delivers the product to the customer and collects the balance owed.

Whatever the sales plan, door-to-door sales workers have some advantages over their counterparts in retail stores. Direct sellers, for example, do not have to wait for the customer to come to them; they go out and find the buyers for their products. The direct seller often carries only one product or a limited line of products and thus is much more familiar with the features and benefits of the merchandise. In general, direct sellers get the chance to demonstrate their products where they will most likely be used—in the home.

There are drawbacks to this type of selling. Many customers grow impatient or hostile when salespeople come to their house unannounced and uninvited. It may take several visits to persuade someone to buy the product. In a brief visit, the direct seller must win the confidence of the customer, develop the customer's interest in a product or service, and close the sale.

REQUIREMENTS

High School

A high school diploma is required for most sales positions, although an increasing number of salespeople are graduates of two- or four-year colleges. In high school, take classes such as business, mathematics, psychology, speech, and economics that will teach you to deal with customers and financial transactions.

Postsecondary Training

The more complex a product, the greater the likelihood that it will be sold by a college-trained person. About 30 percent of all door-to-door sales workers have a college degree.

Some areas of sales work require specialized college work. Those in engineering sales, for example, usually have a college degree in a relevant engineering field. Other fields that demand specific college degrees include chemical sales (chemistry or chemical engineering), office systems (accounting or business administration), and pharmaceuticals and drugs (biology, chemistry, or pharmacy). Those in less technical sales positions usually benefit from course work in English, speech, psychology, marketing, public relations, economics, advertising, finance, accounting, and business law.

Other Requirements

To be a successful sales representatives, you should enjoy working with people. You should also be self-confident, enthusiastic, and self-disciplined. You must be able to handle rejection since only a small number of your sales contacts will result in a sale.

EXPLORING

If you are interested in becoming a sales representative, try to get part-time or summer work in a retail store. Working as a telemarketer also is useful. Some high schools and junior colleges offer programs that combine classroom study with work experience in sales.

Various opportunities exist that provide experience in direct selling. You can take part in sales drives for school or community groups.

Occasionally manufacturers hire college students for summer assignments. These temporary positions provide an opportunity for the employer and employee to appraise each other. A high percentage of students hired for these specialized summer programs become career employees after graduation. Some wholesale warehouses also offer temporary or summer positions.

EMPLOYERS

In the United States, 1.8 million people work as manufacturers' and wholesale sales representatives. About 60 percent work in wholesale, many as sellers of machinery. Food, drugs, electrical goods, hardware, and clothing are among the most common products sold by sales representatives.

STARTING OUT

Firms looking for sales representatives sometimes list openings with high school and college placement offices, as well as with public and private employment agencies. In many areas, professional sales associations refer people to suitable openings. Contacting companies directly also is recommended. A list of manufacturers and wholesalers can be found in telephone books and industry directories, which are available at public libraries.

Although some high school graduates are hired for manufacturers' or wholesale sales jobs, many join a company in a nonselling position, such as office, stock, or shipping clerk. This experience allows an employee to learn about the company and its products. From there, he or she eventually may be promoted to a sales position.

Most new representatives complete a training period before receiving a sales assignment. In some cases new salespeople rotate through several departments of an organization to gain a broad exposure to the company's products. Large companies often use formal training programs lasting two years or more, while small organizations frequently rely on supervised sales experience.

Direct selling usually is an easy field to enter. Direct sale companies advertise for available positions in newspapers, in sales workers' specialty magazines, and on television and radio. Many people enter direct selling through contacts they have had with other door-to-door sales workers. Most firms have district or area representatives who interview applicants and arrange the necessary training. Part-time positions in direct selling are common.

ADVANCEMENT

New representatives usually spend their early years improving their sales ability, developing product knowledge, and finding new clients. As sales workers gain experience they may be shifted to increasingly large territories or more difficult types of customers. In some organizations, experienced sales workers narrow their focus. For example, an office equipment sales representative may work solely on government contracts.

Advancement to management positions, such as regional or district manager, also is possible. Some representatives, however, choose to remain in basic sales. Because of commissions, they often earn more money than their managers do, and many enjoy being in the field and working directly with their customers.

A small number of representatives decide to become *manufacturers' agents,* or self-employed salespeople who handle products for various organizations. Agents perform many of the same functions as sales representatives but usually on a more modest scale.

Door-to-door sales workers also have advancement possibilities. Some are promoted to supervisory roles and recruit, train, and manage new members of the sales force. Others become area, branch, or district managers. Many managers of direct selling firms began as door-to-door sales workers.

EARNINGS

Many beginning sales representatives are paid a salary while receiving their training. After assuming direct responsibility for a sales territory, they may receive only a commission (a fixed percentage of each dollar sold). A modified commission plan—a lower rate of commission on sales plus a low base salary—is also common. Some companies provide bonuses to successful representatives.

Because manufacturers' and wholesale sales representatives typically work on commission, salaries vary widely. Some made as little as $22,010 a year in 2001, according to the U.S. Department of Labor. More successful representatives earn more than $106,560. Most, however, earn between $29,830 and $59,070. The average salary is about $41,510, including commission.

Earnings can be affected by changes in the economy or industry cycles, and great fluctuations in salary from year to year or month to month are common. Employees who travel usually are reimbursed for transportation, hotels, meals, and client entertainment expenses.

Door-to-door sales workers usually earn a straight commission on their sales, ranging from 10 to 40 percent of an item's suggested retail price. The USDL reports that door-to-door sales workers had median earnings of $24,830 in 2001. The lowest paid workers earned $13,220 or less annually, and the highest paid workers earned $53,250 or more.

Sales engineers earned salaries that ranged from $35,730 to $102,090 or more in 2001, according to the Department of Labor.

Sales representatives typically receive vacation days, medical and life insurance, and retirement benefits. However, manufacturers' agents and some door-to-door sales workers do not receive benefits.

WORK ENVIRONMENT

Salespeople generally work long and irregular hours. Those with large territories may spend all day calling and meeting customers in one city and much of the night traveling to the place where they will make the next day's calls and visits. Sales workers with a small territory may do little overnight travel but, like most sales workers, may spend many evenings preparing reports, writing up orders, and entertaining customers. Several times a year, sales workers may travel to company meetings and participate in trade conventions and conferences. Irregular working hours, travel, and the competitive demands of the job can be disruptive to ordinary family life.

Sales work is physically demanding. Representatives often spend most of the day on their feet. Many carry heavy sample cases or catalogs. Occasionally, sales workers assist a customer in arranging a display of the company's products or moving stock items. Many door-to-door sellers work in their own community or nearby areas, although some cover more extensive and distant territories. They often are outdoors in all kinds of weather. Direct sellers must treat customers, even those who are rude or impatient, with tact and courtesy.

OUTLOOK

Employment for manufacturers' and wholesale sales representatives is expected to grow more slowly than the average for all occupations over the next several years, according to the U.S. Department of Labor. Technological advances have reduced the number of sales representatives needed to sell products. Electronic data interchange (EDI), a system that improves communication between computers, for example, allows customers to order goods from suppliers more easily.

Future opportunities will vary greatly depending upon the specific product and industry. For example, as giant food chains replace independent grocers, fewer salespeople will be needed to sell groceries to individual stores. By contrast, greater opportunities will probably exist in the air-conditioning field, and advances in consumer electronics and computer technology also may provide many new opportunities.

FOR MORE INFORMATION

For a list of marketing programs and detailed career information, contact

Direct Marketing Association
Educational Foundation
1120 Avenue of the Americas
New York, NY 10036-6700

Tel: 212-768-7277
http://www.the-dma.org

For referrals to industry trade associations, contact MANA.
Manufacturers' Agents National Association (MANA)
PO Box 3467
Laguna Hills, CA 92654-3467
Tel: 877-626-2776
Email: MANA@MANAonline.org
http://www.manaonline.org

URBAN AND REGIONAL PLANNERS

QUICK FACTS

School Subjects
Business
English
Government

Personal Skills
Communication/ideas
Leadership/management

Work Environment
Primarily indoors
Primarily multiple locations

Minimum Education Level
Bachelor's degree

Salary Range
$30,940 to $48,530 to $74,240+

Certification or Licensing
Voluntary

Outlook
About as fast as the average

DOT
199

GOE
11.03.02

NOC
2153

O*NET-SOC
19-3051.00

OVERVIEW

Urban and regional planners assist in the development and redevelopment of a city, metropolitan area, or region. They work to preserve historical buildings, protect the environment, and help manage a community's growth and change. Planners evaluate individual buildings and city blocks, and are also involved in the design of new subdivisions, neighborhoods, and even entire towns. There are approximately 30,000 urban and regional planners working in the United States.

HISTORY

Cities have always been planned to some degree. Most cultures, from the ancient Greeks to the Chinese to the Native Americans, made some organized plans for the development of their cities. By the fourth century B.C., theories of urban planning existed in the writings of Plato, Aristotle, and Hippocrates. Their ideas concerning the issues of site selection and orientation were later modified and updated by Vitruvius in his *De architectura*, which appeared after 27 B.C. This work helped create a standardized guide for Roman engineers as they built fortified settlements and cities throughout the vast empire. Largely inspired by Vitruvius, 15th-century Italian theorists compiled enormous amounts of information and ideas on urban planning. They replaced vertical walls with angular fortifications for better protection during times of war. They also widened streets and opened up squares by building new churches, halls, and palaces. Early designs were based on a symmetrical style that quickly became fashionable in many of the more prosperous European cities.

Modern urban planning owes much to the driving force of the industrial revolution. The desire for more sanitary living conditions led to the demolition of slums. Laws were enacted to govern new construction and monitor the condition of old buildings. In 1848, Baron George Eugene Haussmann organized the destruction and replacement of 40 percent of the residential quarters in Paris and created new neighborhood park systems. In England, the 1875 Public Health Act allowed municipalities to regulate new construction, the removal of waste, and newly constructed water and sewer systems.

THE JOB

Urban and regional planners assist in the development or maintenance of carefully designed communities. Working for a government agency or as a consultant, planners are involved in integrating new buildings, houses, sites, and subdivisions into an overall city plan. Their plans must coordinate streets, traffic, public facilities, water and sewage, transportation, safety, and ecological factors such as wildlife habitats, wetlands, and floodplains. Planners are also involved in renovating and preserving historic buildings. They work with a variety of professionals, including architects, artists, computer programmers, engineers, economists, landscape architects, land developers, lawyers, writers, and environmental and other special-interest groups.

Chris Wayne works as a redevelopment planner for the city of Omaha, Nebraska. He identifies new project sites—buildings that the planning department wants to redevelop—and helps acquire the property. Before making a purchase, he hires an appraiser to determine the worth of the building and then makes an offer to the building's owner. If the owner accepts and the building is slated for redevelopment, the city may have to vacate the building. "This involves interviewing the residents," Wayne says, "to determine what's necessary for them to move. We determine what amount they'll be compensated." Various community programs assist in finding new housing or providing tenants with moving funds. Once the property has been vacated, the planning department accepts and reviews proposals from developers. A developer is then offered a contract. When demolition and construction begin, Wayne's department must monitor the project and make the necessary payments.

Urban and regional planners also work with unused or undeveloped land. They may help design the layout for a proposed building, keeping in mind traffic circulation, parking, and the use of open space. Planners are also responsible for suggesting ways to implement these programs or proposals, considering their costs and how to raise funds for them.

Schools, churches, recreational areas, and residential tracts are studied to determine how they will fit into designs for optimal usefulness and beauty. As with other factors, specifications for the nature and kinds of buildings must be considered. Zoning codes, which regulate the specific use of land and buildings, must be adhered to during construction. Planners need to be knowledgeable of these regulations and other legal matters and communicate them to builders and developers.

Some urban and regional planners teach in colleges and schools of planning, and many do consulting work. Today's planners are concerned not only with city codes, but also with environmental problems of water pollution, solid waste disposal, water treatment plants, and public housing.

Planners work in older cities or design new ones. Columbia, Maryland, and Reston, Virginia, both built in the 1960s, are examples of planned communities. Before plans for such communities can be developed, planners must prepare detailed maps and charts showing the proposed use of land for housing, business, and community needs. These studies provide information on the types of industries in the area, the locations of housing developments and businesses, and the plans for providing basic needs such as water, sewage treatment, and transportation. After maps and charts have been analyzed, planners design the layout to present to land developers, city officials, housing experts, architects, and construction firms.

The following short descriptions list the wide variety of planners within the field.

Human services planners develop health and social service programs to upgrade living standards for those lacking opportunities or resources. These planners frequently work for private health care organizations and government agencies.

Historic preservation planners use their knowledge of the law and economics to help preserve historic buildings, sites, and neighborhoods. They are frequently employed by state agencies, local governments, and the National Park Service.

Transportation planners, working mainly for government agencies, oversee the transportation infrastructure of a community, keeping in mind local priorities such as economic development and environmental concerns.

Housing and community development planners analyze housing needs to identify potential opportunities and problems that may affect a neighborhood and its surrounding communities. Such planners are usually employed by private real estate and financial firms, local governments, and community development organizations.

Economic development planners, usually employed by local governments or chambers of commerce, focus on attracting and retaining industry to a specific community. They communicate with industry leaders who select sites for new plants, warehouses, and other major projects.

Environmental planners advocate the integration of environmental issues into building construction, land use, and other community objectives. They work at all levels of government and for some nonprofit organizations.

Urban design planners work to design and locate public facilities, such as churches, libraries, and parks, to best serve the larger community. Employers include large-scale developers, private consulting firms, and local governments.

International development planners specialize in strategies for transportation, rural development, modernization, and urbanization. They are frequently employed by international agencies, such as the United Nations, and by national governments in less developed countries.

REQUIREMENTS

High School

You should take courses in government and social studies to learn about the past and present organizational structure of cities and counties. You need good communication skills for working with people in a variety of professions, so take courses in speech and English composition. Drafting, architecture, and art classes will familiarize you with the basics of design. Become active on your student council so that you can be involved in implementing changes for the school community.

Postsecondary Training

A bachelor's degree is the minimum requirement for most trainee jobs with federal, state, or local government boards and agencies. However, more opportunities for employment and advancement are available to those with a master's degree. Typical courses include geography, public administration, political science, law, engineering, architecture, landscape architecture, real estate, finance, and management. Computer courses and training in statistical techniques are also essential. Most masters' programs last a minimum of two years and require students to participate in internships with city planning departments.

When considering schools, check with the American Planning Association (APA) for a list of accredited undergraduate and graduate planning programs. The APA can also direct you to scholarship and fellowship programs available to students enrolled in planning programs.

Certification or Licensing

Although not a requirement, obtaining certification in urban and regional planning can lead to more challenging, better paying positions. The American Institute of Certified Planners, a division of the APA, grants certification to planners who meet certain academic and professional requirements and successfully complete an examination. The exam tests for knowledge of the history and future of planning, research methods, plan implementation, and other relevant topics.

Other Requirements

Chris Wayne pursued a master's in urban studies because he was drawn to community development. "I was interested in the social interaction of people and the space they occupy, such as parks and plazas," he says.

In addition to being interested in planning, you should have design skills and a good understanding of spatial relationships. Good analytical skills will help you in evaluating projects. Planners must be able to visualize the relationships between streets, buildings, parks, and other developed spaces and anticipate potential planning problems. As a result, logic and problem-solving abilities are also important.

EXPLORING

Research the origins of your city by visiting your county courthouse and local library. Check out early photographs and maps of your area to give you an idea of what went into the planning of your community. Visit local historic areas to learn about the development and history behind old buildings. You may also consider getting involved in efforts to preserve local buildings and areas that are threatened.

With the help of a teacher or academic advisor, arrange to interview a working planner to gain details of his or her job. Another good way to see what planners do is to attend a meeting of a local planning commission, which by law is open to the public. Interested students can find out details about upcoming meetings through their local paper or planning office.

EMPLOYERS

There are approximately 30,000 urban and regional planners working in the United States. Seven out of 10 of planners work for local governments; others work for state agencies, the federal government, and in the private sector.

Many planners are hired for full-time work where they intern. Others choose to seek other opportunities, such as with state and federal governments and nonprofit organizations. Planners work for government agencies that focus on particular areas of city research and development, such as transportation, the environment, and housing. Urban and regional planners are also sought by colleges, law firms, the United Nations, and even foreign governments of rapidly modernizing countries.

STARTING OUT

With a bachelor's degree, a beginning worker may start out as an assistant at an architectural firm or construction office. Others start out working as city planning aides in regional or urban offices. New planners research projects, conduct interviews, survey the field, and write reports on their findings. Those with a master's degree can enter the profession at a higher level, working for federal, state, and local agencies.

Previous work experience in a planning office or with an architectural or engineering firm is useful before applying for a job with city, county, or regional planning agencies. Membership in a professional organization is also helpful in locating job opportunities. These include the American Planning Association, the American Institute of Architects, the American Society of Civil Engineers, and the International City/County Management Association. Most of these organizations host student chapters that provide information on internship opportunities and professional publications. (See the end of this article for contact information.)

Because many planning staffs are small, directors are usually eager to fill positions quickly. As a result, job availability can be highly variable. Students are advised to apply for jobs before they complete their degree requirements. Most colleges have placement offices to assist students in finding job leads.

ADVANCEMENT

Beginning assistants can advance within the planning board or department to eventually become planners. The positions of senior planner and planning director are successive steps in some agencies. Frequently, experienced planners obtain advancement by moving to a larger city or county planning board, where they become responsible for larger and more complicated projects, make policy decisions, or become responsible for funding new developments. Other planners may become consultants to communities that cannot afford a full-time planner. Some planners also serve as city managers, cabinet secretaries, and presidents of consulting firms.

EARNINGS

Earnings vary based on position, work experience, and the population of the city or town the planner serves. According to the Bureau of Labor Statistics, median annual earnings of urban and regional planners were $48,530 in 2001. The lowest 10 percent earned less than $30,940, and the highest 10 percent earned more than $74,240. Median annual earnings in local government, the industry employing the largest numbers of urban and regional planners, were $45,300.

Because many planners work for government agencies, they usually have sick leave and vacation privileges and are covered by retirement and health plans. Many planners also have access to a city automobile.

Planners who work as consultants are generally paid on a fee basis. Their earnings are often high and vary greatly according to their reputations and work experience. Their earnings will depend on the number of consulting jobs they accept.

WORK ENVIRONMENT

Planners spend a considerable amount of time in an office setting. However, in order to gather data about the areas they develop, planners also spend much of their time outdoors examining the surrounding land, structures, and traffic. Most planners work standard 40-hour weeks, but they may also attend evening or weekend council meetings or public forums to share upcoming development proposals.

Planners work alone and with land developers, public officials, civic leaders, and citizens' groups. Occasionally, they may face opposition from interest groups against certain development proposals and, as a result, they must have the patience needed to work with disparate groups. The job can be stressful when trying to keep tight deadlines or when defending proposals in both the public and private sectors.

OUTLOOK

The U.S. Department of Labor expects the overall demand for urban and regional planners to grow about as fast as the average over the next several years. Communities turn to professional planners for help in meeting demands resulting from urbanization and the growth in population. Urban and regional planners are needed to zone and plan land use for undeveloped and rural areas as well as commercial development in rapidly growing suburban areas. There will be jobs available with nongovernmental agencies that deal with historic preservation and redevelopment. Opportunities also exist in maintaining existing bridges, highways, and sewers, and in preserving and restoring historic sites and buildings.

Factors that may affect job growth include government regulation regarding the environment, housing, transportation, and land use. The continuing redevelopment of inner-city areas and the expansion of suburban areas will serve to provide many jobs for planners. However, when communities face budgetary constraints, planning departments may be reduced before others, such as police forces or education.

FOR MORE INFORMATION

For more information on careers, certification, and accredited planning programs, contact the following organizations:

American Institute of Architects
1735 New York Avenue, NW
Washington, DC 20006
Tel: 800-AIA-3837
Email: infocentral@aia.org
http://www.aia.org

American Planning Association
122 South Michigan Avenue, Suite 1600
Chicago, IL 60603
Tel: 312-431-9100
Email: APAInfo@planning.org
http://www.planning.org

For career guidance and information on student chapters as well as a list of colleges that offer civil engineering programs, contact

American Society of Civil Engineers
1801 Alexander Bell Drive
Reston, VA 20191-4400
Tel: 800-548-2723
http://www.asce.org

To learn about city management and the issues affecting today's cities, visit this website or contact

International City/County Management Association
777 North Capitol Street, NE, Suite 500
Washington, DC 20002
Tel: 202-289-4262
http://www.icma.org

WRITERS

QUICK FACTS

School Subjects English Journalism	**Outlook** Faster than the average
Personal Skills Communication/ideas Helping/teaching	**DOT** 131
Work Environment Primarily indoors Primarily one location	**GOE** 01.01.02
Minimum Education Level Bachelor's degree	**NOC** 5121
Salary Range $20,570 to $42,450 to $83,180+	**O*NET-SOC** 27-3042.00, 27-3043.01, 27-3043.02, 27-3043.03, 27-3043.04
Certification or Licensing None available	

OVERVIEW

Writers are involved with expressing, editing, promoting, and interpreting ideas and facts in written form for books, magazines, trade journals, newspapers, technical studies and reports, company newsletters, radio and television broadcasts, and advertisements.

Writers develop fiction and nonfiction ideas for plays, novels, poems, and other related works; report, analyze, and interpret facts, events, and personalities; review art, music, drama, and other artistic presentations; and persuade the general public to choose or favor certain goods, services, and personalities. There are approximately 183,000 salaried writers, authors, and technical writers employed in the United States.

HISTORY

The skill of writing has existed for thousands of years. Papyrus fragments with writing by ancient Egyptians date from about 3000 B.C., and archaeological findings show that the Chinese had developed books by about 1300 B.C. A number of technical obstacles had to be overcome before printing and the profession of writing evolved. Books of the Middle Ages were copied by hand on parchment. The ornate style that marked these books helped ensure their rarity. Also, few people were able to read. Religious fervor prohibited the reproduction of secular literature.

Two factors helped create the publishing industry: the invention of the printing press by Johannes Gutenberg in the middle of the 15th century and the liberalism of the Protestant Reformation, which helped encourage a wider range of publications, greater literacy, and the creation of a number of works of literary merit. The first authors worked directly with printers.

The modern publishing age began in the 18th century. Printing became mechanized, and the novel, magazine, and newspaper developed. The first newspaper in the American colonies appeared in the early 18th century, but it was Benjamin Franklin, who, as editor and writer, made the *Pennsylvania Gazette* one of the most influential by setting a high standard for his fellow American journalists. Franklin also published the first magazine in the colonies, *The American Magazine,* in 1741.

Advances in the printing trades, photoengraving, retailing, and the availability of capital produced a boom in newspapers and magazines in the 19th century. Further mechanization in the printing field, such as the use of the Linotype machine, high-speed rotary presses, and special color reproduction processes, set the stage for still further growth in the book, newspaper, and magazine industry.

In addition to the print media, the broadcasting industry has contributed to the development of the professional writer. Film, radio, and television are sources of entertainment, information, and education that provide employment for thousands of writers.

THE JOB

Writers work in the field of communications. Specifically, they deal with the written word, whether it is destined for the printed page, broadcast, computer screen, or live theater. The nature of their work is as varied as the materials they produce: books, magazines, trade journals, newspapers, technical reports, company newsletters and other publications, advertisements, speeches, scripts for motion picture and stage productions, and scripts for radio and television broadcast. Writers develop ideas and write for all media.

Prose writers for newspapers, magazines, and books share many of the same duties. First they come up with an idea for an article or book from their own interests or are assigned a topic by an editor. The topic is of relevance to the particular publication; for example, a writer for a magazine on parenting may be assigned an article on car seat safety. Then writers begin gathering as much information as possible about the subject through library research, interviews, the Internet, observation, and other methods. They keep extensive notes from which they will draw material for their project. Once the material has been organized and arranged in logical sequence, writers prepare a written outline. The process of developing a piece of writing is exciting, although it can also involve detailed and solitary work. After researching an idea, a writer might discover that a different perspective or related topic would be more effective, entertaining, or marketable.

When working on assignment, writers submit their outlines to an editor or other company representative for approval. Then they write a first draft of the manuscript, trying to put the material into words that will have the desired effect on their audience. They often rewrite or polish sections of the material as they proceed, always searching for just the right way of imparting information or expressing an idea or opinion. A manuscript may be reviewed, corrected, and revised numerous times before a final copy is submitted. Even after that, an editor may request additional changes.

Writers for newspapers, magazines, or books often specialize in their subject matter. Some writers might have an educational background that allows them to give critical interpretations or analyses. For example, a health or science writer for a newspaper typically has a degree in biology and can interpret new ideas in the field for the average reader.

Columnists or *commentators* analyze news and social issues. They write about events from the standpoint of their own experience or opinion. *Critics* review literary, musical, or artistic works and performances. *Editorial writers* write on topics of public interest, and their comments, consistent with the viewpoints and policies of their employers, are intended to stimulate or mold public opinion. *Newswriters* work for newspapers, radio, or TV news departments, writing news stories from notes supplied by reporters or wire services.

Corporate writers and writers for nonprofit organizations have a wide variety of responsibilities. These writers may work in such places as a large insurance corporation or for a small nonprofit religious group, where they may be required to write news releases, annual reports, speeches for the company head, or public relations materials. Typically they are assigned a topic with length requirements for a given project. They may receive raw research materials, such as statistics, and they are expected to conduct additional research, including personal interviews. These writers must be able to write quickly and accurately on short deadlines, while also working with people whose primary job is not in the communications field. The written work is submitted to a supervisor and often a legal department for approval; rewrites are a normal part of this job.

Copywriters write copy that is primarily designed to sell goods and services. Their work appears as advertisements in newspapers, magazines, and other publications or as commercials on radio and television broadcasts. Sales and marketing representatives first provide information on the product and help determine the style and length of the copy. The copywriters conduct additional research and interviews; to formulate an effective approach, they study advertising trends and review surveys of consumer preferences. Armed with this information, copywriters write a draft that is submitted to the account executive and the client for approval. The copy is often returned for correction and revision until everyone involved is satisfied. Copywriters, like corporate writers, may also write articles, bulletins, news releases, sales letters, speeches, and other related informative and promotional material. Many copywriters are employed in advertising agencies. They also may work for public relations firms or in communications departments of large companies.

Technical writers can be divided into two main groups: those who convert technical information into material for the general public, and those who convey technical information between professionals. Technical writers in the first group may prepare service manuals or handbooks, instruction or repair booklets, or sales literature or brochures; those in the second group may write grant proposals, research reports, contract specifications, or research abstracts.

Screenwriters prepare scripts for motion pictures or television. They select or are assigned a subject, conduct research, write and submit a plot outline and narrative synopsis (treatment), and confer with the producer and/or director about possible revisions. Screenwriters may adapt books or plays for film and television dramatizations. They often collaborate with other screenwriters and may specialize in a particular type of script or writing.

Playwrights do similar writing for the stage. They write dialogue and describe action for plays that may be tragedies, comedies, or dramas, with themes sometimes adapted from fictional, historical, or narrative sources. Playwrights combine the elements of action, conflict, purpose, and resolution to depict events from real or imaginary life. They often make revisions even while the play is in rehearsal.

Continuity writers prepare the material read by radio and television announcers to introduce or connect various parts of their programs.

Novelists and *short story writers* create stories that may be published in books, magazines, or literary journals. They take incidents from their own lives, from news events, or from their imaginations and create characters, settings, actions, and resolutions. *Poets* create narrative, dramatic, or lyric poetry for books, magazines, or other publications, as well as for special events such as commemorations. These writers may work with literary agents or editors who help guide them through the writing process, which includes research of the subject matter and an understanding of the intended audience. Many universities and colleges offer graduate degrees in creative writing. In these programs, students work intensively with published writers to learn the art of storytelling.

Writers can be employed either as in-house staff or as freelancers. Pay varies according to experience and the position, but freelancers must provide their own office space and equipment such as computers and fax machines. Freelancers also are responsible for keeping tax records, sending out invoices, negotiating contracts, and providing their own health insurance.

REQUIREMENTS

High School

While in high school, build a broad educational foundation by taking courses in English, literature, foreign languages, general science, social studies, computer science, and typing. The ability to type is almost a requisite for all positions in the communications field, as is familiarity with computers.

Postsecondary Training

Competition for writing jobs almost always demands the background of a college education. Many employers prefer you have a broad liberal arts background or majors in English, literature, history, philosophy, or one of the social sciences. Other employers desire communications or journalism training in college. Occasionally a master's degree in a specialized writing field may be required. A number of schools offer courses in journalism, and some of them offer courses or majors in book publishing, publication management, and newspaper and magazine writing.

In addition to formal course work, most employers look for practical writing experience. If you have served on high school or college newspapers, yearbooks, or literary magazines, you will make a better candidate, as well as if you have worked for small community newspapers or radio stations, even in an unpaid position. Many book publishers, magazines, newspapers, and radio and television stations have summer internship programs that provide valuable training if you want to learn about the publishing and broadcasting businesses. Interns do many simple tasks, such as running errands and answering phones, but some may be asked to perform research, conduct interviews, or even write some minor pieces.

Writers who specialize in technical fields may need degrees, concentrated course work, or experience in specific subject areas. This applies frequently to engineering, business, or one of the sciences. Also, technical communications is a degree now offered at many universities and colleges.

If you wish to enter positions with the federal government, you will have to take a civil service examination and meet certain specified requirements, according to the type and level of position.

Other Requirements

To be a writer, you should be creative and able to express ideas clearly, have a broad general knowledge, be skilled in research techniques, and be computer literate. Other assets include curiosity, persistence, initiative, resourcefulness, and an accurate memory. For some jobs—on a newspaper, for example, where the activity is hectic and deadlines are short—the ability to concentrate and produce under pressure is essential.

EXPLORING

As a high school or college student, you can test your interest and aptitude in the field of writing by serving as a reporter or writer on school newspapers, yearbooks, and literary magazines. Various writing courses and workshops will offer you the opportunity to sharpen your writing skills.

Small community newspapers and local radio stations often welcome contributions from outside sources, although they may not have the resources to pay for them. Jobs in bookstores, magazine

Notable Economics Graduates

Name	Job Title	Institution
Earl Graves CEO	*Black Enterprise* magazine	Morgan State University
George H.W. Bush	41st President of the United States	Yale University
Ted Turner	Founder, Cable News Network	Brown University
Sandra Day O'Connor	U.S. Supreme Court Justice	Stanford University
William F. Buckley	Journalist	Yale University
Lionel Richie	Singer/Songwriter	Tuskegee University
Esther Dyson	Software Pioneer	Harvard University
Eileen Collins	Shuttle Commander, NASA	Syracuse University
Jennifer Azzi	Professional Basketball Player	Stanford University
Ronald Reagan	40th President of the United States	Eureka College
Scott Adams	Cartoonist, creator of Dilbert	Hartwick College
Steve Ballmer	CEO, Microsoft	Harvard University
George Schultz	Former U.S. Secretary of State	Princeton University Massachusetts Institute of Technology
Meg Whitman	CEO, ebay Technologies	Princeton University
John Sweeney	President, AFL-CIO	Iona College
Barbara Boxer	U.S. Senator	Brooklyn College
John Snow	U.S. Secretary of the Treasury	University of Virginia
Arnold Schwarzenegger	Actor and California governor	University of Wisconsin-Superior

shops, and even newsstands will offer you a chance to become familiar with various publications.

You can also obtain information on writing as a career by visiting local newspapers, publishers, or radio and television stations and interviewing some of the writers who work there. Career conferences and other guidance programs frequently include speakers on the entire field of communications from local or national organizations.

EMPLOYERS

There are approximately 126,000 writers and authors, and 57,000 technical writers currently employed in the United States. Nearly a fourth of salaried writers and editors work for newspapers, magazines, and book publishers, according to the *Occupational Outlook Handbook.* Writers are also employed by advertising agencies and public relations firms, in radio and television broadcasting, and for journals and newsletters published by business and nonprofit organizations, such as professional associations, labor unions, and religious organizations. Other employers are government agencies and film production companies.

STARTING OUT

A fair amount of experience is required to gain a high-level position in the field. Most writers start out in entry-level positions. These jobs may be listed with college placement offices, or they may be obtained by applying directly to the employment departments of the individual publishers or broadcasting companies. Graduates who previously served internships with these companies often have the advantage of knowing someone who can give them a personal recommendation. Want ads in newspapers and trade journals are another source for jobs. Because of the competition for positions, however, few vacancies are listed with public or private employment agencies.

Employers in the communications field usually are interested in samples of published writing. These are often assembled in an organized portfolio or scrapbook. Bylined or signed articles are more credible (and, as a result, more useful) than stories whose source is not identified.

Beginning positions as a junior writer usually involve library research, preparation of rough drafts for part or all of a report, cataloging, and other related writing tasks. These are generally carried on under the supervision of a senior writer.

Some technical writers have entered the field after working in public relations departments or as technicians or research assistants, then transferring to technical writing as openings occur. Many firms now hire writers directly upon application or recommendation of college professors and placement offices.

ADVANCEMENT

Most writers find their first jobs as editorial or production assistants. Advancement may be more rapid in small companies, where beginners learn by doing a little bit of everything and may be given writing tasks immediately. In large firms, duties are usually more compartmentalized. Assistants in entry-level positions are assigned such tasks as research, fact checking, and copyrighting, but it generally takes much longer to advance to full-scale writing duties.

Promotion into more responsible positions may come with the assignment of more important articles and stories to write, or it may be the result of moving to another company. Mobility among employees in this field is common. An assistant in one publishing house may switch to an executive position in another. Or a writer may switch to a related field as a type of advancement.

A technical writer can be promoted to positions of responsibility by moving from such jobs as writer to technical editor to project leader or documentation manager. Opportunities in specialized positions also are possible.

Freelance or self-employed writers earn advancement in the form of larger fees as they gain exposure and establish their reputations.

EARNINGS

In 2001, median annual earnings for salaried writers and authors were $42,450 a year, according to the Bureau of Labor Statistics. The lowest 10 percent earned less than $20,570, while the highest 10 percent earned $83,180 or more. In book publishing, some specialties pay better than others. Technical writers earned a median salary of $49,370 in 2001.

In addition to their salaries, many writers earn some income from freelance work. Part-time freelancers may earn from $5,000 to $15,000 a year. Freelance earnings vary widely. Full-time established freelance writers may earn up to $75,000 a year.

WORK ENVIRONMENT

Working conditions vary for writers. Although their workweek usually runs 35 to 40 hours, many writers work overtime. A publication that is issued frequently has more deadlines closer together, creating greater pressures to meet them. The work is especially hectic on newspapers and at broadcasting companies, which operate seven days a week. Writers often work nights and weekends to meet deadlines or to cover a late-developing story.

Most writers work independently, but they often must cooperate with artists, photographers, rewriters, and advertising people who may have widely differing ideas of how the materials should be prepared and presented.

Physical surroundings range from comfortable private offices to noisy, crowded newsrooms filled with other workers typing and talking on the telephone. Some writers must confine their research to the library or telephone interviews, but others may travel to other cities or countries or to local sites, such as theaters, ballparks, airports, factories, or other offices.

The work is arduous, but most writers are seldom bored. Some jobs, such as that of the foreign correspondent, require travel. The most difficult element is the continual pressure of deadlines. People who are the most content as writers enjoy and work well with deadline pressure.

OUTLOOK

The employment of writers is expected to increase faster than the average rate of all occupations over the next several years, according to the U.S. Department of Labor. The demand for writers by newspapers, periodicals, book publishers, and nonprofit organizations is expected to increase. The growth of online publishing on company websites and other online services will also demand many talented writers; those with computer skills will be at an advantage as a result. Advertising and public relations will also provide job opportunities.

The major book and magazine publishers, broadcasting companies, advertising agencies, public relations firms, and the federal government account for the concentration of writers in large cities such as New York, Chicago, Los Angeles, Boston, Philadelphia, San Francisco, and Washington, D.C. Opportunities with small newspapers, corporations, and professional, religious, business, technical, and trade publications can be found throughout the country.

People entering this field should realize that the competition for jobs is extremely keen. Beginners may especially have difficulty finding employment. Of the thousands who graduate each year with degrees in English, journalism, communications, and the liberal arts, intending to establish a career as a writer, many turn to other occupations when they find that applicants far outnumber the job openings available. College students would do well to keep this in mind and prepare for an unrelated alternate career in the event they are unable to obtain a position as writer; another benefit of this approach is that, at the same time, they will become qualified as writers in a specialized field. The practicality of preparing for alternate careers is borne out by the fact that opportunities are best in firms that prepare business and trade publications and in technical writing.

Potential writers who end up working in a different field may be able to earn some income as freelancers, selling articles, stories, books, and possibly TV and movie scripts, but it is usually difficult for anyone to be self-supporting entirely on independent writing.

FOR MORE INFORMATION

For information on writing and editing careers in the field of communications, contact

National Association of Science Writers
PO Box 890
Hedgesville, WV 25427
Tel: 304-754-5077
http://www.nasw.org

This organization offers student memberships for those interested in opinion writing.

National Conference of Editorial Writers
3899 North Front Street
Harrisburg, PA 17110
Tel: 717-703-3015
Email: ncew@pa-news.org
http://www.ncew.org

GLOSSARY

assets: what an individual or group owns

bonds: certificate issued by government or corporate entity that pledges the original investment amount plus interest on a specific date

capitalism: economic system that supports the private ownership and trade of goods and services

credit: promise of payment (usually with interest) for goods and services received ahead of time

depression: in economic terms, a period categorized by little to no economic growth, high inflation, and high levels of unemployment

dividends: profits of a company that are distributed to stock shareholders

economics: the study of systems that help to meet people's needs in a world of limited resources

export: to sell goods or services to other countries

import: to purchase goods or services from other countries

inflation: an overall increase in prices brought on by a surplus of money available

invest: to contribute money to a business in the hopes of a larger financial return

macroeconomics: the study of economic systems as a whole and how different parts interact with one another; concerned with issues such as unemployment, input and output levels, and inflation.

microeconomics: the study of small economic systems, such as those within companies or households; concerned with price and income levels and the distribution of goods and services.

monopoly: a market with no competition

profit: the amount of money earned after expenses

recession: less severe than a depression, this is a period of slow economic growth

stock: certificate proving part ownership of a company

tax: a financial contribution to the government required by individuals, corporations, and other groups

FURTHER READING

Bamford, Janet. *Street Wise: A Guide for Teen Investors.* Williston, Vt.: Bloomberg Press, 2000.

Bergen, Lara. *Funny Money: In This Book, You Will Learn All About Pennies, Nickels, Dimes, Quarters and Dollars!* New York: Price Stern Sloan, 1999.

Carter, David M. and Darren Rovell. *On the Ball: What You Can Learn About Business From America's Sports Leaders.* Upper Saddle River, N.J.: Financial Times Prentice Hall, 2003.

Collins, Jim. *Good to Great: Why Some Companies Make the Leap . . . and Others Don't.* New York: HarperCollins, 2001.

Hazlitt, Henry. *Economics in One Lesson.* New York: Three Rivers Press, 1988.

Jaisingh, Lloyd R. *Statistics for the Utterly Confused.* New York: McGraw-Hill, 2000.

Mayr, Diane. *The Everything Kids' Money Book: From Saving to Spending to Investing-Learn All About Money! (Everything Kids Series).* Avon, Mass.: Adams Media Corporation, 2002.

Sowell, Thomas. *Basic Economics: A Citizen's Guide to the Economy.* New York: Basic Books, 2000.

Vallee, Danielle. *Whiz Teens in Business: Enjoy Yourself While Making Money!: A Simple and Complete Guide for Teenagers to Starting and Managing Their Small Business.* Kansas City, Mo.: Truman Publishing, 1999.

INDEX

Page numbers in **bold** denote major treatment of a topic.